The British Cavalry

Some Books by Philip Warner

The Crimean War: a reappraisal
Distant Battle: a retrospect of Empire
The Special Air Service
British Battlefields: the Midlands
British Battlefields: the North
British Battlefields: the South
British Battlefields: Scotland and the Border
Army Life in the 1890s
Dervish: the rise and fall of an African Empire
Alamein
Auchinleck: the lonely soldier
The Special Boat Squadron

The British Cavalry

Philip Warner

J. M. Dent & Sons Ltd
London   Melbourne

First published 1984
Text © Philip Warner 1984

This book is set in 11/12½ Lasercomp Garamond
Printed and made in Great Britain at
the Alden Press, Oxford for
J. M. Dent & Sons Ltd.,
Aldine House, 33 Welbeck Street, London W1M 8LX

British Library Cataloguing in Publication Data

Warner, Philip
  The British cavalry.
  1. Great Britain.   *Army*—Cavalry—History
  I. Title
  351'.1'0941   UA654

ISBN 0-460-04617-9

Contents

List of Colour Illustrations

List of Maps

Foreword

British cavalry is such a large subject that much which is interesting and important must necessarily be excluded from an account of this length. The aim therefore has been to show, from a selection of influences and actions, how the British cavalry evolved, how and where it fought, and what its individual qualities were. Cavalry warfare had been evolving for 3000 years when modern British cavalry came into being, yet in the 300 years of existence of the latter there are feats to rank with the most remarkable in history.

This book is principally concerned with British cavalry in the field and in action. There were, of course, long periods when the cavalry was on domestic duties which varied from hunting smugglers to quelling schoolboy insurrections at Rugby and Winchester. For the life of cavalry in barracks the reader is advised to turn to the Marquess of Anglesey's masterly and comprehensive study of cavalry life from 1816 to the present century. Those volumes also contain many accounts of cavalry in action, and of Indian cavalry, in addition to giving a survey of cavalry at home in peacetime. Barrack life is not entirely excluded from this book, but as it lies outside the main theme of the narrative much of it appears in an appendix. That section also includes the account of the early days as a cavalry trooper in 1877 of the future Field Marshal Sir William Robertson.

Sport was also a large part of cavalry life and included hunting, pigsticking, cricket, hockey, fives and other games. Polo was a recent addition, and in another appendix I have included an account of its introduction to this country which, surprisingly, was as late as 1870.

The appendices also include correspondence relating to the behaviour which made the Earl of Cardigan one of the least popular, even though one of the bravest, military figures of his time. Cardigan was undoubtedly an eccentric, but this interesting correspondence reveals him less as a fanatic than a perfectionist.

Cavalry, it will be seen, was not a mere showpiece; it was probably the hardest worked, most utilitarian arm of the military service. Fortunately, although the horse survives only for ceremonial or recreational purposes, cavalry spirit is as buoyant as ever. The fact that the steed is now of steel rather than flesh in no way diminishes the traditional cavalry virtues of dash, courage, enterprise and nonchalance. Long may it continue so.

In writing this book I have received valuable help and advice from many sources. In particular I would like to thank the librarians and staff of the Royal Military Academy Sandhurst library, the Ministry of Defence library, the National Army Museum, the Imperial War Museum, the Public Record Office, Regimental and Corps Museums, the Royal United Services Institute, and the many kind friends who have lent me papers and photographs.

I

Cavalry Ethos

I had an encounter in single combat this day with a very young French officer between the two lines of skirmishers, French and English, who stood still, by mutual consent, to witness it. The French officer showed great cunning and skill, seeing the superiority of my horse, for he remained stationary to receive me, and allowed me to ride round and round him while he remained on the defensive. He made several cuts at the head of my horse, and succeeded in cutting one of my reins and the forefinger of my bridle hand which was, however, saved by the thick glove I wore, though the finger was cut very deeply to the joint. As my antagonist was making the last cut at me I had the opportunity of making a thrust at his body which staggered him, and he made off. I thought I had but slightly wounded him, but I found on enquiry the next day, when sent on a flag of truce, that the thrust had proved mortal, having entered the pit of his stomach. I felt deeply on this occasion and was much annoyed, as I had admired the chivalrous and noble bearing of this young officer. He was a mere youth, who, I suppose, thought it necessary to make this display as a first essay, as French officers usually do on their first appearance on the field and, indeed I believe, it is expected of them by their comrades. I shall never forget his good-humoured, fine countenance during the whole time we were engaged in this single combat, talking cheerfully and politely to me as if we were exchanging civilities instead of sabre cuts. The cut I received on the forefinger of my bridle hand proved a great grievance for some time, as it prevented me from playing the violin for weeks – a great deprivation, as I always played in the bivouac at night.

The year was 1812; the fight took place outside Salamanca and the writer was Captain T.W. Brotherton. We observe the chivalry which prevailed even in such a bitter campaign as the Peninsular War, the indifference to pain, and the fact that enemies were able to converse fluently in each other's language. Clearly both men were accomplished swordsmen and Brotherton, in addition, was a proficient violinist; the young Frenchman seems to have been an exceptionally talented horseman, so much a master of his profession that he could converse humorously while beating off the attacks of an older and more experienced adversary.

In subsequent years cavalry officers acquired a very different reputation. Later in the nineteenth century they were noted for bone-headed, uncultured arrogance and although there were doubtless still Brothertons and their like in the cavalry regiments, little was heard of them. Instead, the public impression of a cavalry officer was the Earl of Cardigan who led the Charge of the Light Brigade. Cardigan's personal courage was indisputable but his stupidity, his prejudices, his vanities, and above all his indifference to the sufferings of his men, left a stain on the reputation of cavalry officers which was not easily removed. There were, of course, many petty Cardigans, although they were outnumbered by cavalrymen of responsibility and compassion. But once a reputation has been acquired, however wrongly, it has an unfortunate habit of persisting, even when largely untrue. Worse still, it can even attract an unsatisfactory type of officer. The best cavalrymen either refute the slur or profess indifference, but they too, are tainted with it, in the eyes of the public.

'Bad money drives out good.' Thus a bad reputation drives out a good one. This, of course, was Gresham's Law. The statement is undoubtedly true but it is not without interest to recall that Sir Thomas Gresham, a merchant who founded the Royal Exchange in the sixteenth century, never uttered the words, and the term 'Gresham's Law' was not used until three centuries later. For good or bad, much of what was attributed to the cavalry had much the same authenticity.

But, faced with a reputation they only partially deserved, what could the cavalry do about it? The answer was simple: make a joke of it. A popular cavalry story is of the commanding officer who wrote on one of his subaltern's annual report, 'Personally I would not breed from this officer,' and another, 'This officer's troops will follow him anywhere but only out of curiosity.' Or, 'A fine man in a crisis which is just as well for no one but he is more likely to create one.' Much favoured is the old *Punch* chestnut:

> *General* (to foppish young officer): Well, what do you consider to be the purpose of the cavalry on the battlefield?
>
> *Fop* (drawling): Well, I suppose it's to prevent the whole thing becoming rather a vulgar brawl.

Other regiments did not always think the jokes so funny. At the start of the First World War there was a preponderance of cavalry officers in senior positions. They were relentlessly opposed to any attempt to devalue the importance of the horse on the battlefield. The machine-gun, barbed-wire, even trenches were despised. 'I'd like to see the machine-gun which could stop a good cavalry charge,' said one commanding officer. He did. Many senior officers cherished the belief that when things settled down there would be brisk artillery bombardments (preferably by the Royal Horse Artillery), then the cavalry would charge through the bewildered Germans and scatter them, and finally our own infantry would consolidate the victory. We shall, sad to say, have to look at one or two examples of this attitude later in the book, but in presenting the full picture we shall also be able to demonstrate where the best cavalry qualities proved as effective in modern war as they had done in the campaigns of a more leisurely age.

In this survey we propose to begin by defining the function of the British cavalry and from that to proceed to an examination of how that *function* developed. This will involve a brief look at cavalry development in many different countries. It is, of course, not known at what stage in the distant past men first decided that doing battle on horseback was preferable to performing on foot, but it surely goes back to a very early moment in history.

During the Middle Ages in Britain, as in other countries, the performance of the cavalry was influenced by the amount and type of armour which was worn. Through the history of warfare it has been an indisputable fact that if you have strong armour you lose mobility: the choice is therefore between retaining the ability to attack and move rapidly out of danger, or alternatively to lumber forward, an easy target, but with confidence that your armour will protect you from whatever your opponents may aim at you. Today this debate centres on tanks. Towards the end of the Second World War Hitler became so obsessed with the desire to develop an invulnerable tank that he ordered the construction of the Maus, a monster which was almost a mobile fort, but which had a top speed of twelve mph when it could be made to move at all.

But the end of heavily armoured horsemen was brought about by firearms. Although at first they were unreliable and not very effective, firearms did well enough to prove that the day of the lumbering, heavily-armoured knight was over. There had been a hint of this impending doom in the devastating success of the longbow on such occasions as Crécy and Agincourt. In both those battles the French knights and their horses were destroyed by a deadly rain of missiles which could not be warded off. But the longbow could not penetrate thick plate armour; bullets could.

Once armour had been found to be inadequate against firearms it was almost totally discarded, somewhat prematurely. In the sixteenth century stress was laid on the development of swift tactical manoeuvres: There were some spirited cavalry actions in the English Civil War. When the eighteenth century arrived it brought a major continental war and one of history's most brilliant tacticians – Marlborough – whose genius will be examined later. The century saw many other wars and ended during the Napoleonic campaigns, which continued well into the next century.

The nineteenth century saw a wide variety of cavalry actions and some of the less successful received more publicity than they merited. But by now, rifle and cannon were making the life of cavalry increasingly precarious, a development which seems to have been accompanied by obstinacy and resistance to change. The century ended with the South African War, a campaign which emphasized the importance of skilled horsemen though not necessarily of the formal cavalry. Although the present century has seen the end of cavalry (at least for the time being), the earlier years, particularly the First World War, saw its widespread employment.

At the start of the Second World War it was generally assumed that the day of the cavalry was over, but, surprisingly enough, it was still used on occasion in the British army up till 1942, and throughout the war extensively by Russian, German, Polish, Romanian, Italian and Greek forces. The day of the mounted soldier may now seem to be over, completely and finally.

But perhaps not. Two factors may help to keep some form of cavalry in being. First, world oil resources are not unlimited and even before the end of the present century dwindling supplies will put an end to those roseate visions of millions of tanks and other vehicles scurrying across endless plains: there will be insufficient fuel.

Second, the horse can often reach places which no armoured vehicle can climb to and be supplied. This does not of course mean that as armoured vehicles cease to function horsemen will replace them: perhaps the foot-soldier will be the sole inhabitant of the battlefield. But horses will be needed to help transport supplies, and, inevitably, there will be mounted troops. When the infantry emerges from the battlefield, the last line of defence, in contrast to the first line of attack, may be the cavalry.

It may never happen. As fossil fuels disappear, or become too precious to be burnt, robot vehicles run on atomic, electrical, or some as yet undiscovered form of power, may enable man to settle his disputes by mobile warfare. But the hope that man will ever find adequate substitutes for coal and oil may be disappointed. There may be further supplies of both in the world, but if they are under the Antarctic ice, or under the Pacific Ocean, any prospect of a cheap, affordable supply is illusory. Atomic power is available but is as expensive as gold. We merely delude outselves if we imagine that the resources of the world, when exhausted, have adequate, inexpensive substitutes. Where are the reserve stocks or substitutes for whales, salmon, herring or even mackerel? Or of silver? Fanciful though it may seem, man's survival may depend on the revival and re-use of many obsolete methods and crafts. One of the latter may be the breeding and training of heavy horses.

2

The Function and Origins of the Cavalry

The asset of the cavalry was that it was faster and more mobile than the foot-soldier. It could therefore act as the eyes of the army, probing ahead in forward reconnaissance, ensuring that the flanks were not threatened, noting the nature of the countryside over which the foot-soldiers would later be marching. Perhaps it would be engaged in seizing or commandeering supplies, and keeping a wary eye open for ambush positions which, though not occupied by the enemy at that moment, could very well be brought into use before the vanguard of the approaching army appeared. It would report on whether the enemy was close by or at a distance. By questioning the inhabitants of villages it might be possible to make an assessment of the enemy's state of morale, whether confident or dejected, whether they were well-fed and supplied, and above all, whether they seemed prepared for action or vulnerable to a surprise attack. If the enemy army was close by, a commander-in-chief might decide to test the cavalry's observation by a raid or a foray. These would alert the enemy to their presence and intentions, but might be worthwhile if vital information was obtained.

Cavalry raids were by no means haphazard excursions by a few high-spirited volunteers. They usually had specific aims. When the Prussians marched against the French in the Franco-Prussian War of 1871, they used cavalry raids to damage enemy morale. In contrast raids have been used to capture prisoners, particularly important ones, to seize or destroy convoys of food, supplies, or money, and, not least, to give an impression of great vigour and determination.

If an army was advancing through enemy territory the purpose of the cavalry would be to test whether the local population could be persuaded – or intimidated – into co-operation, or represented a threat. If the latter, the cavalry would employ terrorist tactics, burning and destroying, leaving a few bodies hanging on conspicuous gibbets as a warning against any form of resistance. In some areas the local population detested all armies, their own or foreign ones, with equal intensity. They wished to be left alone and to continue their primitive existence without interference. Attempts to coerce them into co-operation might have the unfortunate effect of making them more friendly to the opposing army, which they had not yet encountered, than to the one disrupting their lives. Provided the army observed 'correct' behaviour, which meant leaving their homes, their crops and, above all, their women, unmolested, there would be sullen, though unenthusiastic acceptance of the army's presence: on the other hand, cavalry troops dashing here and there, damaging crops, enticing a woman or two, could lead to the ham-stringing of horses, the murder of stragglers, and the betrayal of tactics and strength to the enemy.

The cavalry was a hard-worked arm of the service. As the main force moved forward, two or three miles ahead and also out to the sides would be 'videttes'. They consisted of less than a dozen men patrolling as an early warning system against strong resistance ahead or a flank attack. They would belong to what were known as outlying picquets – detachments of up to fifty men. If the videttes reported trouble, the picquets would come forward to help. Sometimes these larger forces would clash with their counterparts from the enemy army who were also playing their part in screening. The result might be a brief but bloody skirmish. Videttes and picquets continued to function when the army was static. They were essential but led to a constant dribble of casualties among men and horses. The numbers would mount up quickly when the outlying picquet decided that it had taken on more than it could manage and thus needed the help of the inlying picquet. The inlying picquet was held in reserve for just such an emergency. In the great French retreat from Moscow in 1812, the French picquets were so harassed, outwitted, and exhausted by Cossacks operating on their own terrain that the French screening system often broke down entirely. A nineteenth-century army extended approximately twenty-one miles from vanguard to rearguard; that meant that at any given time the cavalry had the task of screening at least 42 miles of flank, in addition to forward reconnaissance and the protection of rear areas. When Napoleon set off to Moscow his wagon train had to supply food for 400,000 men and oats for 50,000 horses. Transport broke down frequently on the poor roads and the cavalry faced an almost impossible task in trying to protect a straggling, slow-moving, undisciplined baggage train.

Another important function of cavalry was communication. Before modern forms of signalling were invented the eyes and the ears of the commanders, and the method of transmission of information, was the cavalry. Successful generals were often found to be those who made the best use of cavalry for communication with their subordinates or allies.

It is not, perhaps, generally realized how haphazard warfare was before the development of reliable portable timepieces and compasses. Armies could arrange to meet at a certain point on a certain day. In trackless country, or when progress was hampered by rivers, flooding, forests, or broken bridges, such meetings might never take place. Froissart quotes examples of medieval armies vainly searching for the enemy, often passing within a few miles of each other, yet never coming to a confrontation. In developed countries this was less likely to happen but until the nineteenth century there were many occasions of acute suspense when commanders wondered if their allies would appear at all. Inaccurate estimates of time sometimes resulted in armies not appearing till the main battle was almost or completely over. Some newcomers then prudently joined the winning side, whether it was the one they had set out to help or not. The best hope of avoiding such lapses was for the horsemen with the best mounts to skirmish far and wide and learn all that might be learnt about timing and terrain.

Although all these ancillary functions were immensely important, they took second place, in the minds of the cavalry at least, to the set-piece battle. Here the distinction between heavy and light cavalry would become apparent. In the early stages light cavalry would be used on the flanks in a series of harassing and disruptive moves. These would not have a decisive effect but they could cause unwanted delays to any army manoeuvring into what it felt was a favourable attacking position. Once the battle lines were adopted the heavy cavalry would come into its own: weight and impetus might enable it to smash its way into the heart of the enemy formation. While this bloodbath was taking place, the light cavalry would be relatively inactive. Their turn would come again when the issue was resolved. Either their own army would be in retreat and they would have to do their best to cover its withdrawal, or they would be on the winning side and given the opportunity of trying to prevent an orderly retreat by the enemy. After a major battle the cavalry would be expected to turn victory into rout. One of the criticisms of Lord Raglan after the battle of the Alma in 1854 was that he failed to order the cavalry to pursue the defeated Russians. In Raglan's defence it has been suggested that he thought that the cavalry were too ill-disciplined and unco-ordinated for such a move to be feasible. Judging by the subsequent behaviour of some of his cavalry leaders, he may well have been right. Raglan, of course, had little influence on the course of the battle, for he managed to get himself cut off from his own army: nevertheless when a pursuit could have been ordered he was in a position to make the appropriate decision. The order – if pursuit was the correct decision – could have ended the Crimean War within a month, for beyond the Alma heights the way to an undefended Sebastopol was almost clear.

Military history abounds with examples of successful cavalry pursuits and of unmitigated disasters. On successful occasions, the cavalry has galloped past defeated armies and captured fortresses and towns from commanders who had no idea that they were in danger. With an army between themselves and the enemy they had made no effort to close gates or man defences. The result was the easy capture of towns and forts which could otherwise have made the life of the invader very difficult.

In contrast there have been total disasters, some of which will be described later, when the cavalry had assumed a battle was won and galloped after a portion of an apparently routed enemy. Many hours later that same cavalry has straggled back, tired and blown, expecting to find victory celebrations in full swing, only to discover that in their absence the battle has gone to the enemy and the people celebrating that victory are the ones they hoped would now be lying dead on the battlefield.

A curious but explicable fact about early battles was that more people were killed after the battle was over than when it was taking place. Once a battle had been deemed won, the unfortunate losers faced the alternatives of being slaughtered where they stood or making an attempt to escape. Prisoners were only taken if they were rich enough to merit ransoms: the common soldier would be slaughtered as a prevention against his ever bearing arms again. And, of course, there was minor booty, blood lust, and in some wars, long-nurtured hatreds to influence conduct. The dead or dying were usually stripped by the ghouls who followed the armies; a battlefield the following day would consist solely of naked corpses: all arms, clothes, and possessions would have been removed. Yet, incredibly, wounded men, stripped naked and left on a battlefield in winter, have been known to survive.

But between the height of the battle and the macabre scenes which followed there might be a turning-point which a thoughtful commander would have kept in mind. With his main army defeated, and probably surrounded, and waiting a final massacre, there might be little for him to hope for. But on the flanks there would still be that light cavalry which had been resting during the battle and now would be available to cover those lucky enough to find a path of retreat. To it he might be able to add a small reserve from another part of the field, held back for this very moment. Now, with the original battle lines badly disrupted, with the victors breaking through recklessly and either not hearing or not heeding the words of their commanders, the victorious army could be in a very vulnerable state. That would be the moment when the cavalry, frustrated, impatient and desperate, in a mood of suicidal despair, could suddenly be launched into the disrupted armies. As like as not, the effect on the victors could be overwhelming. In the very moment of triumph they are suddenly dealt a swift devastating blow from an unexpected quarter. It must be a new army coming on to the field; it cannot be a part of the one they have just defeated. The effect at least would be confusion, enabling some of the defeated to escape; at best would cause the victors to turn back into their own lines, thereby creating chaos and dismay.

Cavalry, therefore, could always introduce a note of uncertainty on the battlefield. They could lose a battle which had apparently been won but they could also snatch victory out of the jaws of defeat. The possibility of their doing either was entirely influenced by their commanders, their training, and their discipline.

So much for the functions: we shall see examples of them later. The origins are more complex. British cavalry did not of course develop on its own, it derived from many other forms of cavalry, and near cavalry, and even when it had fully established its own traditions it needed to keep an eye on what was happening elsewhere and to learn from it. Unfortunately it did not always do so. Douglas Haig, then a Major-General, wrote a book entitled *Cavalry Studies* which was published in 1907. In it he wrote: 'The Boers succeeded on more than one occasion in executing tasks pronounced by our military experts to be quite impossible . . . and if we endeavour to deduce from the study of campaigns the causes which at certain epochs have extended or diminished the role of cavalry we find that these causes have no strict relation to the changes of armament but depend almost exclusively on the principles which have governed the training and employment of the arm – in a word, *on the character of those who have had command.*' (One might of course think that if Haig can describe as 'in a word' a phrase of nine, he may have been as muddled in his ideas as some of the people he is criticizing.)

For the most part, cavalry through the ages has learnt its lessons the hard way. In one sense the evolution of cavalry has turned full circle. The earliest known use of horses in war was with chariots. The horse, driven by a very skilled charioteer, supplied the speed and manoeuvrability; behind was the platform from which various death-dealing devices were launched. The modern tank – the iron cavalry – mirrors this function exactly. Chariots were used in many countries: ancient Egypt, Greece,

India, Assyria, Persia, ancient Britain. It is, not unnaturally, a matter of pride to us, that when the Romans came to Britain they found that the British charioteers had skills unknown in other countries. There is a widespread though probably incorrect belief that the ancient Britons had long scythes projecting outwards from the vehicle. This seems most unlikely as any substantial obstacle would cause the chariot to swing round, upsetting the horses and possibly throwing out the charioteers. A more likely practice was to have a long pole separating the horses and for the charioteer to run along this. (It is always necessary to draw a line between what an enemy was said to be able to do and what he actually did.)

The reason for the use of chariots was that the horse could not be used in any other way. Neither saddles nor stirrups had been invented at this stage and it does not take an accomplished horseman to demonstrate how difficult it is to control a horse without these two aids. Bareback riders with feet dangling may accomplish remarkable feats in the circus, and American Indian horsemen performed moderately well under such conditions, but half-controlled horses would be a dangerous liability in conventional warfare.

There are enough references to chariots in ancient literature for us to realize that they were widely and skilfully used. But undoubtedly they had their limitations. The horses were much inferior, both in speed and strength, to their successors. The

Babylonian chariot, from which cavalry developed.

Greek cavalryman – a long lance, sword, axe, small shield and spur, but no stirrups.

vehicles themselves were crude and clumsy by modern standards. But the one feature of this form of warfare which leaves an indelible impression is the agility and resource of the charioteers. Xenophon reports them as dashing in and out of action, too wily to allow themselves to be swallowed up by the enemy but capable of administering quick, painful shocks before disappearing from view. The measure of their success is the respect with which they are described and the apprehension they created.

Neither the date nor the originator of the first cavalry proper are known. Identifying the first nation to originate a form of warfare is rarely possible for, if successful, it was quickly and widely copied; often the imitators claimed the new invention as their own. Herodotus says that the Scythians fought as mounted archers; clearly this was an important step in the development of the cavalry arm. It was effective enough in its day too, for that day lasted seven hundred years, from 900 BC to 200 BC. The Scythians seem to have originated near the Carpathians, but eventually settled between the Black Sea and the Caspian. They used bronze arrowheads and wore bronze armour, and their technique was to ride close to the enemy, launch their arrows and retire at speed. But they fought as individuals, not as organized groups.

The Assyrians may well have been the originators of cavalry warfare: they were forerunners in many other military arts. It is often assumed that their monopoly of iron, which they kept a closely-guarded secret, was the key to their success but it is only part of the story. They built siege towers and military catapults; their missiles carried incendiary material. In early sculpture the Assyrian warrior appears with a horse wearing a collar, a headstall and a snaffle. But there were no saddles and they appear to be going to the battle clinging to the horse's neck, two men to each horse. One of the men carried the bow, the other the arrows. Later sculptures show a horseman sitting in a relaxed position on a square saddlecloth. He has helmet, trousers and boots and carries a sword. The bows were said to be four feet in length and to discharge a three-foot arrow. This was a powerful weapon but in order for the rider to handle a weapon of this kind the horse would need to be still; it is closely akin to the English longbow which, with its 70 lb pull, required several hours practice a *day* if efficiency was to be maintained. But early warriors did not expect to do anything except practise their skills. If you rely on bow or sling for hunting or survival you do not begrudge the time you spend perfecting an art, in fact you do not make a distinction between training and relaxation. Perhaps the fact that bareback riding was the only form of riding known meant that the horsemen achieved a greater degree of control than nowadays we imagine possible.

The lance, so much a part of British cavalry tradition, appears to have been pioneered by Cyrus the Great in the fifth century BC. His Persian cavalry, armed with heavy spears and protected by armour, were used as shock troops. This worked very well until the following century when heavily armed Persians were unable to stave off the attacks of more lightly-equipped but very mobile Greeks. This moment of truth came at the Battle of Marathon (490 BC).

By the fourth century BC cavalry were displaying an amazing variety of skills. Xerxes, the Persian commander, was said to have an army of 160,000, of whom half were cavalry. The cavalry included Sargatians, who advanced on fast horses, lassoed their opponents and then stabbed them, and Medes, who carried short- and long-range bows. Although their opponents, the Greeks, were renowned for the Phalanx, which was an infantry formation composed of 'hoplites' – well-armoured men carrying an eight-foot spear and short sword – they were well experienced in the use of cavalry, too. The corps d'élite of cavalrymen in this Greek army was composed mainly of Thessalonians, who were said to have originated the art of cavalry warfare in their own district. The Thessalonians became so expert and so renowned for cavalry tactics that they were often hired as mercenaries by other countries. The Spartans, too, developed cavalry skills but the Greek army as a whole was slow to encourage this arm. Well aware of the Persian prowess and experience in cavalry warfare, the Greeks decided that they themselves would do better to continue to specialize in infantry tactics, at which they knew they were very effective. But eventually they decided that for modern warfare (of their day) they, too, must have a strong cavalry arm. They learnt this lesson by harsh experience. Before the Battle of Plataea in 479, with the Persians (as usual) for their opponents, the Greeks found the attentions of the Persian cavalry more than they bargained for. The Persian squadrons disrupted the Greek supply lines, harassed the marching infantry, and created a constant sense of uneasiness. When the battle was joined the Greek infantry proved more than a match for the Persians and defeated them, but the Persian cavalry, which had nearly tipped the balance in the battle several times, then protected their retreating army and prevented the Greeks from taking full advantage of their victory. The lesson was appreciated. In the future Greece had a more balanced army, and cavalry contributed its share to that balance.

Ironically, it was not against the arch-enemy Persia that Greek cavalry came into its own, but against their own neighbours. The Persian threat was eliminated in the naval battle of Salamis in 450 BC. By that time what were known as the Peloponnesian Wars had already begun; the contest was between Athens and the Peloponnesian League. The Athenians took some pride in their cavalry but soon found that these were no match for their opponents who had an expert force drawn from Thessaly and Macedonia (now part of Yugoslavia). The Athenian response was to create three distinct types of cavalry themselves: heavy, medium and light. Heavy cavalry were protected by armour, as were their horses, and carried lances, swords and spears. Medium cavalry wore less armour, and were thus less suitable for shock tactics but were particularly well-protected about the head. They dispensed with the spear. Light cavalry (the 'Tarentines') merely wore a leather jerkin and buckler. They were armed with bows and javelins and were mainly employed in skirmishing. They seem to have something in common with the British yeomanry regiments of which we shall be speaking later.

As the Greek cavalry had neither stirrups nor saddles there were clearly limitations on what it could do. The Tarentines were scarcely organized at all, but the remainder of the cavalry were grouped in 'iles' – blocks of sixty-four with a front of sixteen (four deep). The tactical method was for one wing to deliver a crushing blow while the other merely held the enemy. Any gain would be reinforced and these tactics could often turn a small advantage into a rout. The traditional maxim of the British Staff College: 'Always reinforce victory, never reinforce defeat', seems to stem from this long-distant period.

When Alexander the Great ruled Greece from 336 to 323 BC, his reign was memorable in many ways, not least for his employment of cavalry in his great victories. Prior to this the ratio of cavalry to infantry had been one to fifteen; Alexander changed the ratio to one to five. He quadrupled the numbers in the iles but never made them more than eight deep. Light infantry was interspersed between the iles in battle. The Tarentines were increased in numbers and given very fast horses.

Alexander himself often led the cavalry in the attack and his methods seem to have influenced military theory for the next 2000 years. The right was clearly the most important part of the battle line and, led by Alexander, would deliver a devastating blow, while the centre held and the left retreated slightly. Then it would be the turn of the left who would come in an enveloping movement or, on occasion, straight through the enemy centre. Almost inevitably the enemy would either be surrounded, or uncertain where the next attack would come from.

It is not without interest that when the German Count Schlieffen conceived the master-plan to defeat France in 1914 (he made the plan in the 1890s but it was not put into operation till long past his retirement and a year after his death) he emphasized the point, 'Keep the right very strong'. In fact he is supposed to have muttered those very words with his dying breath. The Schlieffen Plan visualized the entire German army pivoting on Metz and destroying the French as it swept round on the right like a

Alexander the Great (from a bust found on a site of Villa Piso, Tivoli, 1779). He was a cavalry commander of vision and genius.

closing door. In the end the right was not kept strong enough and the army also outran its supplies.

In Alexander's battle at Granicus, in 334, his plan went exactly as he intended except that the blow from his right was so devastating that the enemy opposite disintegrated and began to flee. A less intelligent commander would now have decided the battle was won and followed in pursuit. However, Alexander knew that there was still much to be done in the centre, to which he now turned his attention. In consequence complete victory was won with minimal casualties to the Greeks.

The emphasis on the importance of the right wing in battle seems to have led to a persistent military mystique. So valued did a station on the right become – even though it was the most likely to produce an early demise – that regiments would refuse to take part in a battle if they were not given their honourable place on the right, to which they felt entitled. The Camerons were exceedingly displeased when they were refused their place of honour on the extreme right at Culloden. It may even have affected social behaviour: the place of honour is on the right, a convention normally observed in the placing of guests at a dinner table.

To appreciate Alexander's influence on cavalry warfare millenia after his death, we must take a quick look at the battle of Gaugamela in 331. Knowing what to expect from Alexander tactically, the Persians deployed an extended line overlapping his position. When he drove forward they would therefore be able to fold inwards and envelop him. Alexander had learnt their plans from spies and was not therefore surprised when he saw this demonstration of new tactics. He proceeded with his plan but kept a cavalry reserve. When the Persians fell on his flank they found themselves attacked by this reserve force. But Alexander's opponent, Darius, was almost as skilled as Alexander himself. He rallied his forces and dealt the Greek cavalry a severe blow. Alexander, checked at all points, concentrated his forces in a solid wedge and broke through the Persian line. Darius left the field but Alexander was too wary to pursue him. His caution was justified, for the Persian cavalry had now found a gap in the Greek position and were pouring through it; they reached the Greek rearguard and were proceeding to destroy it when Alexander, gathering up his best troops, counter-attacked and after a bitter struggle gained victory.

Not surprisingly these tactical battles became a model for later cavalry commanders in the ensuing centuries. For the most part the ancient battles were fought under admirable cavalry conditions with plenty of room for manoeuvre, and with vast numbers of disciplined and well-led men. Such conditions were rarely to be found when the British cavalry fought their battles later, but something of the same subtleties may be detected, particularly in India. Alexander, too, learnt something from the Battle of Gaugamela. He himself was a master of deceptive tactics, of leaving apparent gaps whose purpose was really to break up enemy cohesion, and of appearing to commit an entire wing to the battle while in fact keeping a corps d'élite in reserve: however, Darius was scarcely less a master of the art of war. He also could feign a retreat and tempt the enemy into rash pursuit; he also had an instinct for picking the right moment to switch an attack.

Another of Alexander's legacies which proved very popular with other armies later was the use of sport to develop military skills. He encouraged all forms of sporting activities, provided they had a military application. Vaulting over obstacles, archery, running, javelin-throwing, contests requiring horsemanship – these were Alexander's favoured leisure activities. A wrestling match was often used to determine who, finally, was the best man on the field. Polo, hunting, sabre-fighting, and pistol-shooting became their later counterparts.

Another notable cavalry commander was Hannibal. Hannibal's use of elephants, and his brilliant handling of infantry, have somewhat obscured his skill as a cavalry commander, but there is no doubt at all that he was a cavalry commander of the first rank. Ironically, his final defeat was brought about by Roman cavalry, although it was the latter's least important arm.

The Romans, however, did much to create the impression that the cavalry was an élite. Their first cavalry was made up of the sons of rich patrician families. Although rich they did not have to provide their own horses. They wore a distinctive badge and a gold ring. Periodically they were inspected by a 'censor' who would transfer them to the infantry if he was not satisfied with their turnout, attitude and character. It was no idle threat, but it did nothing to check their self-esteem. In the third century 400 were demoted for refusing to obey an order by Cotta, the consul, to help build fortifications in Sicily. One can imagine the scene and the words. 'We are the *equites*; we do not handle shovels and bricks like common workmen.' 'You, my conceited young puppies, will obey an order.' And so on. Their protest was a foolish one, for the success of the Roman armies had relied almost as much on the spade as on the spear and sword. When on the march in unfriendly or unknown country the Roman army gave up at least half of its day to fortifying its camp for the night. Experience had taught the danger of a tired army being caught by surprise. And a Roman conquest was firmly tied together by a series of linking and durable roads, as we know full well.

But their attitude seems more understandable when it is realized how pampered these young men were by the system. Although the Roman army was extremely democratic, almost a people's army, the cavalry was given a status which it did not deserve by any military prestige or value. Yet we find that cavalry officers holding a rank equivalent to infantry officers were in fact one stage higher. Furthermore, promotion to the highest posts in the army was easier for the cavalry than the infantry. On leaving the army, cavalry officers moved easily to the higher civil service posts, such as Chief Magistrate. In the circumstances the fact that the cavalry believed that the world owed them a living, and would defer to them, does not seem surprising. But throughout the ages the deference paid to cavalry has persisted, often enduring in circumstances when scorn and censure would have been more appropriate.

As far as we know, Livy being our main source, cavalry fought with lances but, if necessary, would dismount and fight as infantry. In the later stages Roman cavalry was divided between lightly armed skirmishing troops and heavy cavalry which was merely a form of mounted infantry. Mounted infantry is not, of course, classed as cavalry, though very often it bears a close resemblance to it. Mounted infantry use their horses to approach the battle area, then dismount and fight on foot. Horses are merely a form of transport but the essential point is that the riders are armed as infantry, not as cavalry. A mounted infantryman would never carry a lance, unless it was to be used to repel cavalry charges in the way that pikes were used.

Roman cavalry had one of its severest tests in the wars against Carthage during the second century BC. The Carthaginian commander was the redoubtable Hannibal, but he was ill-supported by his own people and eventually was defeated. He is best known for his ingenuity in using elephants, which he marched over the Pyrenees, over the Alps, and into northern Italy. But from the cavalry point of view his most notable achievement was in his use of Numidian troops. Although these were only a small part of his cavalry, which in turn made up a quarter of his army, they were a remarkable asset, said to be the finest troops in the world at the time. They appear to have had every conceivable disadvantage, small horses, no saddles, reins or bridles, and the horsemen themselves were entirely unprotected. Some contemporary engravings depict them as naked apart from a short cloak. Their only means of control, apart from their bony knees, was a short whip. They carried javelins and each man had a small, round shield.

Astonishingly, these poorly armed, ill-equipped troops were the terror of their opponents. With virtually nothing to assist them they had remarkable control over their mounts. No ground was so rough that they could not traverse it with ease; their speed and mobility made them a constant threat. Sometimes they would appear from nowhere and launch their javelins with deadly accuracy at the vanguard; soon afterwards they would be harassing the flanks or plundering the rearguard, and then be back at the vanguard again. So rapid, unpredictable, yet lethal, were their attacks that they were a threat to the morale of the solid Roman legions, who began to wonder if these naked demons could really be human. Their commander was an inspired general named Maharbal.

Although Hannibal suffered heavy losses on his arduous and audacious marches, he usually defeated the Romans, who had superior numbers, by enveloping them in his cavalry. In consequence the Romans always tried to meet him in battle in a place where he could not use this devastating arm. It was in vain. Hannibal's Numidian scouts always knew exactly where the Romans were and what they seemed likely to do. If necessary the Numidians could goad the Romans into coming out and attacking them; these moves disrupted Roman plans. There is no space here to go into the details of Hannibal's battles, fascinating though they are. Not the least of his achievements was his ability to blend a variety of troops – Gallic, Spanish, African and Carthaginian – and maintain morale under circumstances where other armies would have disintegrated. Had he been properly supported it would have been Rome which would have been destroyed, not Carthage. In his final battle he was defeated by a general who had copied his tactics and – most bitter of all – acquired Hannibal's 6,000 Numidians by a timely treaty with the Numidian king.

Thus far we have established that cavalry has a long history and was used with intelligence and success long before the days of stirrups, saddle and bit. Although it is common knowledge that Julius Caesar invaded this country in 55 BC., it is not often realized that when he returned the following year he brought a force of 2,000 cavalry with him. Although these were probably for reconnaissance duties rather than for fighting, their presence is ample evidence of their importance in Roman military plans. In order to reach Britain they had to cross at least twenty-one miles of sea. Horses are notoriously bad sailors and have the unfortunate disadvantage that they cannot be seasick. Apart from these considerations, their size alone makes them difficult to transport. Yet Caesar felt that they were important enough to justify the shipping and trouble required to transport them. In the event a storm destroyed most of the shipping in port soon after their arrival; had that storm arrived when the horses were at sea the results would have been catastrophic.

In the later Roman period, we find generals experimenting interestingly with their cavalry. In the year 48 BC Julius Caesar and Pompey fought the decisive battle of Pharsalia. Pompey had almost double Caesar's numbers and decided to vary traditional tactics by concentrating his main cavalry disposition on the left wing. This would then, he assumed, overwhelm Caesar's right wing which was a mixed force of cavalry and infantry. Pompey was correct in assuming that he would drive Caesar's right wing back but he did not realize that this was partly by Caesar's own orders, so that Pompey's men were then faced by Caesar's most experienced infantry. As Pompey's all-conquering cavalry swept down on to this resolute infantry force they were met with a solid defence of infantrymen using their javelins much as pikes would have been used. Their casualties were high but so was the toll among Pompey's horsemen. This unexpected turn of events left Pompey's cavalry confused and at a standstill. It is an axiom of cavalry warfare that when in doubt you should do anything but remain still. A horse, or a tank, which hesitates, can easily be assessed as a target by a watchful marksman. At Pharsalia Caesar had been hoping for this very moment and proceeded to launch the remainder of his cavalry at Pompey's dispirited and bewildered force. There were other tactical moves of importance in the battle but this was the main one: it is particularly interesting because it was the first recorded example of 'decoy, surprise, and crush', using reserves whose function might have been thought to have been quite different. Although we do not know for sure, Caesar's cavalry may have been of better quality than Pompey's. Gaul (France) from which he drew many troops, abounded with natural cavalry fighters. They were heavily armed and wore an iron cuirass (breastplate and backplate); they would charge opposing infantry, smash a way forward, and then move aside to let lighter cavalry through to the pursuit.

The Germans also provided the Romans with some cavalry. They were scantily dressed and crudely armoured and their weapons consisted of a short lance only. Their main weakness was the poor quality of their horses. The Goths were rather better and carried battle axes. The Spaniards were very good indeed. They carried short lances which were occasionally thrown as javelins; they had swords and daggers and they wore leather cuirasses. Some of these early cavalrymen bore a close resemblance to the troops that British cavalry would meet in wars some 1700 years later, as we shall see.

In the period of the expansion of the Roman Empire one of its most formidable opponents had been the Parthians. The Parthians were unusual in that they rated cavalry as their greatest asset, far more valuable than infantry. When they confronted the Roman general Crassus, in what is now Iraq, their heavy cavalry wore chain mail, scale armour and iron helmets. They carried long lances but felt themselves well enough protected to dispense with shields. They could also fight dismounted using swords, daggers and heavy bows. There was a proportion of light cavalry which was not unlike the Numidians mentioned earlier. Although this light Parthian cavalry carried a sword and dagger, the principal weapon was a bow. This was a powerful weapon, not unlike the English longbow centuries later. The arrows were long, heavy, barbed and in apparently unlimited supply: camels were used as a supply train.

The Parthian technique was to harass armies on the march by endlessly circling around them and inflicting considerable damage by high-flighted arrows which fell into the heart of the advancing column. When the Romans came out to beat off their tormentors there were two possibilities: either they never came to grips with the Parthians at all, or they ran into well-prepared ambushes where they were often cut off and massacred. One of the more notable achievements of the Parthians was the renowned 'Parthian shot'. When they were being driven off they would suddenly swing round and deliver a final arrow shot. It was often the more effective through being completely unexpected – even by those who knew the ways of the Parthians by experience. In Britain, until recently, a final remark in an embittered conversation, made when one of the speakers was departing, would be described as 'a Parthian shot'.

The Romans had little success against the Parthians who, it is said, were probably the best cavalry the world has ever seen. Whatever method the Romans tried against them proved quite ineffective, rather like a man trying to beat off an attack by angry wasps. Even if they killed a few Parthians, others got through and inflicted damaging blows. The Romans could not destroy all their camps: there were too many. Against this it must be remembered that the Parthians were fighting on their own terrain, in a countryside which suited their tactics. They were too wise to be drawn away into lands which would not suit their tactics.

3

The Evolution of British Cavalry

As we have seen, cavalry took a prominent part in warfare in what is broadly dismissed as Ancient History. Our survey covered a period of nearly a thousand years and included a wide variety of different countries and peoples. The period produced some remarkable and innovative generals, and the performance of cavalry was undoubtedly influenced as much by the temperament of the people as by the tasks they faced. Our review brought us up to Caesar's use of cavalry and he will always be remembered, in cavalry annals at least, as the man who brought formal cavalry to Britain. But cavalry of a different type was, as we saw, already here. It was the cavalry of the charioteer and the most formidable of its kind yet seen.

The Roman occupation of Britain, which did not begin till AD 43, does not appear to have included any notable cavalry actions. Britain, during that period, was infantry country, with a landscape of forest, swamp, scrub and hillock. Horses were, of course, widely used but not as formal cavalry. Cavalry manoeuvres need space for them to be effective; it was many years before land clearance and drainage had advanced sufficiently in Britain to make it suitable for cavalry actions. The only form of cavalry action which the Romans could successfully employ in Britain was with videttes to guard against surprise attacks; as we have seen earlier, the Romans took every precaution against surprise attack and were rarely discomfited.

But the later inhabitants of Britain were not left entirely without cavalry experience, for the Roman legions, into which many Britons were conscripted, fought intense cavalry battles in Germany and Gaul. By the second century AD the German cavalry, though still primitive, had improved considerably. Their control of horses was remarkable: the rider would leap to the ground, take part in the action and return to his horse with the justified confidence that it would be standing exactly where he had left it. This enabled the Germans to advance to the battle area, conceal themselves in woods, ambush their enemy, move on foot among the opposing troops killing or disabling the horses, then return to their own mounts and pursue the fleeing remnants of the defeated army. Caesar admired the warlike qualities of these Germans and recruited cavalry from them. Re-equipped with better horses, and trained by experienced Roman cavalrymen, they became a very formidable force.

Another German race was the Vandals. They were armed with sword and lance and consisted entirely of cavalry. They obtained their enduring reputation from the rapid destruction which they practised. Their technique was to embark horses on coastal vessels, land, range over the entire countryside destroying everything they encountered, and then return and re-embark. Several centuries later the Vikings used similar techniques in Britain except that they did not bring their horses with them. Instead they captured horses near the coastal towns and used these on wild forays inland.

Gallic and Spanish cavalry became widely esteemed, the former being especially well-mounted. Their courage and horsemanship was impressive, but their tactical ability less so. However they produced an interesting innovation. This was to group horsemen in bands of three, one of whom was the principal. If the principal was killed one of his assistants would take his place. This formation was the precursor of the medieval 'lance' (a formation consisting of a knight and two esquires).

The Roman Empire lasted longer than most empires have done and in its decline became one of the most degenerate. The cavalry, which had once been an élite, became a conscript force drawn from the poorest classes. Patriotism, which had once distinguished the Roman citizen, became virtually extinct. Military service became so unpopular that, according to Gibbon, young men used to cut off the fingers of the right hand in order to avoid it. Attempts by a few public-spirited generals to regenerate the army proved ineffective. In the reign of the Emperor Gratian Roman soldiers declined to wear armour at all, saying it was too heavy. As armour was being adopted by their future opponents, the outcome was inevitable.

Meanwhile in the east a new and awesome threat was emerging. This was the Hun invasion. The Huns, who came from far distant Asia, were to set their mark on the pattern of European warfare for the next thousand years. Their speed and mobility made them seem invulnerable. But other warriors had had these qualities too. What made the Huns the most devastating form of cavalry the world had yet seen was not their speed, endurance or ruthlessness, but the fact that they also had saddles and stirrups. Curiously enough, it was not the use they themselves made of these which had the most lasting influence, but the difference they made to other forms of cavalry. Previously there had been no point in increasing the weight and power of heavy cavalry because everything which made that cavalryman heavier made him more likely to overbalance. But now, with saddle and stirrups, he would develop an almost rock-like stability. Heavy cavalry would now dominate the battlefield, with their bone-splintering knee-to-knee charges, until a suitable counter-weapon was found. That eventually proved to be the pike – over a thousand years later. The longbow had made life difficult for heavy cavalry, and early firearms had shown that the long reign of armour was approaching its end, but it was the pike which stopped heavy cavalry in their tracks, in every sense of the word.

The Huns proved to be the best cavalry since the Parthians. Led by men of remarkable efficiency and sense, the Huns earned the name 'the Scourge of God'. They appeared to live in the saddle, eating and sleeping there, and when on the move would cover as much as a hundred miles in a day. They were hideously ugly and this made them even more terrifying to their victims. Most of them had iron swords they had picked up in their conquests, a few had lances, yet others had nets and lassoes, and nearly all carried a bow, in the use of which they were highly skilled. Fortunately for their opponents, the period of their domination was relatively short. But in that brief horrific time they had set new standards of endurance and with their revolutionary innovation in the form of saddle and stirrups they had changed the pattern of warfare world-wide. The nineteenth-century British cavalryman might not have cared much for the suggestion that he owed his professional skills to barbarians whom their opponents thought were scarcely human, but his debt was there none the less.

The next stage in the evolution of cavalry came from the Byzantines in the second half of the sixth century. The Byzantines had an outstanding general named Belisarius. Belisarius built up an army which consisted almost entirely of cavalry and mounted it on a breed of horse which was a considerable advance on its predecessors. Previously, horses had tended to be nimble but too frail to carry much weight, or strong but ponderous. Belisarius managed to breed an adequate blend of agility and strength.

His troops were not merely well-mounted: they were also armed with a remarkable diversity of weapons. They carried a lance for the charge and a sword for close-quarter work; they also had a bow and a small javelin. The bow was a powerful weapon and Belisarius's tactical approach to battle would often be with a shower of arrows from long distance, a follow-up by javelins from a shorter range, a charge with lances and the clinching of victory with the sword. The last phase was seldom necessary as by then the enemy was either demoralised or dead. Clearly, such manoeuvres require tight discipline, or the javelins are thrown too soon and fall short, or the charge with lances is met by a still resolute adversary. Belisarius insisted that his cavalry should possess all the virtues and none of the potential weaknesses of the form of attack. He therefore trained it with meticulous and unstinted throughness. Everything had to be accurate, speedy and precise. Arrows and javelins must always find their targets; endless hours were therefore spent in practice. A suspended, swinging figure, rather like the medieval quintain, was used. The quintain was a medieval device consisting of a figure on a fulcrum: if the lance did not hit the target squarely, the lancer would be given a damaging blow by the quintain's arm as it swung round. It was very good for training and gave much amusement to spectators. Centuries later, tent-pegging and pig-sticking put a high premium on accuracy. A faulty aim could lead to disaster or death.

Belisarius captured Rome when it was occupied by the Ostrogoths. His contribution to cavalry development did not stop at tactical training for battle. The Byzantine world in which he lived, under the Emperor Justinian, has probably never been equalled in the complexity of its bizarre intrigues, many of them centring on women. It is not without significance that Belisarius's Chief of Staff was an Armenian eunuch. A fellow-general, and rival, of Belisarius was another eunuch, Narses. Narses was not only a brilliant general who swept all the Ostrogoths, Franks, and Gepids out of Italy, he was also somewhat unusual in that he did not reach the peak of his powers till he was eighty years old.

According to Procopius, a historian who accompanied Belisarius on his campaigns, the Byzantine cavalry could discharge their bows and find their targets while riding at full speed. Nothing like this would be seen again until the South

Medieval horsemen were taught to ride straight by attacking the quintain. A misdirected lance brought havoc to man and horse.

African War of 1899–1902, when the Boer farmers displayed an astonishing ability to shoot straight from a fast-moving horse. Belisarius's troops also used incendiary arrows. The Byzantines had either invented or developed the mysterious substance known as 'Greek Fire'. Nobody to this day knows exactly what constituted Greek Fire but it is thought it was some blend of petroleum, pitch and phosphorus. It could be blown from cannon or attached to arrows; it would burn even more fiercely on water than on land. During the Middle Ages it was widely used, but at the end of that period the secret of its manufacture was lost. In the nineteenth century a fresh development occurred with the invention of the incendiary bullet and this, of course, has been popular, though not with the recipients, ever since.

The staying power and courage of horses continued to improve under the Saracens, who had been a powerful military force from the seventh century onwards. The term 'Saracen' which became well-known in Britain from the Crusades, was applied to all non-Christians and therefore included Arabs and Turks. The Arab horse is too well-known to need description here but it remains to say that this faster, stronger and more mobile mount had an inevitable effect on warfare. Saracen methods of warfare were akin to the Byzantine, described earlier, but the Saracens spent more time harassing and encircling. They were also adept at cutting-off, i.e. isolating, small groups. This was a practice which became popular with British cavalrymen many years later.

An interesting contrast in styles appeared when the Saracens' light cavalry encountered Charlemagne's heavy cavalry in the ninth century. Charlemagne placed his faith in heavy cavalry and, as he considered his mission in life was to fight and subdue non-Christians, this gave him ample opportunity for conflict. Charlemagne appears to have been a slightly unorthodox Christian in that he had eight wives and numerous mistresses; and he once ordered the massacre of 5,000 Saxon hostages.

This period, which is known, with good reason, as 'the Dark Ages', had its effect on warfare for the next thousand years. Charlemagne's vast, ungainly empire contained many remote areas where local lordlings felt they were beyond the jurisdiction of their feudal superior. They therefore set themselves up with fortifications on mounds. These mounds, with steep sides, a barricade on top, and a wide ditch at the foot, were reckoned to be a match for any punitive expedition consisting of cavalry, as they were too steep for a warhorse to climb. After a brief period of frustrating siege the punitive force would, in theory, become bored and depart. The device might not have worked with lighter horses, such as the ones the Saracens used, but it seemed to frustrate Charlemagne's heavy cavalry.

Warfare and the apparatus of state were now becoming a burden. Previously, armies had cost little: soldiers had been able to live off the country and had manufactured much of their own equipment. But now there was an element of cavalry warfare which would bedevil it evermore. It was becoming increasingly expensive. Cavalrymen were no longer expendable; they valued their own lives and therefore protected their bodies with armour; their equipment was not a simple spear or bow but a heavy lance which might easily break on impact. The expense of an adequate supply of lances, swords, properly trained horses, helmets, breastplates, gauntlets and so on gave the Dark Ages cavalrymen the expenses and problems which would be all too familiar in the later cavalry regime, and find an echo in the Defence Review of the 1980s, when the staggering cost of main battle tanks, missiles, rockets and even body-armour, are considered.

The increasing cost of warfare led to various expedients for offsetting it. An early and long-lasting one was taxation. The section of the population least able to resist taxation was, of course, the peasantry, but there was a limit to what could be squeezed out of the serfs even by the most ruthless and overbearing landlord.

Other devices for raising money and soldiers had to be found. The most productive was feudal tenancy. The essence of it was that all land was held to belong to the monarch. The monarch granted tenancies to the most important people in the kingdom and they in turn granted land holdings to lesser beings. The rent of land held in this way was carefully assessed. Each large landowner would have to furnish a body of his own vassals, which would contain knights with their armour, weapons, and horses, and a number of armed foot-soldiers. The foot-soldiers were drawn from the peasantry whose only 'rights' were to work without reward. In time, however, many serfs, by virtue of stealing, saving, prowess in battle, or ingenious trading, managed to haul themselves up into a more privileged position. Successful campaigning was a profitable and popular activity to all concerned: however, as campaigning costs money, each feudal lord ground the faces of his underlings in order to produce the necessary equipment. Great store was set on wealthy prisoners, whose ransoms would keep their captors in comfort for decades. In the Middle Ages prisoners were often held for many years while their unfortunate tenants and relations amassed their ransom money. Caister Castle, Norfolk, was built with the ransom of a French knight who had been captured at Agincourt.

When we look at cavalry custom and attitude in the eighteenth and nineteenth centuries – or earlier – it is easy to see the traces of feudalism. Until the Cardwell reforms of 1870, commissions in the British Army were by purchase, on a fixed scale. Promotion was also by purchase, although in wartime it could also be gained by prowess in the field. This practice was often thought to date back to the Free Companies of the Middle Ages but, as we can see, it had its origins much earlier. At the worst the purchase system meant that an infant could hold the Lieut-Colonelcy in a regiment, and in consequence of the investment he, or his relations, would obtain the lion's share of any plunder. There were many such scandals. Somewhat better, though not without its grave faults, was the system in which a regiment became a rich man's toy. It would be dressed spectacularly but absurdly in order to gratify the egotistical whim of its owner; Cardigan's 'Cherrybums' were his pride and joy. However, uniform which looked magnificent on the parade ground was often cold, constricting and, in general, totally unsuitable for soldiering. Feudal levies were spared such idiocies and were only too glad to have a smock and some footwear.

As with modern warfare, economics were a limiting factor. The economic health of a country rested entirely on the sequence of sowing and reaping. Unless the peasants were available to plough the land and sow it in the spring, and again to harvest the crop, no warfare was feasible. Warfare was not in any case practicable in the winter months. That left the period from May to August. In consequence feudal service was originally set at forty days a year. If it lasted longer the soldiers – who were also the peasants – would miss the late sowings or early reapings. A compaign which cannot last for more than forty days has obvious limitations: it must take place near at hand, it must not involve lengthy sieges, and it must end promptly even though victory might be in the near future. In consequence feudal service was often commuted by payment – 'scutage' – 'shield money' which could pay for mercenaries. Mercenaries will, usually, fight for as long as they are paid to fight.

In this pattern we discern the regional associations and loyalties of British regiments, particularly cavalry regiments. Very often their members, officers and men, came generation after generation, from the same family. In many ways this was mirrored by the way the Indian army received its recruits: to serve in *the* regiment was a great honour.

But the system had its drawbacks. In medieval times (which may be described as the ninth century to the fifteenth), the cost of being a soldier was not high. Once you were horsed and equipped your expenses were few. It was very different with the cavalry regiments later. It became impossible in peacetime to enjoy life in a cavalry regiment unless one had ample private means. Of this, more later.

Feudalism also introduced what was known as the Age of Chivalry. Chivalry was the code of conduct observed by a chevalier, a caballero, or a gentleman. He was entitled to a coat of arms, but he was not classed as nobility. Chivalry was, in theory, practised by everyone, including the sovereign. The French had Orders of Chevaliers; the British had Orders of Knighthood. Medieval chivalry is often regarded with some cynicism nowadays, as being something which was applied to the privileged and denied to those most in need of it. A knight who had been unhorsed or disarmed could make an honourable surrender to someone of equal rank. (Welsh archers often made themselves very unpopular by despatching fallen knights and robbing the corpses; they felt that this was as sensible as sparing their lives and telling them to surrender to someone else who would make a profit from the ransom.) A member of an Order of Chivalry could ask for, and receive, hospitality, even when in an enemy country. The Saracens were reputed to be more chivalrous than the Crusaders. It seems, however, that chivalry only functioned above a certain social level. Peasants, being inferior beings, could be massacred, starved, tortured, beaten or humiliated at will. It is significant that the French Knights at Agincourt rode down their own allies, the Genoese crossbowmen, because the latter were thought to have been a failure.

This code of conduct has lasted into modern times, sometimes with improvements, sometimes with exceptions. Pauses in fighting have often occurred in order for the wounded to be recovered: the treatment of prisoners-of-war is theoretically governed by the Geneva Convention, which is the expression of a certain form of chivalry.

Chivalry and the Orders of Knighthood brought in an astonishing variety of developments, including heraldry. The mystique attached to knighthood, shown in the taking of vows, swearing of oaths of loyalty and acceptance of the idea that they were set apart and superior to their fellow-men, was very evident in the attitude of many later officers. In itself that was not entirely to be deplored. Although it led to certain conceits, it did incorporate the principles of loyalty, courage and sacrifice.

Heraldry became enormously complicated. Until the end of the eleventh century it was not customary to wear symbols or shields; the Bayeux tapestry shows none at all. At that period men, although armoured, were recognizable. A few years later when armour had increased, it often included an iron helmet which obscured the wearer's face. This led to an interesting incident which gave considerable stimulus to the establishment of heraldic recognition. In 1087 the aged William I (the Conqueror) was engaged in a battle against rebel forces led by his turbulent son, Robert, Duke of Normandy. During one of the brisker exchanges two unidentifiable knights met, and one was unhorsed. The victor, Robert, was about to despatch his opponent by a dagger-thrust through a chink in his armour when he heard a voice he recognized calling for help. It was his father, William I, whom he had unhorsed and was about to kill. Subsequently both men were said to bear an identifying symbol on their shields. Nobody nowadays knows what they adopted, but it seems possible they might both have borne the two lions of Normandy, which subsequently became part of the Royal Arms. However, arms earlier than the reign of Richard I (1189–99) are thought to owe more to the imagination of later heralds than to authentic use.

Nevertheless, once the custom of painting identifying arms on a shield had been adopted, it quickly became universal. Soon it was also the custom for a man's followers to bear his arms; the leader's own rank shown by the crest he wore. The crest of the Plantagenet kings was originally a sprig of broom, 'a planta genista'. Now the identification of living – and dead – on a battlefield could be established by heralds, who had computer-like memories for these matters. The word herald means literally 'strength of an army'. Soon heralds became indispensable. Leading noblemen all had personal heralds. Newly created knights who wished to bear arms had to discover from the royal heralds whether the coat was available or already in use. Heraldic design became an immensely complicated matter with quarterings on marriage, 'differences' for descendants, and so on. Its importance was closely tied to the feudal concept of rank. A man was either 'gentle' – derived from the Latin *gens, gentilis*, meaning a man – or a non-man, i.e. a serf. Middle class did not exist: traders counted as serfs. The test of being a gentleman was the tenure of land. There was, originally, no implication of gentle or courteous behaviour. This accounts for the somewhat arbitrary nature of chivalry, as mentioned above. Chivalry was applied merely to other 'gentlemen'. Needless to say, many coats of arms were adopted without reference to the crown, and although efforts were made to prohibit these they were not invariably successful.

But, once begun, the association of land with arms and rank and privilege was not allowed to diminish, even though later some of the armigerous families lost all their lands through folly, treason, or bad luck. The significance of being heir to estates and of ancient lineage, however villainous one's ancestors may have been, became deeply enshrined in English military tradition. In the Middle Ages it was impossible for a man-at-arms, i.e. a common soldier, to challenge a knight to single combat. If a knight offered single combat in front of his own army, the heralds in the opposing army examined his coat of arms and crest and decided who in their army was of equal rank and could therefore accept the challenge. During sieges, archers were very careful to pick their targets from unimportant people. At the siege of Rochester in 1216 King John came within easy crossbow range and an archer asked the castle commander, William D'Albini, for permission to put an arrow through him. D'Albini refused permission. Subsequently, when John captured the castle he executed all the garrison, including the archer who had been ordered to spare his life. Of course, in battles or sieges when the contestants were mixed up together in close-quarter fighting, serfs might kill knights, but this was not encouraged. The invention of the crossbow which could kill, anonymously and indiscriminately, from a distance was not popular, and it was banned at the Lateran Council of 1139 as a 'barbarous and inhuman and unChristian weapon'. It was all those things because it could kill the wrong people.

There were, of course, flagrant breaches of convention. In 1461 at the Battle of Towton, during the Wars of the Roses, Lord Dacre paused and took off his helmet in order to get a breath of fresh air. His coat of arms was spotted by a young archer on the other (Yorkist) side, who had good reason to hate the Lancastrians and Dacre in particular. He had stationed himself in the branches of a tree and neatly put an arrow through Lord Dacre. Most of Dacre's fellow-soldiers were tumbled into grave pits but Dacre, although a member of the losing side in what was considered the bloodiest battle in British history, was buried in the nearby churchyard, sitting on his horse. His tomb is there still to be seen.

These conventions and beliefs survived undiminished well into later centuries. The bullet, unfortunately, took no notice of rank and lineage when entering its target but that was one of the unfortunate aspects of military science. The hazards of the battlefield were accepted. But within the army itself it was fully realized that command could best be executed by the landed gentry. And even the landed gentry would be graded in a strict order of precedence. Many people were astonished to learn that when Robert Graves joined the Royal Welsh Fusiliers in 1914 (a regiment to which he was always proud to belong) it was the custom to address junior officers as 'Warts'. Nobody spoke to him when he went into the Mess. When the Colonel saw Graves and another newly joined officer at lunch, he said to the Adjutant:

'Who are those two funny ones down there?'
'New this morning. Answer to the names of Robertson and Graves.'
'Which is which?' asked the Colonel.
'I'm Robertson, sir.'
'I wasn't asking you.'

The meal concluded with the two being sent to the regimental tailor for 'not being properly dressed'. They moved up into the trenches the same night. A year later Graves and one other officer were the sole survivors of that entire officers' mess. The Colonel would not, of course, have expected otherwise. However, he would not have his junior officers going into action improperly dressed or speaking before a senior officer had given them permission. Standards must be maintained. The cavalry would have shared his point of view.

The Royal Welsh Fusiliers even contrived to have a polo ground in France, in spite of their being often sent up to the trenches. Polo matches took place between the battalions. Newly joined officers who were unable to ride had to attend a riding school every afternoon when they were not in the line. They were kept trotting round the field on pack saddles with crossed stirrups.

But in action the RWF were superb; officers, warrant officers, NCOs and fusiliers were second to none. 'With both battalions it was a point of honour to be masters of No Man's Land from dusk to dawn.' That meant constant patrolling. In battles they were no less efficient. Graves considered that their efficiency and reliability were based on drill rather than leadership. Drill gave a man a routine to follow when he was unable either to see or hear a leader.

If this was the situation with the infantry, it was even more notable with the cavalry. Graves was quickly made aware of the fact that although he came from an upper middle-class background he simply did not belong to the same social strata as the regular officers of the regiment. In peace-time a candidate for a commission in the RWF had not only to distinguish himself in the passing-out examination of the Royal Military College, Sandhurst, and be strongly recommended by two officers of the regiment, but he had to have a guaranteed independent income that enabled him to play polo and hunt and keep up the social reputation. 'In wartime these requirements were not insisted on', said Graves, 'but we were to understand that we did not belong to the regiment in the "special sense". We were warned that we were none of us to expect to be recommended for orders or decorations . . . they would be reserved for professional soldiers.'

These feudal views survived the horrors of the First World War and were not unknown, though somewhat softened, in many regiments in the Second World War. In the 1980s such sentiments would no longer be voiced, but this does not mean that they are entirely extinct. Although we have quoted an example from an infantry regiment a dozen cavalry regiments could match it. But the interesting question is: did this attitude, born in the eleventh century, produce greater fighting efficiency than any alternative? Possibly it did. It does not, incidentally, appear to be an exclusively British tradition.

4
Problems in the Field

The supremacy of the cavalry in the eleventh century in Britain – and even earlier overseas – had an interesting consequence. The armoured horseman, however crude his accoutrements, was clearly master of the battlefield. This was demonstrated at Hastings, on 14 October 1066, when William of Normandy's mail-clad horsemen swept through the English peasant levies and killed his opponent Harold. Having achieved his somewhat surprising victory, William was in no mood to be robbed of it. He did not wish to fight any more pitched battles, and still less did he wish to see his temporary encampments swept away by Saxon counter-attacks. In order to consolidate his victory he introduced into Britain that device which Charlemagne's distant and rebellious supporters had used to discourage disciplinary action by their overlord. It was to build a castle of wood on an earth mound. William had already seen the value of this type of fortification in Normandy and Anjou, and proceeded to create a network of similar structures all over Britain, at fords, important crossroads, entrances to valleys, and various other places of strategic or tactical importance. He made huge grants of land to the knights who had fought with him at Hastings and these feudal magnates secured their grip on these with their cavalry-proof castles. Later, some of the motte and bailey castles (motte=mound, bailey=surrounding enclosure) were abandoned but others developed into vast, prestigious strongholds. William was careful not to grant his followers land grouped in one area; he scattered their holdings all over the country so that any would-be rebel would have an impossible task if he tried to rally all his followers.

Four hundred years later, castles had become palatial and luxurious (by the standards of the day) and armour immensely elaborate and sophisticated. There is a widespread belief that a knight in armour could do little but waddle about if unhorsed. On the contrary he could be extremely mobile, climbing scaling ladders in sieges, or jousting on foot. In a contest between the Earl of Crawford and Lord Wells in 1398, Wells was knocked clean out of his saddle on the first course. Spectators thereupon protested that Crawford must be tied to his saddle. Crawford listened impassively to their complaints and then disdainfully vaulted from the saddle to the ground and back again. After that it came as no surprise when Wells was knocked out of his saddle again on the second course.

An enormous advantage of being mounted, in medieval battles, was that one could see what was happening on the battlefield. After the advent of cannon,

Norman cavalry winning the battle of Hastings, 1066.

Crusaders and Saracens locked in close combat at the battle of Jaffa in 1199.

King Edward I at the siege of Berwick in 1300. In medieval times the advantage of being on horseback was considerable.

Robert Bruce, lightly armoured, despatching the heavily-armoured Sir Henry de Bohun in the opening stages of the battle of Bannockburn, 1314. Bruce's more agile horse wheels away from the charge and enables him to deliver an effective counter-stroke.

battlefields were often covered by rolling smoke in which it was neither possible to see or be seen. In medieval battles the fact that the leader was mounted and close to his banner meant that his followers could keep him in view and obey his orders. In certain civil wars, such as the Wars of the Roses, there was a natural tendency to distrust anyone you could not actually see. This was soon extended to distrusting those who had a quicker means of leaving a battlefield than yourself, if the other side appeared to be at the point of gaining a victory. In consequence, at the Battle of Towton, mentioned in the last chapter as being so unfortunate for Lord Dacre, the opposing commander-in-chief, Edward IV, killed his horse in sight of his army before the battle as an earnest of the fact that he had no intention of making a premature departure from the conflict should his army be unsuccessful. His example was followed by subordinate commanders. Edward IV would have been conspicuous in that he was unusually tall for that time, being over six feet at the age of nineteen. Many of his followers were little over five feet. Such a ploy as killing one's horse was undoubtedly a gamble. Ten years later, when the Earl of Warwick was taking his force to battle at Barnet, he left his horse well to the rear, though still alive. Unfortunately for him, when the battle went against his side he left his departure too late and was killed before he could reach his horse again.

Two battles in the Middle Ages gave a preview of the disasters which can occur from having undisciplined cavalry. The first was at Lewes in 1264. The reigning king was Henry III, and he with his troops was lined up facing north, with their backs to Lewes Castle. Opposite was the rebel leader, Simon de Montfort. Occupying the position of honour on Henry's right was his son, Prince Edward, later to be the redoubtable Edward I but at this stage an inexperienced headstrong youth. Opposite Prince Edward was de Montfort's weak left wing; it consisted of half-trained Londoners for whom Edward had a special dislike, believing they had insulted his mother.

The battle began with a brisk cavalry charge by Prince Edward which drove the opposition before it. The Londoners quickly decided they had had enough and would return to their native city. Edward sped after them. It is said that some had even reached Croydon by the time he caught up with them. At the end of the day, flushed and victorious, with his horses completely blown, he returned to the battlefield. To his dismay he found the other side in possession and was quickly taken prisoner.

An equivalent disaster took place at Barnet in 1471. In the opening stage of the battle the Earl of Oxford, on the Lancastrian right, made a powerful drive towards the opposing (Yorkist) left wing. He drove them before him and the contestants disappeared into the early morning fog which hung over the battlefield. The troops in the Lancastrian centre were not over-pleased at finding their right wing now completely exposed, and moved across into the space vacated by the pursuing Lancastrians. Meanwhile a steady slogging match, toe-to-toe, was taking place over the rest of the field. Oxford's men, having chased their opponents off the field, now settled down to a little quiet looting in the houses of Barnet. Oxford made desperate attempts to collect them up but only succeeded in recovering about a quarter of their original numbers. With these he moved back to his former position, quite unaware that this was now occupied by troops sent over from the Lancastrian centre. When therefore Oxford's men came whooping and yelling out of the fog they were given a brisk reception by their former fellows, who were not sure whether Oxford's men were genuine Yorkists or Lancastrians who had decided to change sides at this critical moment in the battle. Changing to what men thought might be the winning side was a frequently used expedient in the Wars of the Roses. Some part of the confusion seems to have derived from the Oxford badge which, in a poor light, was easily mistaken for the white rose of York. The upshot was a battle within a battle, defeat for the Lancastrians after an initial undisciplined success, and the death of their commander, the renowned Earl of Warwick.

This sort of disaster might well have seemed excusable, or even inevitable, in the Middle Ages when commanders were less experienced and troops only partially trained. However, we find it also occurring nearly 200 years later during the Civil War. In the opening battle at Edgehill (1642) Prince Rupert, commanding the Royalist right wing, drove the opposing Roundheads off the field and pursued them for two miles. He would, no doubt, have gone further but just outside Warwick ran into some Roundhead reserves commanded by a dour but quick-thinking man, named Captain Oliver Cromwell. Ominously this little force checked the Royalist thrust which then wheeled off, disengaged, and amused itself by trying to plunder the Roundhead baggage-train. Meanwhile on the Royalist left wing an equally promising cavalry success was completely wasted by eventually swinging too wide. However, the

A medieval joust – a serious form of practice for warfare in the Middle Ages.

Roundhead cavalry was not much more effective, for when it had charged right into the Royalist centre and reached their guns it could not spike them because nobody had thought of bringing along the appropriate nails. The Roundhead cavalry, unsupported by infantry and therefore unable to hold its hard-won gains, retired. This battle was eventually indecisive, mainly due to the fact that the Roundheads were not astute enough to exploit the opportunity which Rupert's impetuosity had presented to them.

This was not the only occasion when Rupert nearly lost a battle through lack of discipline. At Naseby, just under three years later, on 14 June 1645, Rupert was once more commanding the Royalist right wing. He began proceedings with a vigorous charge. This drove back his opposite numbers, although Cromwell, now commander of the whole Roundhead army, had prepared for just this sort of contingency by concealing a troop of dragoons, commanded by one Okey, behind a hedge from which they could emerge to attack Rupert's right flank. However, the flank attack did not stop Rupert; perhaps nothing would have done. After his initial success he drove forward, looking for another target to attack but not finding one. During his absence from the field the Royalist infantry in the centre were hard pressed, not least by a charge from Okey's dragoons who, having failed to check Rupert, were now trying to make up for it and doing very well in the process. At this point Cromwell, personally commanding the main Roundhead cavalry force, sent them hurtling onto the hard-pressed Royalists. Rupert, when he returned with horses blown and ineffective, could do nothing to help. For a time he watched with dismay and then, with the King, left the field.

These were, unfortunately, not the last occasions when the cavalry pushed on too far and fast and returned unable to influence the battle, which they had helped to lose. Nor, of course, as we have seen, was it the first. Ever since men first began confronting each other on the battlefield in pre-Christian times, right up to the present day, it had been made abundantly clear that, unless one is very wary, the moment of apparent victory can be the turning-point to eventual defeat.

During the seventeenth century cavalry encountered cannon, musket, halberd and pike, any of which might have been said to portend its doom. Of these the pike and halberd were probably the most disliked. Both seem to have been developed and perfected by the Swiss, who frequently served as mercenaries. The halberd was basically an axe on an eight-foot handle. Jutting out behind the axe-head was a spike, often combined with a hook. Swung by an experienced infantryman the axe could shear through armour: at close quarters the hook could be used to drag a rider from his saddle.

1422–61. Chain mail, some plate armour, battle axe.　*Over the next twenty years both the knight and his horse became much more heavily armoured.*

The battle of Naseby, 1645.

Battle of Dreux, 1562, won by François de Guise over the Protestants – a good example of the way in which cavalry often had to confront pikes.

The pike was up to twice as long as the halberd. Owing to its length it required disciplined drill, for a carelessly handled pike could do more damage to a fellow-soldier, who was nearer, than to an enemy knight who was approaching. Held steady by a kneeling pikeman, a pike would check any horse and, as it reared or fell, another pikeman in the rank behind – or perhaps a halberdier – would be driving home a point or an axe-head. In the fifteenth century, pikes had eighteen-foot shafts with ten-inch steel heads. A phalanx of pikes, bristling with points, was an obstacle indeed.

However, the pikemen were not invariably successful, as was shown at the Battle of Pinkie on 10 September 1547. Pinkie is on the outskirts of Edinburgh. On the death of Henry VIII the ten-year-old Edward VI had become king. His position was 'Protected' by Lord Seymour who had married Henry's widow, but the political situation looked too vulnerable for the Scots and French, the 'auld alliance', to leave unexploited. Seymour decided to nip the trouble in the bud and arrived in Berwick with an army of 17,000, which included 2,000 light cavalry, and some mounted Spanish arquebusiers. Arquebuses were handguns and these Spaniards were very experienced in their use. The cavalry screened the army as it advanced. On the day before the battle when the English were in camp at Falside, Lord Home rode up and down in front of their position with 1,500 troopers and taunted the English to attack him. Lord Grey asked Somerset's permission to accept the challenge and when he received it went out with 1,000 men-at-arms and 500 demi-lances (cavalry lancers). It was an unequal contest for the English were fully armoured while the Scots had scarcely a breastplate among them. Home was mortally wounded; his son was unhorsed and taken prisoner. It was all in the best romantic tradition.

But it was not the only example of obsolete convention on that day. Late on the night before the battle Seymour received a medieval-type challenge to stake the issue on a tournament of ten or twenty men, the Scots contingent to be commanded by the Earl of Huntly. The Earl of Warwick, one of Seymour's commanders, was keen to accept but Seymour would not allow it. 'For', he said, 'the Earl of Huntly is not the equal of your lordship.' It did not occur to anyone that saving the lives of thousands might perhaps offset the effrontery of a minor Earl daring to challenge a major Earl. The Scots, incidentally, were already gambling with the ransoms of the prisoners they planned to take the next day.

With considerable tactical cunning Seymour moved his army in the general direction of the Firth of Forth. This was interpreted by the Scots as an ultra-cautious manoeuvre decided on in order to put him within easy reach of the ships, in case a hasty embarkation might be necessary. The assumption was incorrect, as the Scots quickly realized. As they came across to confront the English army, they came within range of the combined fire of the ships' guns and the English artillery. Before they had even been able to strike a blow the Scots were being torn to pieces by murderous and accurate gunfire. As soon as the Scots realized they had been decoyed into a highly dangerous position, Arran, their commander, adopted the only course left him which was to direct his entire army towards the centre of the English position.

So rapidly did he advance that the English army, thus far happily engaged in watching their own artillery and ships destroying the enemy, was surprised to find the

Scots hurtling towards them. Not liking the look of this, Seymour ordered an immediate cavalry attack. This went in with some force, in spite of the going, but as it reached them the Scots took up position with their eighteen-foot spears and contemptuously held it off. Time and again the English horse crashed into the charge but were checked; time and again the remnants retired, regrouped and came forward again. Behind that impregnable wall the Scots jeered at them as 'loons, tykes and heretics'. Lord Grey, the cavalry commander, received a spear thrust straight through his face, in through one cheek and out of the other. Nearly choked with blood, he reeled in the saddle, and his aides rushed to take him out of action. He would have none of it. 'Give me a drink to wash this muck away,' he gulped. He was given a flask of beer, the only drink available, and he swallowed a quart of it. 'I'm all right now,' he said. (This event occurred at Barbacklaw, just to the west of what is now the A6094.)

Nevertheless, in spite of considerable personal courage by individuals, the day was not going well for the English. Had the Scottish cavalry commander, Angus, known his business he would have put in a charge there and then with everything he had on to the flustered and frustrated English centre. But Angus felt that the infantry had been so mauled by the preliminary gunfire that there was no certainty they would be able to follow up and hold ground. He hesitated, and the delay was fatal. Warwick, meanwhile, was thrusting forward quickly and flexibly. He called off the abortive cavalry charge and instead instructed the artillery to lob cannon balls into the closely packed Scottish centre. His archers were told to reinforce the effect of this with a

Charge of the English cavalry at the battle of Pinkie, 1547.

steady steam of arrows, lifted high and falling obliquely. Meanwhile the Spanish arquebusiers galloped up to the pikemen, wheeled and discharged their pistols into their faces. Then they returned to do the same, occasionally supplemented by German mercenaries who were also arquebusiers but were operating on foot. (The technical name for this manoeuvre was a 'caracole'.) This combined onslaught on the Scots, who had held out long and gallantly, was more than they could bear; the line began to give and to fall back. Again sensing the right moment, Warwick ordered another cavalry charge. As it came forward there was hardly a pikeman to receive it in the torn and shattered Scottish line. It brought a savage and bitter ending to the battle. In the first stages of the Scottish advance some barbaric cruelties had been perpetrated on the wounded English; these were now discovered and triply revenged (leading, of course, to much subsequent bitterness). It was 'Black Saturday of Pinkie'. The Scots had made a fine fight of it against impossible odds for they had been fighting with a badly led, poorly equipped, medieval-type army against a well-drilled and well-equipped, balanced force. But Pinkie had demonstrated that cavalry could use the new-fangled weapons as easily as infantrymen, and future battlefields would see new and interesting tactics.

The war which would give the cavalry the chance to demonstrate how much it had learnt, or failed to learn, since medieval times, was the English Civil War. Although most of this was concentrated between 1642 and 1646, there were fierce and bloody battles in the second phase which began in 1648, and hostilities were not concluded till 1651. We have already taken a preliminary look at two battles, both of which proved unfortunate for Prince Rupert, but these, it must be emphasized, are not typical of the way in which cavalry was handled during the war. In fact, throughout the campaign, cavalry played a significant, often decisive, part. Furthermore, in spite of his mistakes at Edgehill and Naseby, Rupert was a brilliant tactician who had first commanded a cavalry regiment at the age of sixteen. At the start of the Civil War he was twenty-three. He had spent three years in captivity after a lost battle in Germany and had apparently spent most of the time studying cavalry tactics. After the Civil War he became an Admiral and showed himself as extremely capable in that post, too. Not all cavalry commanders were as versatile but Rupert was not entirely alone in his adaptability: Blake, a colonel of horse on the opposite side, made an equally impressive venture into command at sea.

Oliver Cromwell, who eventually became commander-in-chief of the Roundhead (Parliamentarian) army, never had any illusions about the rôle of the cavalry from the beginning. Cromwell is normally thought of as a dour man of the people, probably working-class: in fact he was a country gentleman, Cambridge educated, a Justice of the Peace, and Member of Parliament. When the Civil War began he, like many of the contestants, had no personal experience of war, but he was a student of the art and made shrewd appraisals. After the sorry showing of the Roundhead army at Edgehill he made up his mind very firmly over what the Parliamentary army required and said so in a conversation with John Hampden:

> Your troopers are most of them old decayed serving men and tapsters and
> such kind of fellows. Their troopers are gentlemen's sons, younger sons and

Prince Rupert of the Rhine. He won many victories but often tended to be impetuous.

persons of quality. Do you think that the spirits of base and mean fellows will ever be able to encounter gentlemen that have honour and courage and resolution in them. You must get men of a spirit that is likely to go as far as gentlemen go, or else I am sure you will be beaten still.

However, after the first year of the war Cromwell decided that the cavalry commanders needed more than gallantry and high spirits: they needed conviction and determination:

I beseech you to be careful which captains of horse you choose, what men be mounted; a few honest men are better than numbers. Some time they must have for exercise. If you choose godly honest men to be captains of horse, honest men will follow them. I had rather have a plain russet-coated captain that knows what he fights for and loves what he knows than that which you call a gentleman and is nothing else. I honour a gentleman that is so indeed.

The word 'exercise' meant training. Having stated firmly what he needed in the way of troopers for his cavalry, Cromwell was now beginning to see that dash and courage were not enough. What he needed was spirited, highly motivated commanders who would study their profession and, when in action, press home attacks regardless of cost.

As Cromwell was well aware, the cavalry had a prestige which the infantry, at that time, lacked. Of all the branches of the army a man could be in, which included infantry, artillery, pioneers, and engineers, cavalry was the most consistently dangerous. During the Middle Ages knights on horseback had enjoyed considerable immunity because of their armour, but this had been first eroded by the longbow, then disposed of by firearms and pikes. Service in the cavalry was once more highly dangerous. But this, and the fact that it was the place for the enterprising, the swift, and the fearless, gave it an air of distinction. And of all the rôles in the army, that of the cavalry was the most varied and interesting. Their job kept its members constantly on the move, and if they got into a difficult situation they usually had the mobility and speed to extricate themselves. This was not so with the infantry who, once locked in combat, could only emerge through defeat, death or victory. The fact, too, that the cavalry had the job of protecting the flanks while the army marched gave it a feeling of independence and responsibility.

Cromwell was trying to get the best of all worlds. 'Plain, russet-coated captains' implies a professional outlook. That professional outlook is extremely desirable if it includes a dash of unorthodoxy and charisma. Troopers will respond to a dashing, daring leader. He may frighten them to death but they will follow him. Furthermore the horse will know as much about his rider as anyone does, and respond accordingly. Horses are adept at judging the character and courage of their riders. An interesting feature of the horse, which was frequently demonstrated in medieval warfare (and apparently occurred in biblical times too) is that it enjoyed battle, being ready at all times to kick and bite the enemy.

Oliver Cromwell, 'warts and all', but a brilliant cavalry commander.

Although the cavalry of the Civil War had long since discarded the heavy armour of their predecessors, they still wore a considerable quantity of protective metal and material. There were, broadly speaking, four main groups of horse at this period. They were cuirassiers, lancers, (h)arquebusiers, and dragoons. Cuirassiers were quite heavily armoured and were almost a medieval survival. The cuirassier wore a helmet with a visor, a gorget (like a metal collar) to protect his neck, a breastplate, overlapping plates of armour to cover his stomach and thighs, and heavy leather boots. The construction of the helmets gave cuirassiers the nickname of 'lobsters'. This armour was not bullet-proof at close range, but was a match for anything further off; it could also protect very satisfactorily against lance thrusts or sword cuts. The disadvantage was that it robbed the wearer of mobility and, of course, required a heavy, and therefore slow, horse. Cuirassiers seem to have been less adept at wearing armour than medieval warriors were, for once unhorsed they seemed to find it very difficult to remount. Lancers were rather scarce. The reason was mainly lack of time and knowledge to train them. We shall return to the subject of training lancers later. Most of the mounted troops were arquebusiers. They wore a breastplate and a backplate, a triple-barred helmet, and a leather coat. A properly prepared leather coat, usually boiled in the process, would turn a sword cut. The arquebuses consisted of two pistols, but some of the troops also possessed carbines. They carried straight swords. A few had pole-axes. There was no rigid scale for equipment; a man carried what he knew would serve him best (if he could obtain it).

Dragoons were really mounted infantry and took their name from the 'dragon' – the small pistol they carried (it spouted fire like a dragon was supposed to do). Mounted infantry rode to the scene of battle, then dismounted and fought on foot.

Regiments in theory numbered 500, and were divided into six troops; later their numbers dropped to between 300 and 400 (except in the Roundhead army). Organization was approximately the same for both sides. There were four officers in each troop. In the major battles several thousand horses would be in the field. Many of the horses would be less than perfectly trained and it is not difficult to visualize the problems of command with runaway or riderless horses on all sides, horses frightened by gunfire, and riders who were too occupied with the effort of controlling their mounts to pay much attention to orders from their senior officers.

One of the more surprising aspects of cavalry development was the ease with which the cavalryman took to firearms. Later, there were examples of lancer regiments refusing to carry carbines, but this was due to obstinacy rather than lack of adaptibility. The arquebus had been invented in the fifteenth century, so was a familiar weapon by the time the Civil War broke out. It had a matchholder and a trigger and was reasonably reliable. The wheel lock was a later development but did not entirely supersede the arquebus.

Pistols took their name from Pistoya in Italy (just as the bayonet is said to originate from a siege of Bayonne). They represented a step forward for the cavalry, who were battling hard to recover lost ground, as far as effectiveness was concerned. In the early sixteenth century cavalry seemed to have lost the main quality which in the past had made it so formidable, the ability to produce a shattering charge. Even after

Arquibusiers with snap-hance carbines, from Instructions for the Cavallrie, *1632.*

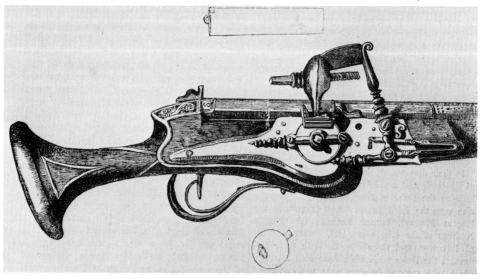

Breech-loading wheel-lock pistol (about the time of King Henry VIII), with a stock of ivory.

the advent of the pistol, cavalry charges were painfully slow and ponderous. It was only when less well-equipped forces, a couple of centuries behind in military thought, impetuously charged better armed forces and knocked them apart, that cavalry tacticians began to realize that their survival lay in a combination of the speed and dash of the past with the weapons of the present and the future. Many of these lessons were learnt in the Continental wars of Europe, and the knowledge came to England second-hand. On occasion, cavalry had been intermingled with infantry, and this had proved disastrous to both. But it would happen again.

The problem of how cavalry should be deployed in battle was a matter of considerable argument. The traditionalists believed that cavalry should charge in line (*en haye*). Others believed that the squadron should be several lines deep, perhaps ten or more. The latter formation was clearly weightier and more devastating in a charge, but if the charge was not effective the two front lines would be locked in combat while the others sat idly by. Even the 'caracole', mentioned in connection with Pinkie, did not always lead to the defeat of the infantry or pikemen. Sometimes the tables were turned by the foot-soldiers charging with their pikes. If taken by surprise cavalry could suffer horribly from a charge of pikemen.

A technique for making the best use of cuirassiers had been developed by Prince Maurice of Nassau, who is said to have invented this type of cavalryman because in the Netherlands neither horses nor ground were suitable for lancers. Prince Maurice's cuirassiers would advance, fire two shots, i.e. one from each pistol, then fan out and envelop the enemy, slashing away at his flanks. If the shots had found targets, this often led to a swift victory. But if the aim had been uncertain it was equally likely to be a prelude to a defeat.

The term 'hussar' was now coming into use. Hussars were originally Hungarian irregular light cavalry of dubious reputation. The light lances which some Continental cavalry employed were known in England as 'demi-lances'. Another term which came into common use, though with a changed meaning, was 'carbine'. 'Carabins' had originally been mercenary forces fighting under the French flag. They consisted of Basques and Gascons and carried arquebuses and pistols. Later a carabineer had a larger and more reliable weapon. During the Civil War much was heard of 'cornets' to describe a formation of horse. The 'cornet' was the standard which, like the medieval banner, distinguished each corps. It gradually came to be used to denote the 300 men of a cavalry unit. From this it became a rank and a 'cornet', like an infantry ensign, carried the regimental flag in battle. To this day certain infantry regiments call their 2nd lieutenants 'ensigns'.

The seventeenth century was a time of rapid development in warfare. Immediately before the English Civil War the redoubtable Gustavus Adolphus of Sweden, who had spent the early years of his reign fighting Danes, Poles, and Russians, found himself drawn into the Thirty Years War (1618–48). Gustavus Adolphus was a military genius who, because of his country's limited resources, had to make each part of his army more than usually effective. He was a student of military history but was flexible in outlook and not afraid of change. It was Gustavus who first introduced the idea of uniform. He also increased the proportion of officers to men, so that his orders were quickly relayed and executed. He lightened the amount of armour on all his cavalry: light cavalry were given no protection whatever and had to rely for survival on speed, manoeuvrability, and the sword. He also lessened the weight of firearms, which, as we saw, were improving dramatically in this period. The wheel lock eventually gave way to the flint lock which sprang a flint on to a steel plate which was near the flash pan. The spark then set off the charge. (The flint lock was originally called the snaphaunce; it owed this peculiar name to its origin in the Netherlands where it was seen to resemble a chicken pecking.) Gustavus Adolphus's tactics, weapons and methods were widely admired and imitated. Among those who derived much from studying the Swedish king's campaign strategies was Oliver Cromwell. Prince Rupert was also a great admirer of Gustavus.

Cromwell's 'professionals' won him a useful success at Winceby in Lincolnshire in October 1643, nearly a year after Edgehill. It was only a small battle but was important in its effects. Cromwell (now a Colonel) led a charge on some lumbering Royalist dragoons, but a pistol shot brought down his horse and him with it before he had gone a few yards. At that moment, Fairfax, commander of the Roundhead centre, suddenly noticed that the Royalist army had moved in an unco-ordinated way and there were gaps in it. He hurled his cavalry onto the flanks of the leading Royalist troops and tumbled them off the field. The rest of the Royalists decided that enough blood had been shed pointlessly that day and there was no point in adding theirs to it in a battle which had been so misdirected as to be past recovery. But for the Roundheads it was a vastly different story. Initiative, speed, perfect timing and tremendous vigour had brought them the first of what they hoped would be many cavalry victories.

Winceby was all the more gratifying because of the defeats they had sustained from the Royalists the previous July. In that month they had been beaten out of a strong position at Lansdown Hill, near Bath, on the 5th, and then had a worse thrashing at Roundway Down, Wiltshire, on the 13th. The latter victory was against heavy odds. After Lansdown the Royalists were short of ammunition and particularly so of match (to take the light to the powder). This last problem was overcome by the army commander commandeering all the bedcords in Devizes. These were then boiled in resin and made an adequate substitute for the normal issue.

Roundway Down is an open plain but on one side drops sharply on to ground well below. Wilmot, commanding the Royalist cavalry force of some 1,800, opened the battle by attacking the two wings of the opposing army. This left the infantry in the middle as puzzled spectators. The cavalry charges soon came to a halt. We have an account of a personal battle in one part of the field from the pen of Richard Atkyns, a cavalier. He wrote:

> Twas my fortune in a direct line to charge their general of horse [Sir Arthur Hazelrigg]; he discharged his carbine first, and afterwards one of his pistols, before I came up to him; and missed with both; I then immediately struck into him and touched him before I discharged mine, and I am sure I hit him for he staggered and presently wheeled off from his party. Follow him I did and discharged the other pistol at him and I'm sure I hit his head for I touched it before I gave fire and it amazed him at that present but he was too

well armed all over for a pistol bullet to do him any hurt, having a coat of mail over his arms and a headpiece musket proof.

Hazelrigg's force were cuirassiers and Atkyns felt greatly frustrated at not being able to inflict a suitable wound on his distinguished opponent. However, he was not to be put off:

> I came up to him again and having a very swift horse stuck by him for a good while and tried him from the head to the saddle and could not penetrate him or do him any hurt; but in this attempt he cut my horse's nose that you might put your finger in the wound and gave me such a blow on the inside of my arms amongst the veins that I could hardly hold my sword: he went on as before and I slackened my pace again, and found my horse drop blood, but not so bold as before.

Atkyns stuck to his task and now tried to pull Hazelrigg off his horse. Hazelrigg slashed at Atkyns's horse, cutting its cheek and half the headstall from the bridle. Reluctantly Atkyns decided that his only course was to kill Hazelrigg's horse. He stabbed at it with his sword. As Hazelrigg's horse began to stumble Atkyns aimed a further blow at his opponent and managed to prick him behind his helmet. Atkyns was then joined by two other cavaliers and thereupon demanded Hazelrigg's surrender. Hazelrigg had no option but was reluctant to give up his sword. Just as he had done so, a troop of Roundhead cavalry saw what was happening and charged up. Hazelrigg was rescued and in the process Atkyns was wounded in the shoulder by a pistol shot. Later, when Atkyns returned to the field he found his horse still alive. Within a few days it had recovered and he was riding it again.

Confusion was widespread in this battle and Waller, the Roundhead commander, who should have won an easy victory in view of his superior numbers, was the greatest victim of it. Finding that the battle had gone against him, he realized he must leave the field promptly if he wished to preserve his cavalry: at a safe distance they could regroup and return. Unfortunately for them, the point at which they had decided to gallop off the battlefield contained the cliff-like edge mentioned above. As they galloped away they went over the edge in a moment.

The catastrophe still left the Roundhead infantry stolidly waiting in the middle of the field, unaware of what had happened elsewhere. They were soon to learn their fate. On one side they were attacked by dour Royalist infantry from Cornwall; on the other by a charge from Wilmot's excellent cavalry. There was no hope for them. The Royalists had won a devastating victory on a scale which they would never emulate again; the Roundheads were stunned by their two rapid and unexpected defeats. They certainly needed a Winceby after that.

Atkyns seems to have been a tenacious fighter. He probably enjoyed the Civil War. He was about twenty-eight at the time of the fight at Roundway and, as he was reported to be rather fat and given to hard drinking, it is surprising he lasted the pace. In his youth he had been a student at Oxford for two years, had not done well, and then proceeded to Lincoln's Inn where he had done little better. However, a substantial legacy from his father had removed the need to try to earn a living and soon afterwards he married an heiress. All looked well for Richard Atkyns but before the end of his life he was in Marshalsea prison for debt, for he and his wife had dissipated his fortune by stupid extravagance. By that time they hated each other. He might well have wished he had fallen at Roundway in the days of his triumphs.

Another major battle of the Civil War took place almost exactly a year after Roundway. That was the battle of Marston Moor of 2 July 1644. The numbers on both sides were substantial, the Royalists probably mustering 13,000, but the Roundheads 9,000 more. Surprisingly, Rupert decided to leave York from which he could have preyed on the Roundhead communications, to give battle on a field which has probably not changed greatly in appearance from that day to this.

As any modern visitor will appreciate, Marston Moor was an ideal site for a cavalry battle. It would have been wise for Rupert to have attacked before the Roundheads had completed their disposition, but he had too many troubles to consider doing that until the best opportunity was lost. Some of his followers were busy looting abandoned Roundhead equipment, others had refused to come out until they received their arrears of pay. Although it might not seem important for a man's pockets to be filled with his due pay before he risks his life on the battlefield, it is in fact a matter which relates directly to morale. An unpaid soldier begins to lack faith in his own cause.

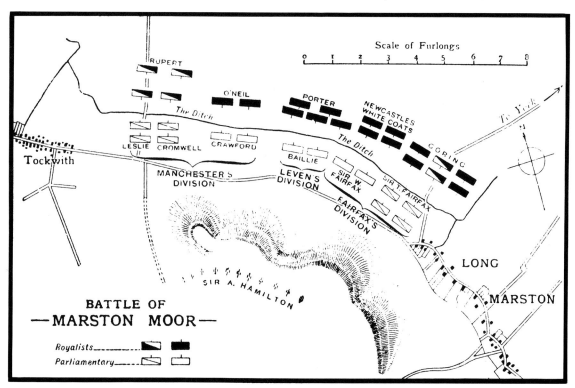

1 *Plan of the Battle of Marston Moor, 2 July 1644.*

Having missed their early opportunity to catch the Roundheads by surprise, the Royalists then waited for a second chance to present itself. Heavily outnumbered as they were, there seemed little point in battering themselves against superior forces. By the end of the day no opportunity had presented itself and the Royalists therefore lit fires and began their evening meal. Darkness had come early for July. This opportunity of catching the Royalists unawares seemed to the Roundheads to be too good to miss. On the sound of a single cannon shot, their army moved forward, achieving complete surprise. The reason for the early nightfall now became apparent. The failing light was the prelude to a thunderstorm.

At first the Royalists did well. Fairfax, on the Roundhead right wing, pushed back his opposite numbers, commanded by Lord Goring, and were off in pursuit. But unluckily for him, he was only pursuing a portion of Goring's force; the remainder saw the gap created by Fairfax's move, charged into it and went on to maul the Scottish infantry next to it. Fairfax then returned, saw the hopeless confusion all over his part of the field, despaired of collecting his forces, and promptly gave up further hope of playing an influential part.

On the Roundhead left it was a different story. Cromwell had come forward with some 3,000 troops and smashed into the opposition. Instead of letting their musketeers take the charge, the Royalist cavalry had tried to combine with them in a counter-charge. The musketeers found they could not fire without risking hitting their own men and as a result Cromwell gradually got the upper hand in a closely fought contest.

In the dark, the rain, and the confusion, men from both sides were under the impression that the battle was lost, and from both sides therefore, incongruously, men began to flee. At this point Fairfax came across and reported to Cromwell on his own disastrous failure. The situation at that moment was a drawn battle. Goring's men were now plundering the Roundhead baggage; in the centre the infantry were stolidly confronting each other with the Roundheads getting marginally the better of it; on the Roundhead right Cromwell, who had been slightly wounded earlier but was now apparently without ill effects, was surveying a conclusive but limited cavalry victory.

It was a moment for initiative and luck. Cromwell hastily assembled a cavalry force from the troops around him. He came forward, wheeled sharply, and then drove hard into the rear of Goring's forces who were happily celebrating their victory by choosing trophies from the battlefield. Few developments could be more disconcerting than those now presented to Goring's men. The one direction from which an attack was seemingly impossible had produced one; so surprised were they that they put up little fight. However, small parties of Royalists fought to the end; they included the Whitecoats and the Bluecoats.

The conflict, though it began so slowly, now turned into a particularly savage and relentless battle. Royalist casualties were very high: Marston Moor was second only to Towton in being the biggest and bloodiest battle ever fought on English soil. By this stage in the war, chivalry and mercy were much-dwindled commodities. The Roundheads stripped the Royalist corpses so thoroughly that by the following day every body on the battlefield was completely naked. Neither side, at this juncture, had much inclination to grant quarter. Why spare an enemy who might fight against you again in the future?

The above accounts describe but a few of the engagements of the Civil War which contained numerous battles, sieges and skirmishes. The war ended, not with the execution of Charles I in January 1649, but with the battle of Worcester in 1651. In the final battle Cromwell confronted troops led by Prince Charles, the future Charles II. Here again it seemed for a long time as if either side might win. Then, at a critical phase in the gruelling battle, Cromwell launched an attack on what he sensed was Charles' weakest point. Three more hours of fighting passed before he was proved right, but the victory was complete and the war over.

Civil Wars are, as the Romans knew, 'unholy wars', and this one caused much misery and destruction with little in real gain. The fight for government by consent ended with government by military dictatorship. But in the purely military sense it was a time of great progress. At the beginning of the following century Britain would be launched on a long, difficult Continental campaign. Without the experience of the Civil War she might have fared much less well.

5

A New Army

The defeat of the Royalists had largely been due to the 'New Model Army' of 1645. This was a creation of Cromwell and had been planned as a permanent standing army and not one which would disappear in the winter. In medieval times, as we know, it was usual for armies to disperse at harvest time and not reassemble until the following spring; the custom had continued with later armies going into 'winter quarters' until the weather improved and movement over roads and fields became easier. The 'New Model' was to have eleven regiments of horse, each of 600 men, twelve of foot, numbering 1200 each, 1000 dragoons and an artillery train. The Commander-in-Chief was Sir Thomas Fairfax, whose rank was Captain-General, the infantry was commanded by Skippon with the rank of Sergeant-Major General (out of which the word Sergeant was later dropped), and the cavalry was commanded by Lieutenant-General Oliver Cromwell. However, the cavalry was the senior arm and this is why a Lieutenant-General today is senior to a Major-General, anomalous though that sounds.

The 'New Model' adopted Gustavus Adolphus's idea of a uniform and all troops now wore scarlet. Up till this time the troops had worn the livery of the officers who raised them. However, traces of the former practice were continued in that each regiment wore the colours of its colonel as facings. These facings often gave regiments nicknames, which they later took pride in perpetuating. Thus the 5th Dragoons were known as the 'Green Horse' from the colour of the facings. Fairfax's own colour was dark blue and this may now be seen as a prominent feature in royal regiments, a curious feature when one thinks of its origins. The 'New Model' survived to cheer Prince Charles when he arrived in London as Charles II, although many in the ranks had fought against him. It was disbanded soon after, as Parliament was strongly opposed to standing armies. However, just before the disbandment was complete there was a minor insurrection against the monarchy in London. It was obvious that some form of regular standing force must be maintained to preserve the King's safety, and approval was given for a regiment of guards, a regiment of horse, and a regiment of horse guards. There was already in existence the Duke of York's troop of guards, which was overseas; it was soon to be brought back as the 2nd Life Guards. The Life Guards were thought to be former royalists, but the Royal Horse Guards were known to be from the New Model Army. To them was added the regiment of foot brought by Monk. It was marched to Tower Hill where it paraded. It then became General Monk's

51

English cuirassier at the time of King Charles I.

Regiment of Foot Guards or 'Coldstream Guards'.

The establishment of a standing army, however small, was viewed with disfavour and dismay by Parliament, which felt it had its hands full of problems with the new king; the army was therefore kept separate from the militia which was a Parliamentary responsibility through Lord Lieutenants of counties.

Twenty-five years after his accession, Charles II decided that the Grenadiers should be given precedence as the first regiment, and the Coldstream Guards made the second. By then a number of other regiments had been created. These were known as regiments of the line to distinguish them from Guards regiments. Subsequently the function of Guards regiments was not limited to garrison duties and they fought in the line with as much distinction as anyone.

In 1670 there was a development which, although made in the name of progress, almost ensured the superiority of cavalry over infantry. This was the plug bayonet. The bayonet did what its name implied: it plugged into the end of the musket, thus immobilizing it for firing though converting it into a replica of a pike. The time lost in plugging and unplugging was disastrous, but the plug was discontinued on the invention of the socket bayonet, twenty-three years later. The socket bayonet could be screwed on to the barrel of the musket and therefore did not interfere with firing.

After the initial founding of the regular army in 1660 little was done to add to it for some twenty-five years. However, just as the Foot Guards were acquiring distinctive names so was the cavalry. The cavalry regiments were designated the 1st and 2nd Life Guards and the Royal Horse Guards. To them was later (in 1684) added the Royal Dragoons. This last had begun somewhat humbly as the Tangier Troop. Charles II's wife was Catherine of Braganza and she had brought with her a useful dowry. One part of it was the port of Bombay, another was the fortress of Tangier. The Tangier Troop was created in order to defend the fortress. It returned to England in 1684 and became the 1st Royal Dragoons. These regiments preserved their distinctive titles until they were amalgamated and called 'The Blues and Royals'. The Royal Horse Guards had always been known as 'The Blues' from the colour of their uniforms.

In the following years, for the Dutch Wars of 1665–72, twenty-two new regiments were created but these saw little action and were disbanded by 1674.

The year 1685 saw a sudden burst of military expansion. It was the year of Monmouth's rebellion and James II used the occasion to create twelve more infantry and eight more cavalry regiments. Once the process of raising regiments had begun again, the military situation in Europe made further creation inevitable. One of the more impressive was the Black Horse in 1689. It was raised by the Earl of Devonshire and became the 7th Dragoon Guards. It had various titles, such as Ligonier Horse and the Black Irish Horse, and finally became part of the 4th/7th Dragoon Guards.

All the early cavalry regiments were dragoons. The Royal Scots Greys, now amalgamated with the 3rd Carabiniers (who were themselves original dragoons) to form the Royal Scots Dragoon Guards, were originally the Royal Regiment of Scots Dragoons. Because they wore grey they were known as the Scots Greys. In 1751 they became the 2nd Royal North British Dragoons, but in 1921 the Royal Scots Greys (2nd Dragoons). On this last amalgamation it was clear to all that the word 'dragoons' should once more be given place; however, as they were already Royal the presence of a Royal Scots regiment and a Royal Scots Dragoon Guards obviously had possibilities of confusing friends even more than enemies. For everyday purposes therefore the word Royal is omitted, the regiment is normally referred to as the Scots Dragoon Guards, the SDG. There is, needless to say, much sad head-shaking about the disappearance of the evocative titles 'Scots Greys' and 'The Greys'.

In 1689 another awe-inspiring title began to be heard. This was 'The Black Dragoons', otherwise Cunningham's Regiment of Dragoons. Less than a hundred years later they were the 6th (Inniskilling) Dragoons. In 1922 'The Skins' amalgamated with the 5th Dragoon Guards to create a regiment known as the 5th/6th Dragoons, but this mish-mash of a title was too much for the members of either regiment to bear; it omitted the word 'Guards' dear to the 5th, and 'Inniskilling' equally cherished by the 6th. Five years later a new title was given, the 5th Inniskilling Dragoon Guards. In 1935 the word 'Royal' was added, and there the title has stayed although, of course, within the service the regiment is usually referred to as 'the 5th D.G.' or 'The Skins'.

Meanwhile, from 1685, there had been a regiment known as 'The Queens' or '2nd Regiment of Horse'. In 1714 this suddenly became the King's Own Regiment of Horse; later in the century it became the 1st King's Dragoon Guards. In 1959 it was amalgamated with the Queen's Bays to become the 1st The Queen's Dragoon Guards.

The Queen's Bays had begun in 1685 as the Earl of Peterborough's Regiment of Horse. In 1711 it was the Princess of Wales' Own Royal Regiment of Horse. It became the Queen's Bays in 1721 and was usually referred to as 'The Bays'.

The 3rd Dragoons, which eventually formed part of the Scots Dragoon Guards, was at first the Earl of Plymouth's Regiment of Horse. The 4th Royal Irish Dragoon Guards began as the Earl of Arran's Cuirassiers, the 5th as the Duke of Shrewsbury's Regiment of Horse (in 1685), and the 6th, or Carabiniers, as the Queen Dowager's Regiment of Horse, also in 1685.

A trooper in the Royal Regiment of Horse, c. 1684.

The Hussar regiments had a no less striking set of origins. The 3rd began as the Queen Consort's Own Regiment of Dragoons in 1685. They remained Dragoons till 1861 when they became the 3rd (King's Own) Hussars. In 1958 the 3rd amalgamated with the 7th to form the Queen's Own Hussars, the QOH. The 7th were five years younger for they had begun in 1690 as Cunningham's Dragoons. They became Hussars in 1805.

The 4th Hussars had begun, in 1685, as Princess Anne of Denmark's Dragoons, and did not become Hussars till 1861. In 1958 they were merged with the 8th Royal Irish Hussars to form the Queen's Royal Irish Hussars. The 8th had once been Cunningham's Regiment of Dragoons (1693).

The 10th Hussars began later. They were formed as Gore's Regiment of Dragoons in 1715, and stayed as dragoons for nearly a century, that is till 1806. They joined with their friends and rivals, the 11th, to form the Royal Hussars in 1969. The 10th had been a Prince of Wales Regiment, whereas the 11th had been Prince Albert's.

The 13th had also been a later creation, as Munden's Regiment of Dragoons. They remained dragoons till 1861, after which they were Hussars. In 1922 they amalgamated with the 18th as the 13th/18th. The 14th, in 1715, were raised as Dormer's Regiment of Dragoons and they, too, became Hussars in 1861. Dormer's name was dropped five years later when the regiment became the 14th Dragoons. In 1861 they became the 14th (King's) Hussars. In 1922 they merged with the 20th Hussars to become 14th/20th Hussars, which in 1936 became the 14th/20th King's Hussars.

The 15th was raised in 1759 to take part in the Seven Years War, in which it distinguished itself. It began as the 15th Light Dragoons but became 15th (King's) Hussars in 1806. In 1922 it amalgamated with the 19th Royal Hussars to become 15th/19th The King's Royal Hussars.

The 18th Royal Hussars, whom we saw amalgamated with the 13th in 1922, had begun life in 1759 as the 19th Light Dragoons. In 1910 they became 18th (Queen Mary's Own) Hussars and took the QMO into the amalgamated regiment.

The 19th (Queen Alexandra's Own), whom we saw in the merger with the 15th, were also raised in 1759, and as Light Dragoons. In 1783, at the end of the American War of Independence, they were disbanded, but reappeared in 1786 still with the original title. However, in 1817 they became the 19th Lancers. Four years later they were disbanded once more and stayed in abeyance until 1858 when they were enrolled again as the 1st Bengal European Cavalry (East India Company). Three years later this lengthy and ponderous title was changed to 19th Hussars. They remained Hussars until the 1922 amalgamation with the 15th.

The 20th began in 1759 as the Inniskilling Light Dragoons but the word Inniskilling disappeared on their disbandment in 1763, at the end of the Seven Years War. However, in 1791 they reappeared as the 20th Jamaica Light Dragoons, were renamed the 20th Light Dragoons in 1802 but were disbanded again seventeen years later. In 1858 they became the 2nd Bengal European Light Cavalry (East India Company) but three years later were more simply the 20th Hussars. As we saw above, they merged with the 14th in 1922.

So much for Dragoons and Hussars: we turn now to Lancers. The first in sequence were the Royal Irish Dragoons, who were raised in 1689. In 1704 these became even more impressively titled as the Royal Dragoons of Ireland, but in 1756 became simply the 5th (Royal Irish) Dragoons. In 1799 they were disbanded but in 1858 reappeared as the 5th Royal Irish Lancers. The fact that they were originally dragoons, and fifth in sequence of dragoons, meant that when they became Lancers they were still numbered the 5th, although there were no 1st, 2nd, 3rd or 4th Lancers. In 1922, when the Army was reduced to peacetime strength with the accompanying financial restrictions, the 5th amalgamated with the 16th to form the 16th/5th Royal Lancers. The reason that the regiment was the 16th/5th, rather than the 5th/16th as might have been expected, was that the 16th had been Lancers since 1815. In order to clarify this point we have to take the 16th out of normal sequence. They, too, had begun as Light Dragoons, numbered 16th, as early as 1759, but had become Lancers in 1815. In 1815, as we saw above, the 5th was disbanded and did not reappear till 1858. The word 'Irish' has disappeared from the joint title and their full designation is 16th/5th The Queen's Royal Lancers.

The 9th Lancers began their life in 1715 as Wynne's regiment of Dragoons. Wynne's encouraging name had disappeared by 1751 when the regiment became simply the 9th Dragoons. They became Light Dragoons in 1783 but Lancers in 1816. In 1830 they became the Queen's Royal Lancers, being granted this title by Queen Adelaide, wife of William IV. However, in 1960, when they amalgamated with the 12th to form the 9th/12th, Queen Adelaide disappeared and they became Prince of Wales's. The Prince of Wales was not the present holder of the title but George IV before he acceded to the throne. The 12th had begun its life in 1715 as Bowle's Regiment of Dragoons, but received Royal patronage in 1768 from the future George IV when he was Prince of Wales. This title clearly took precedence as it was over sixty years older.

There remains the 17th/21st Lancers. The 17th were raised in 1759, but as the *18th* Light Dragoons. Four years later they became the 17th Light Dragoons. In 1822 they were redesignated Lancers and in 1876 became 17th Lancers (Duke of Cambridge's Own). H.R.H. the Duke of Cambridge was a somewhat eccentric personage who served for many years as Commander-in-Chief of the British Army. His language was noted as being particularly colourful and strong even in a period when vigorous expression was commonplace, but this characteristic does not seem to have transmitted itself to the 17th/21st any more than to any other cavalry regiment, in spite of the term 'to swear like a trooper'. The Duke of Cambridge gave his name to Camberley, the little township which grew up along the present A30 to see to the needs of the Royal Military College Sandhurst. The eastern part of the town was called Cambridgetown and the western Yorktown. However, the fact that much of the mail addressed to R.M.College Sandhurst, Cambridgetown, was delivered in error to Cambridge University caused the title to be changed to the less confusing one of Camberley. The Duke's name is now commemorated by the local hotel: Yorktown on the other hand has preserved its name but is a small part of its more prosperous neighbour.

The 21st, having begun in 1759, subsequently had three periods of disbandment, though never changing its title of 21st Light Dragoons until it became the 3rd Bengal

European Cavalry (East Indian Company). It will be observed that the 1st and 2nd Bengal European Cavalry had both been Hussar regiments. However, the 21st did not remain Bengal European Cavalry for long, for three years later they were 21st Hussars. In 1897 they became 21st Lancers (with which name they fought in the Battle of Omdurman) and in 1899 became the 21st Lancers (Empress of India's). The Empress of India was, of course, Queen Victoria. In 1922 the 21st and the 17th became 17th/21st Lancers.

In order to show the sequence and development of cavalry regiments we have run somewhat ahead of our survey of the battles in which the regiments took part. However, while these regiments are fresh in mind we might look at another, less formal, aspect of them.

It is, of course, well known that the most impressive, awesome title is liable to be derided or scoffed at by those who do not care to show respect for such matters. During the Second World War one of the most fiendish weapons, the flying bomb, was nicknamed the 'doodlebug' even by those likely to be incinerated by its arrival. Thus in the Army the distinguished regiments of Foot Guards were liable to be referred to disparagingly as 'the wooden tops', the Royal Corps of Transport as 'the jam stealers', and the cavalry collectively as 'the donkey wallopers'.

Although the other regiments of the British Army are well aware of the fighting record of the Household Cavalry (the Life Guards and Blues and Royals), this does not prevent their being nicknamed 'the Piccadilly Cowboys', solely because they are

'An Incident of Sedgmoor. A Private Gentleman of the Life Guards, 1685.'

stationed in London. An additional nickname, based on the fact that they still wear cuirasses for ceremonial occasions, is 'the tin bellies'. Visitors who observe the Household Cavalry performing their ceremonial guards or parades, immaculately accoutred, may pause to reflect that these most loyal soldiers are in direct descent from Hazelrigg's Cavalry which fought at Roundway Down, when their leader was in the running fight with Richard Atkyns described earlier. Nobody, these days, calls them 'lobsters', because their helmets are now different in design.

It is said that an insulting nickname is really a sign that your contemporaries regard you with warmth and affection. Whether the QDG consider the term 'the Queen's Dancing Girls' reflects these emotions is liable to doubt. Sometimes the nickname may reflect the fact that although you regret someone's misfortune you cannot help but laugh at it – the banana-skin syndrome. Many years ago, after the Bays had produced a boastful series of recruiting posters, their appearance was seen to fall somewhat short of their claims. They therefore tended to be dismissed as 'the Rusty Buckles'. But no one disparaged their fighting qualities.

The fact that numbers of Irish cavalrymen had connections with farming before they joined, or settled down to it afterwards, if they survived, gave rise to the agricultural nicknames. The 4th/7th became known as 'the Buttermilks', and the 5th DG as 'the Old Farmers' (in addition to being 'the Green Horse'). The 7th in their early days acquired the unusual title of 'The Virgin Mary's Bodyguard'. The title dates from the mid-eighteenth century when the regiment was sent to assist in protecting Maria Theresa, the Archduchess of Austria. In 1740 the Emperor Charles VI had died leaving a vast inheritance of territory to his daughter, Maria Theresa. The fact that an inexperienced woman had inherited a huge, sprawling empire was too much of a temptation for her neighbours and she was promptly attacked by Prussia, France and Spain. Britain, less perhaps for humanitarian reasons than from a desire to frustrate their European rivals, decided to aid Maria. The use of the word 'virgin' seems to have been somewhat jocular. She had been married four years but had not had any children. However, one was born the following year, the future Emperor Joseph II, and was followed by fifteen more.

Many former nicknames have now disappeared from the minds of all but regimental historians, but a few survive, although those who use them have little idea of their origins. The Queen's Own Hussars, for example, are sometimes referred to as 'the Saucy Seventh'. The term dates back to the days when part of the regiment was the 7th Light Dragoons. As we have seen, most regiments adopted a less than modest tone about their own merits when outlining prospects on a recruiting poster, but the 7th outdid them all.

The 8th Hussars acquired their nickname in more meritorious circumstances. At Saragossa, in the Peninsular War, the 8th captured the belts of the opposing cavalry. On the strength of this they were granted the privilege of wearing the sword belt over the right shoulder, as opposed to wearing it round the waist. In consequence they became known as 'The Cross Belts'.

Needless to say, the Lancers have acquired nicknames from their prowess with their principal weapon, which other regiments sometimes disrespectfully refer to as 'their spears'. The 9th performed with macabre distinction in the Indian Mutiny in

1857 and became known as 'The Delhi Spearmen'. Their partners, the 12th, enjoyed a somewhat different nickname, one based on their skill at manoeuvring into favourable attacking positions in battle. It was 'The Supple Twelfth'.

The 21st Lancers became known as 'The Grey Lancers'. The title came from their facings, and was not to be confused with 'The Greys' (now the Scots Dragoon Guards). 'The Greys' now derived their title[1] from their horses which were of pure white. White horses are never white in equestrian circles: they are always grey. The 21st Lancers, incidentally, rode black horses.

The 21st acquired a further title at Omdurman in 1898 – 'the Death or Glory Boys'. The occasion, of which we shall have more to say later, was a charge into the centre of a large number of fanatical dervishes. Winston Churchill, although not a member of the 21st, but of the 4th Hussars, had managed to get himself attached and took part. Three Victoria Crosses were awarded. The regiment appears to have been lucky to have survived, for the charge was ordered without adequate understanding of the nature of the ground ahead.

Not surprisingly the Hussars have taken pleasure in acquiring some rather unusual nicknames. The 10th Hussars wear chain mail on their pouches and for this reason became known as 'the Chainy Tenth'. This expression seems to have been confused with 'the Shiny Tenth'. When regiments are christened 'shiny' by their contemporaries it is less in admiration of their high standard of turnout than an implicit criticism that anyone can waste so much time on making himself elegant. Should it be suggested that the critics are equally culpable in this respect, the accusation will be smartly refuted: when another regiment goes to enormous trouble over turnout it is pure swank; if you do it yourself it is in the cause of greater military efficiency.

The 11th certainly attracted attention when the Earl of Cardigan commanded them, having bought himself the appointment. He was enormously rich and spent well over £100,000 for their horses and equipment. They wore cherry red trousers. Either this, or the fact that some of the regiment were captured in the Peninsular War while picking cherries in an orchard, has given them the name 'The Cherrypickers'. Lord Cardigan is said to have referred to them as his 'Cherrybums'.

The Peninsular War produced a peculiar but, in fact, highly creditable nickname for the 13th/18th. The 13th, then Light Dragoons, had always been proud of their immaculate appearance. However, they were in action so long and continuously in the Peninsula, losing approximately half the original regiment and numerous horses as they fought through murderous battles, that their appearance suffered badly. They became known as 'The Ragged Brigade', but it was a title of honour. As soon as they emerged from the campaign they became impressively smart almost immediately, but cherished the nickname 'The Ragged Brigade' as a proud memento.

The 14th/20th have a somewhat bizarre nickname as 'The Emperor's Chambermaids'. The term came from the Napoleonic Wars. When Napoleon's eldest brother, Joseph Bonaparte, was departing in some haste from the battlefield of Vittoria, where his forces had been routed, he had to abandon the coach in which he had planned to

---

[1] The original facings were no longer worn.

travel in favour of a quicker conveyance. The coach fell into the hands of the 14th, who were delighted to discover in it a handsome silver chamber-pot. This rapidly found its way to the officers' mess where, after appropriate cleansing, it became a mazer for champagne. There is, undoubtedly, a certain cachet in drinking champagne out of a silver chamber-pot; it is probably easier than drinking it out of a lady's slipper.

Champagne is, of course, a popular drink in the cavalry. Cardigan is said to have consumed a bottle of it during his solitary dinner after the Charge of the Light Brigade. It was considered a very health-giving drink, stimulating to all the senses. As a wedding drink it had replaced mead. (Mead, which is brewed from honey, was considered especially suitable for newly-weds, giving the word 'honeymoon' its special significance.) The cavalry, which was probably able to afford champagne more easily than certain other regiments, developed a ritual for opening the bottles with a sabre. The neck is not chopped off but snapped off by running the sabre up the seam of the bottle (the wire and foil having first been removed). The Scots Greys were noted for their fondness for champagne and were sometimes referred to as 'the bubbly Jocks'. However the word bubblyjock has another less flattering meaning in Scotland where it denotes a turkey cock!

6
The Clash of Battle

The year 1689, when the Jacobites made a last desperate attempt to put James II back on the English throne, was a time of great tension and uncertainty. As we have seen, it was a year in which many regiments were raised; it also produced the unexpected victory of the Highlanders at Killiecrankie. This last was a considerable setback for military planners, for the Highlanders, with sword and target (shield), charged and routed regular troops who were armed with muskets. The failure of the redcoats lay in the fact that once they had fired their muskets their only means of fending off the Highlanders was with their plug bayonets. Once these were fitted, and fitting a plug bayonet with a wild, naked Highlander bearing down on you with gleaming sword, required more time and nerve than was generally available, the muskets had ceased to be firearms. Unfortunately for the Scots the Jacobite leader, John Graham of Claverhouse, was killed in this battle and there was nobody to replace him and to prevent his army falling apart. The war lingered on in the depths of the Highlands but was overwhelmed by far more serious troubles in Ireland where the French were assisting with officers, arms, and money.

Somewhat surprisingly there was also a Frenchman serving on William III's side. This was the Duke of Schomberg. He had been expelled from France for refusing to become a Roman Catholic. In 1690 he took command of the future 7th Dragoons, 'the Black Horse' which we saw earlier had been raised as the Earl of Devonshire's Regiment of Horse (also the 10th Horse!). Under the French Duke it became the Schomberg's Horse, or the 8th Horse, fifty years later it was the 4th Horse, and eventually became successively the 7th Dragoon Guards and 4th/7th Dragoon Guards. The war in Ireland produced many embittered and desperate struggles, notably the Battle of the Boyne (where 6,000 out of James II's 30,000 troops were French) and the siege of Limerick. At the conclusion of hostilities 11,000 Irish went overseas to serve in the French army. There were, at this time as at many others, large numbers of Irish fighting with the British army; therefore, in the following century, there were many occasions when Irish were fighting Irish, although on paper English were fighting French.

In the present century, when our minds have been taken up first with the threat from Fascist Italy, Nazi Germany, and totalitarian Japan, and then with the steady menace euphemistically described as 'the Cold War', it may come as a surprise to realize under what shadows our ancestors lived. In the 1690s Louis XIV of France wished to dominate Europe, to capture the Netherlands and to invade England. The fact that he was forced to sign a peace in 1697, after a series of military and naval defeats, did nothing to deter the ambitious 'Sun King'. Four years later his armies were in the field again. The reason for this war was that the throne of Spain had been left to a young Frenchman, the Duke of Anjou, who was Louis XIV's grandson. The legacy was the defiant act of a dying man who was tired of hearing people quarrel over what would happen to his possessions after his death. However, any arrangement which put France into alliance with Spain, which was already occupying a good portion of the Netherlands (now Belgium) and Italy, was bound to produce immediate reaction from Britain. William III thereupon assembled as strong an alliance as he could from the other European powers before he, too, died (1702). The fact that the dispossessed monarch, James II, had also died, and his son, James III, been promptly proclaimed rightful King of England by Louis XIV, did little to endear the French to the British at that moment.

William III's alliance had a slightly ramshackle air to it, being composed of England, Holland, Austria, and many small European states (Portugal and Savoy joined later) but it had a general of outstanding quality in the person of John Churchill, later to be 1st Duke of Marlborough. Louis was in the unusual position of being allied to his traditional enemy Spain, although not all the Spaniards were whole-heartedly in favour of having a Frenchman for their king.

The war did not begin properly till 1703: the fact that there were four separate theatres made it particularly interesting from the cavalry point of view. Marlborough was a general with views on warfare which any enthusiastic cavalryman could not but view with favour. He knew exactly where he wanted to go and what he wanted to do when he got there. He believed that surprise was virtually essential if victory was to be achieved, and that it should best be employed in a constant programme of offensive actions. Force should be concentrated where it was needed but never wasted in unplanned actions. He would never take unnecessary risks, realizing that spectacular gambles which cost lives for little gain were always to be avoided. He was quite happy to share his triumphs with his allies, unreliable and undeserving though some of them were. Finally, there was nothing rigid about Marlborough: he would have been as happy commanding a Roman cohort under Julius Caesar as he would a tank division in the Western Desert in 1943. He was criticized for alleged duplicity in politics but was implicitly trusted by the soldiers who served under him. Perhaps the greatest factor in his popularity was not that he cared for soldiers' welfare, although undoubtedly he did, but that he was a military genius with a special aptitude for winning battles with minimal casualties.

In order to give an intelligible and coherent account of the cavalry actions in the ensuing war, which became known as 'The War of the Spanish Succession', we shall first trace the events of the main campaigns, then put certain selected cavalry actions into context.

At the outset Marlborough was handicapped by having with him two Dutch deputies, of no talent except in obstruction and delay. This was the price exacted by the Dutch government for accepting an English general as Commander-in-Chief. Marlborough's first task therefore was to outwit these two before they could frustrate

The Battle of Warburg 1760.

10th Hussars in the Seven Years War (1756–63).

10th Hussars at the beginning of the Napoleonic Wars. Uniform of 1783–1803.

5th Dragoons in 1780.

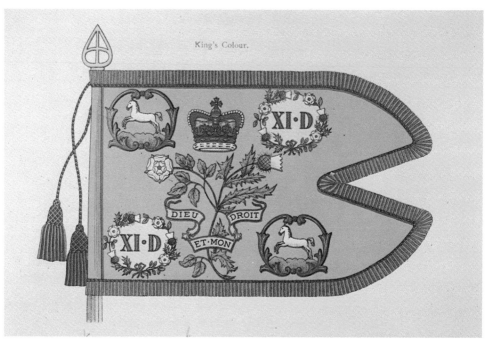

Standard of the 11th Hussars (then Dragoons) 1788 (King's Colours). The white horse, top left and bottom right, was common to all cavalry regiments, as the special badge of the Hanoverian dynasty. The entwined roses and thistles represents the union of England and Scotland.

The Battle of Willems 1794. The 7th Dragoons to the front.

7th Hussars engaged in a lively skirmish while on picquet duty in the Napoleonic Wars.

12th Light Dragoons at Salamanca, 1812.

Waterloo, June 18th, 1815. Final stages: 'The Whole Line will Advance'.

1820   17   1824   18   1826   19

17TH LANCERS   DRAGOON GUARDS   HEAVY DRAGOONS

1832   25   1835   26   1835   27

15TH KING'S HUSSARS   HUSSARS   LANCERS

Cavalry helmets of different periods.

John, 1st Duke of Marlborough. A commander of genius who was at the front of many battles.

his plans. The British army contributed a mere fifth to the army of 60,000 which was under his command; and he faced superior numbers of French. However, the French dispositions, as Marlborough noted with satisfaction, were very extended and trying to cover too much ground. His Dutch colleagues wanted Marlborough to take up defensive positions along their frontier; instead Marlborough made a sequence of rapid offensive marches towards the French who retreated in some surprise while trying to guess his intentions. When it became clear that the French were in considerable disarray, Marlborough was in an ideal position to deliver an attack on their weakest point, but his Dutch assistants vetoed the move and the French escaped unhurt.

Marlborough then tempted the French to come north and when they were there slipped behind them and cut them off from their bases. A full-scale attack might well have ended this part of the war but the Dutch objected; Marlborough's only satisfaction was to have captured all the French fortresses along the Meuse.

Much of 1703 was spent in planning for 1704. Marlborough knew only too well that the best move the French could make would be to join forces with the Bavarians and together to attack Vienna, the heart of the Austrian empire. Somewhat inconveniently for the 'Grand Alliance', as Marlborough's forces were called, the Elector of Bavaria had joined his fortunes with the French, taken the field with a French army, and already helped to defeat an Austrian force. This situation was highly perilous to the Grand Alliance for, if the forthcoming move against Vienna succeeded, Austria would collapse and the French be on their way to complete victory. While Marlborough could see the urgent need for him to intervene in this quarter, his Dutch colleagues were equally determined that he should not. They wished his army (and theirs) to remain in Holland, defending the country against any French attack. All Marlborough's brilliant tactical plans for drawing on the French, cutting them off, and defeating them, came to nothing against the resolute refusal of the Dutch to co-operate.

He decided therefore that it was necessary to deceive his friends as well as his enemies. He persuaded the Dutch, not without difficulty, that the best course for all concerned would be for the army to move on to the Moselle with the ultimate aim of pushing the French back to Paris. The Dutch agreed, though not without misgivings; at least from this position Marlborough could double back and intercept any French thrust into Holland. He left a token force for the necessary delaying action. It was an interesting move tactically, to no one more than the French king who wondered whether Paris or Alsace might now be in the greater danger. Marlborough had, rather surprisingly for a man with his normal attitude to security, mentioned his options quite openly, even writing down one in a letter which was certain to be 'leaked'. Next he marched to Coblenz, and made one or two diversionary moves which set his French opponents on the defensive. Then, in a moment of apparent madness, he set off briskly to Heidelberg, his cavalry smoothing the path ahead. At Mannheim he met Prince Eugène, a talented and venturesome commander, and Prince Louis of Baden, a man of no ability but good resources of troops. The entire march took six weeks; to have covered 250 miles over the roads and with the transport of that day was an astonishing achievement. It was the more so because the men arrived fit, well-fed, and well-equipped. Marlborough had made his preparations well in advance.

In order to capture the vital town of Munich, Schellenberg hill must first be occupied. The critical battle took place in the afternoon, after the soldiers had marched fifteen miles. But their blood was up. Many regiments distinguished themselves on that day, none more so than the 5th Dragoons and the Scots Greys. The joint French-Bavarian army were said to have lost 10,000 in the battle.

But it was a step, not the end of the campaign. The remaining Bavarians fell back, waiting for French reinforcements. Within a few days these had arrived. Prince

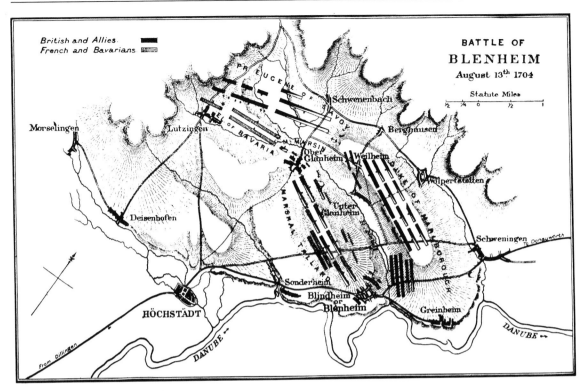

2 *Battle of Blenheim, 13 August 1704.*

Eugène's army now joined Marlborough's. The French-Bavarian army, under Marshal Tallard, was strongly established around a village named Blindheim (later corrupted to Blenheim) on the Danube, in western Bavaria. The French had superior numbers and were too well prepared for a successful attack to be possible. The Allies were also outnumbered two to one in guns. By marching twenty-four miles and crossing three rivers on the previous day Marlborough had arrived at a point three miles from Blindheim. That was April 11th. By 3 am the next day his army was on the move again and had reached the outposts of the French army by 6 am. Marshal Tallard's position was indeed an excellent one. His right wing was protected by the Danube; his left by wooded hills. The centre, including Blindheim, was full of experienced infantry, and there was a huge cavalry force of eighty squadrons poised ready to charge the Allies if they tried to cross the Nebel river and the surrounding marshland. And there, in positions from which it would be difficult to dislodge either side, the two armies inspected each other, eyeball to eyeball.

The attack began slowly round about midday. The intervening time had not been wasted. During the morning preparations had been made for crossing the Nebel, which ran across the front of the French position. When the crossing took place Marlborough's tactics surprised and disconcerted the French. Cavalry and infantry were intermingled and, advancing in line, were playing havoc with the defence. The

French cavalry tried to turn to attack but their efforts to interfere were frustrated by brisk fire from the British muskets. Eugene, on the extreme right, was not so happy and was badly mauled by the French cavalry. Blenheim looked like becoming a steady pounding battle of attrition in which victory would eventually go to the army with the greatest numbers. But that was not Marlborough's idea. In mid-afternoon he launched almost all his cavalry force with one headlong burst into the French centre. This was a departure from his usual tactics which were to enfold with his wings, but it was dictated by the lie of the ground. The French cavalry were knocked back on to their infantry, then forced back to the Danube, while the infantry tried to make their escape through the flanks. But Marlborough had anticipated the move to escape and had the Scots Greys and 5th Dragoons heading the infantry off. Tallard himself was captured by the 5th DG and delivered to Marlborough. Marlborough was very polite and considerate to his defeated opponent.

Allied losses were surprisingly small for a victory of this magnitude: 13,000 was the figure given against the surprising round number of 40,000 quoted for the Franco-Bavarian army. Among the regiments receiving Battle Honours were the KDG, the 3rd DG, the 5th DG, the 6th DG, the 7th DG, the Royal Scots Greys and the 5th Lancers.

The most astonishing aspect of this fierce and bloody battle as far as the Scots Greys were concerned was that, although many had sustained wounds, not a single officer or man had been killed.

In the history of the British army, and no doubt of many armies, there were several occasions when women enlisted and served as men without being detected. One such case occurred with the Scots Greys at this time. The wife of a man who had enlisted in the Scots Greys decided, when he had gone, that she would pass herself off as a man and enlist too, with the aim of reaching her husband and fighting side by side with him. This she did, and was in action with him at Schellenberg, where she was wounded in the leg. She was not, however, discovered; the medical attention of those days did not extend to much more than clapping a dressing on a wound. She recovered and continued to serve. Her unmasking came two years later at Ramillies where she was again wounded, but the regiment was so touched with her story that she was allowed to continue as a sutler – a follower with permission to sell provisions to the regiment. When she died in 1739 the regiment buried her with full military honours.

The year 1705 dawned full of promise for Marlborough but his hopes were soon to be blunted by the unreliability of his allies. The Dutch were less pleased with his victory at Blenheim than they would have been if they had not felt he had left them exposed in order to achieve it. Prince Eugène had now departed to Italy; the Austrians felt secure and had no interest in fighting in northern Europe. Marlborough made several feints at the French in northern France but any whole-hearted attempt to exploit their confusion was defeated by his Dutch colleagues who were unwilling either to help him or let him out of their sight. The year passed tediously in a series of minor skirmishes. The brightest spot as far as Marlborough was concerned was when he personally led a charge of the Scots Greys. After a night march, the Alliance had made a dent in the French lines but was hard pressed when the French quickly rallied reinforcements. The cavalry charge, in which several regiments in addition to the

Greys took part, turned the scales and enabled the Alliance to capture many trophies from the French.

At the beginning of 1706 Marlborough felt so frustrated that he decided to attack the French again whether he received Dutch aid or not. This meant a thrust into Flanders, where the French were well-positioned, near to a village named Ramillies. His opponent was the French general Villeroi, a man who was well aware of what had happened to the French dispositions at Blenheim and had no intention of letting a similar disaster occur at Ramillies. Marlborough obligingly gave him every indication that a replica of the Blenheim battle was all that was in his mind. He noted that Villeroi was very strong in the centre, with ample supplies of cavalry and infantry. The remainder of the French cavalry was concentrated on the right, except for a reserve lying behind the infantry on the left. Each army numbered approximately 60,000. As at Blenheim the French were relying on marshy ground in front of their position to slow down any advance by Marlborough's army. Ramillies lay in the centre of the French position, to the right was Tavières and the river Meheigne, and to the left was Offuz and the somewhat oddly named Autre Eglise.

Marlborough took until midday to assess his options, then suddenly launched the Dutch troops on his left into the general direction of Tavières. They did well and captured the township. However, the move was not interpreted by Villeroi as the main threat, and, as the rest of Marlborough's army now began to press on the French centre and left, Villeroi concentrated his defence in those areas. The fact that large numbers of British infantry were positioned on the right wing created the impression that whatever happened elsewhere the final thrust would be from that quarter. But that theory reckoned without Marlborough's devious tactical thinking. The dispositions of the two armies were in the shape of a crescent with the tips inclined back towards the Alliance. It was therefore a quick and relatively uncomplicated matter for Marlborough to switch his cavalry from one wing to the other. This he now proceeded to do. While keeping Villeroi apprehensive about the next threat to his left (from the Allied right), Marlborough transferred the bulk of his own cavalry from right to left.

The next blow came with stunning force from the Allied left. Marlborough used the majority, but not all, of his cavalry. His technique was to smash down the opposition with momentum rather than to fight a way through with sword and pistol. Before the French realized what was happening the onslaught had engulfed them. Then the Allied cavalry swung right and moved in behind Ramillies, driving their enemy before them and leaving them broken in their tracks. As the bewildered French army tried to withdraw or flee, Marlborough's reserve cavalry was now launched after them, cutting them to pieces and pressing home the pursuit. Inevitably, French losses were high: they amounted to a quarter of their army; in addition they lost the majority of their guns. This breakthrough enabled Marlborough to capture one fortress after another as he cleared the Netherlands of French. Louvain, Brussels, Ghent, Menin, and Ostend all fell into his hands. Marlborough had demonstrated beyond all possible doubt that he was one of the world's great cavalry commanders. He had won a battle before the French had realized what was happening, and he had done it under their noses, for their army had had every opportunity of observing his moves from the Ramillies heights. Later in the year the Allied army had further encouraging successes in Spain, so much so that Louis XIV offered peace. Unwisely, the Allies rejected the offer, the acceptance of which would have saved many lives. The Alliance considered that the year 1706 had been so successful that a few more victories during the next campaigning season would have the French begging for peace at any price.

This view reckoned without two factors which could upset any calculation. The first was the weather: a wet winter was followed by an equally wet summer. The second was the relentless determination of Louis XIV, who was driven by an incurable obsession to conquer and humiliate the Dutch. He watched with satisfaction as the Dutch prevailed on Marlborough not to begin hostilities again in 1707; in consequence by the beginning of the following year he had two substantial armies in the field. One was deployed in the Netherlands, the other on the Upper Rhine. Marlborough confronted the first, Prince Eugène the second.

The French opened the 1708 campaign by capturing Bruges and Ghent; they then marched to Oudenarde which Marlborough had captured two years before. This move threatened Marlborough's communications with Britain. As the presence of a large, unpredictable French army in the area also posed an obvious threat to Brussels, Marlborough had to take steps to make sure that that city was adequately defended. He was cheered to learn that Eugène was now heading towards Maastricht and an early junction between their two armies now looked probable. He therefore decided to turn the tables on the French who had been threatening to cut his communications, by advancing and cutting theirs. The French soon realized their danger and began to move back to a safe position in Flanders. However, Marlborough was hard after them, marching his army of 80,000 men twenty-eight miles in twenty-four hours. He sent his advance guard to cross the Scheldt on pontoons close to Oudenarde; the French crossed at Gavre. Marlborough's advance party was commanded by the Earl of Cadogan and included fifteen squadrons of cavalry. This had a brisk encounter with the French who had just crossed the river. The commander of the French in this area was the young, reckless but inexperienced Duke of Burgundy. Burgundy decided to stake everything on a full-scale attack on Marlborough's army, although he would have been wiser to choose ground more favourable to himself. The ensuing events were an interesting proof of the thesis that a battlefield is not simply a place where two armies meet and fight, but a site onto which one commander, probably the victorious one, has manoeuvred his army so that every advantage of the ground will lie with his own troops.

Marlborough deployed his infantry on the left, Cadogan and his mixed force of cavalry and infantry in the centre, and a strong body of the British cavalry, with Eugène's troops, on the right; he also stationed another cavalry force on the extreme left. The battle was then won by stealth. While the rest of the army was engaged in an indecisive battle, Marlborough's cavalry manoeuvred around the French right flank, a tactic which they were able to execute unobserved as they were sheltered by high ground. At the end of the day the French were not merely surrounded but also completely cut off from their line of retreat. Most of their forces had no option but to be taken prisoner. Marlborough would have liked to further this success with an advance into France but, as he had learnt to expect, such a proposal found no favour with his allies. He therefore decided to capture Lille, as this would be a powerful obstacle to any future invasion. Lille, said to be impregnable, certainly proved a powerful nut to crack; its investment required a siege train of close on two hundred guns which had to be brought by road from Brussels. The escorting cavalry discharged their duties with such belligerent efficiency that the French were deterred from making more than half-hearted attempts to delay the convoy. However, as the siege dragged on from August to September, the need for more ammunition became urgent. To satisfy this, yet another convoy set out, this time from Ostend where the British ships had unloaded the all-important cargoes. This time the French made a more thoroughgoing attempt to disrupt the convoy, and the cavalry were hard pressed to protect it. In one engagement, at Winendaele, there was a brisk battle in which the casualties were numbered in thousands. The convoy got through in the nick of time. Other convoys followed, though now with less difficulty. Meanwhile the French in the north tried to divert attention from Lille by threatening Brussels again, but that move was quickly disposed of by a surprise attack from Marlborough. Lille eventually fell on 10 December.

The war, which had now drifted on into its seventh year, had exhausted the resources of both sides. The Allies were too suspicious of Louis XIV to offer him any terms but those too humiliating for him to accept, and he, in his turn, gave no sign that several years of unsuccessful war had, in any way, distracted him from his ambition of ruling most of western Europe. It seemed the end of the conflict could only come if the Allies rode into Paris, whenever that might be. Nobody in his wildest nightmares imagined that the war would drag on for another five years. In what he thought was a final desperate throw, Louis XIV summoned all the resources France could offer, and appointed a new commander, the Duke of Villars, a man not unlike Marlborough himself. Villers took the field with 80,000 men. The combined Allied force had a numerical advantage in that Marlborough and Eugène's joint army totalled 120,000. With the capture of Paris in mind the Allied army had no option but to destroy the fortresses standing in the way. As with Lille, this task proved more difficult than anyone had thought possible. Tournai lost the Allies 5,000 men. Mons was the next stop, but as the Allied forces invested it Villars copied the switch tactics in which Marlborough normally specialized. Villars' next move would be to lift the siege, but first he had to decoy Marlborough's army out of position to defend it. Having posed his threat to the Mons besiegers, he drew back into the woods, fortified his position and waited to see what Marlborough would do.

Marlborough, for his part, realized that his own best course was to continue towards Paris and then, when Villars had been drawn out of his chosen position, to turn on the Frenchmen in an attack over ground of his own choosing. But Marlborough, aware of growing intrigue against him at home, and being anxious to annihilate what must surely be France's last army, decided to finish the war without further delay, by facing Villars at Malplaquet.

When he came up to the French position he realized they were more strongly entrenched than he had visualized. Villars was in heavily wooded country and had used some of the available timber to construct defensive positions. As many soldiers have learnt, advance through wooded country is usually much slower and more dangerous than senior commanders appear to appreciate. Opponents are rarely seen until they have seen you first. The main body of the Allied army advanced from the north-east, fighting every foot of the way. Marlborough had advised caution, but his words fell on deaf ears. On the left, where the Prince of Orange had thirty regiments, he hurled them forward, apparently unaware that he was crowding them into a narrow defile of which both sides were occupied by the enemy. From this nightmare predicament they had to be rescued by Marlborough himself but the rescue was not completed until the toll of casualties had made that wing of no further value in the battle. As further troops came up, they went into the battle piecemeal.

Across the entire battlefront, the two armies were now locked in desperate combat, each trying to break through the other. The cavalry on each side put in charge after charge but without making more than a dent in the opposing lines. Finally,

The battle of Dettingen, 1743, between France and England and her allies, was the last in which an English monarch personally took part.

although his losses had been high, Marlborough still had enough cavalry in reserve to smash in one last thunderous attack on the French right. Villars was wounded; Boufflers, who had succeeded him, seemed to have no other tactical thought than to batter away with cavalry charges which were making no headway. The French line began to give, and then fall back. It had been a desperate battle with unexpectedly large losses on both sides: the Allies, although victors, had lost 20,000 against the French 12,000. This battle took place on 11 September and Mons capitulated on the 23rd. The way to Paris was open, but it was too late in the year for Marlborough to collect a fresh army and take on such a bitter and costly campaign.

Marlborough's skilful handling of his cavalry had been a striking feature of all these battles. The list of cavalry regiments gaining Battle Honours at Ramillies, Oudenarde and Malplaquet was exactly the same as that for Blenheim; no one failed to live up to expectations. But Battle Honours were only half the story. The rest was made up of the endless picketing, convoy work, reconnaissance and patrolling. Morale was at its peak: Marlborough appreciated the cavalry and the cavalry appreciated Marlborough.

Unfortunately these were times in which political favouritism played a greater part than at almost any other period of history. Marlborough's position as Commander-in-Chief depended less on his ability in the field than on the influence his wife had on Queen Anne. As that influence declined, so did Marlborough's chance of finishing off this strung-out conflict. Nevertheless, during the year 1710 he continued with his policy of reducing those French fortresses which could impede his army's drive to Paris. Douai, Béthune, St Venant, and Aire all fell to him in that year. Villars, forced back from his outer ring of defences, built and strengthened an inner chain. These, if nothing else, should check Marlborough's apparently unstoppable advance.

The new fortifications were undoubtedly a formidable obstacle. Villars had linked together everything likely to delay an invading army. Marshes and canals lay between cleverly sited forts and strongpoints. Villars had good reason to be proud of his military engineering. Although now on the defensive, the French army looked to be in a position to give a very good account of itself. Marlborough, on the other hand, had a fresh series of frustrations and handicaps to contend with. Five battalions had been withdrawn from his army for service in Canada, Eugène had departed to deal with potential trouble in his own domains, and Marlborough's German allies were increasingly uneasy about the length of time their forces were campaigning abroad in a struggle which seemed to have no end.

As Marlborough moved forward to Villars' ring of defences, which had been christened the 'Non plus ultra' lines, he observed that the fortress of Bouchain could not be invested while Villars' army stood in his path. His immediate task, therefore, was to lure the French commander out of position. He occupied the nearby town of Arleux and proceeded to fortify it. He left a token force there, having told Cadogan to come up and assist if Arleux was threatened by the French. The threat materialised but Cadogan was unusually dilatory. The French recaptured the town, which was almost empty, and systematically demolished its fortifications; they destroyed not only the British-built defences but the more formidable ones which had existed long before. This, as Marlborough noted with satisfaction, meant that if Villars now decided to try to check the British advance at Arleux he would have no fortifications to assist him, for under his own orders all the fortifications had been reduced to rubble.

Marlborough now became more than usually communicative. He vowed vengeance on Villars for frustrating him, and his threats were duly reported to Villars. However, Marlborough's next moves were so erratic that they baffled not only Villars but his own troops as well. He announced that he would make a frontal attack on Villars' army but did not concentrate adequate supplies and artillery to make it possible. Then he changed his mind. He reviewed his troops and sent his cavalry heading westwards. Night fell. Soon after dark he struck camp and set off east with his remaining troops. As soon as this latest move was known the French set off to follow. Meanwhile news came to Marlborough that the other half of his army had now driven a gap through the enemy lines near the now unfortified town of Arleux. He doubled back behind Villars' army in order to join up with his other force, between the French army and the fortress of Bouchain. This strategy involved a march of forty miles in nineteen hours, but left Bouchain at his mercy, for Villars could do nothing to help. Paris was now within a few days' march. It was the culmination of years of strategic, diplomatic and tactical thinking. All he now needed to do was to replace the losses in his veteran army, collect adequate supplies, and launch the final offensive the following spring.

It did not, of course, happen. Louis XIV, aware that France was on the verge of a defeat which would probably bring him down with it, began secret negotiations for peace. The war had now been going on so long that every participant was heartily tired of it. At the English court his political enemies were assiduously persuading the Queen that Marlborough was too powerful and too popular. She was persuaded that it was necessary to diminish his power. On 11 January 1712, the year which he felt would bring him the reward for all the setbacks of the past decade, she dismissed him. He was replaced by the Duke of Ormonde, a general whose degree of ineptitude was almost inversely proportioned to Marlborough's skill. Faced by Ormonde the French had little difficulty in recapturing many of their former positions, and the war dragged on for yet another year. Finally, when the peace was signed in 1713, it was less favourable to Britain than it would have been in 1711.

Marlborough died in 1722, mourned by no one more than by his troops, whose welfare was always to the forefront of his mind. To them he was not a remote figure, but one of themselves whom they had marched with, fought with, and trusted. Their nickname for him was 'Corporal John'. That pleased him.

It will be clear from this brief account of Marlborough's campaigns that much of his success depended on his cavalry. In his sudden deceptive marches, it was the cavalry which reconnoitred ahead, reported on the state of bridges, roads and rivers, and advanced on points at which severe resistance might be expected. When the army was in camp, often in little known and potentially hostile territory, it was the cavalry which kept up incessant patrolling, intercepting spies, making occasional forays, indicating where much needed supplies might be found. After a victory, it fell to the cavalry to consolidate it. However, the campaigns were not invariably successful and there were occasions when the cavalry had to stage feint attacks on a dangerous enemy thrust in order to let their comrades extricate themselves from potential death traps.

The life of the cavalryman was one of constant excitement and danger but also one of considerable strain and weariness. At this point in the history of warfare the balance of power was beginning to tilt against the cavalry. Up till this time the cavalry had possessed an enormous advantage by being able to plunge into a battle at speed, shocking and crushing its opponents by weight and impetus. There had been, as we saw, various means of restricting this advantage, such as offering battle on broken or marshy ground, or confronting the horsemen with long pikes, or picking off horses from a distance with flighted arrows. Pikes were discarded when muskets became reliable, for pikes were heavy and cumbersome. But as long as musketry remained slow and erratic, the cavalry could more than hold its own. Yet at the beginning of the eighteenth century it was becoming ominously clear that improvements in muskets, combined with greater expertise in handling them, would require the cavalry to make sweeping changes in its tactical approach. A closely packed squadron of horse presented a solid target which even the most erratic musketeer could scarcely miss. Opening the ranks would provide more space for bullets to fly through but at the same time would remove much of the effect of the concentrated charges. Clearly, there must be an entirely new approach to the handling of cavalry in warfare or the arm would disappear from the battlefield as surely as the sling, the battleaxe, the mangonel, and the archer had done before it.

But the improved musket was not the only threat the cavalry would face in the future. An equally dangerous opponent was the economist. Cavalry was so much more expensive to train and maintain than infantrymen that the value of cavalry in relation to cost was beginning to be closely examined. An infantryman moved on his feet, and that cost next to nothing; a cavalryman needed a horse which required equipment, bulky food, farriers to attend to veterinary needs, blacksmiths for shoeing, shelter, and training. Nor could every recruit ride a horse, although those from Ireland showed remarkable aptitude. All in all, if the function of the cavalry could be performed by someone else more cheaply, there would be no valid reason to keep the arm in existence at all. Consequently, the number of cavalry in proportion to other arms gradually began to shrink. It was a feature common to all armies, and was not by any means more marked in the British army than in others.

Clearly, the most vulnerable was the heavy cavalry. Their horses were larger, slower, and altogether less suitable to reconnaissance and skirmishing than those of their lighter comrades. They themselves went some way to meet this criticism by reducing their body armour, abandoning their heavy helmets in favour of hats, and relying on long coats and leather boots for protection in battle. Leather coats, curiously enough, could sometimes be effective against musket balls, particularly if the range was not too short. Reasonably light clothing was essential for a dragoon as he might at any time be called to resume his function of being mounted infantry. It was one thing to wear heavy equipment, and carry heavy weapons, if you were going to fight in the battle on horseback, but it was a different matter altogether if you merely used your horse as transport and then dismounted and fought as a foot soldier. Dragoons were liable to find their horses encumbered with extra equipment and stores, perhaps forage or the fascines which were an essential part of eighteenth- and nineteenth-century warfare. Fascines were bundles of long sticks which had a multiplicity of uses. They were used as temporary barricades, as linings for trenches, as camouflage for guns, and for filling rivers and ditches. When a body of men marches through a stream, however small, the crossing-point rapidly becomes slippery and dangerous. A few fascines put down by a leading squadron of dragoons will shore up the banks and make the crossing safer. In marshy country fascines were invaluable for making the foundations of a road. They were as essential to the steady progress of an eighteenth-century army as the spade had been to Julius Caesar's. However, their general usefulness was not always appreciated by the dragoons who carried them, and who suggested, usually rightly, that they were looked down on by the rest of the cavalry as mere baggage-men. To add injury to insults, the dragoon's pay was usually less than that of his more glamorous contemporary. Furthermore, in spite of the fact that the 1st Dragoons had been founded many years before them, the Kings Dragoon Guards and Dragoon Guards generally tended to look upon themselves as older and in every way more distinguished that the plain dragoons. This deep feeling lasted for centuries; we noted earlier that when the 5th Dragoon Guards were amalgamated with the Inniskilling Dragoons in 1922 their fury at losing the word 'Guards' in their new title was only matched by the apoplectic rage of the Inniskillings at losing that word. However, while the Horse looked condescendingly on the Dragoon Guards and the Dragoon Guards on the Dragoons, they were in complete accord in despising the hussar regiments, who were rated as little more than legalized bandits.

Command of cavalry was more complicated than command of infantry. Success required an instinct for giving the right order at the right time – and a good deal of luck. Marlborough often took risks, any one of which could have lost him a battle. At Blenheim he was lucky that Tallard did not attack immediately after the British had crossed the Nebel. At Ramillies Marlborough kept up the momentum by using reserves and squadrons from the wings, but if the French had managed to check his drive forward he could have found himself locked in a fierce struggle and in danger of being surrounded. At Malplaquet Marlborough used cavalry against entrenchments, which is a very risky procedure. Marlborough's art was to assess what his opponent must be thinking. At Namur, in 1703, he knew that the strongest point in the French lines would be the least well defended by troops for it had a series of ditches to protect it.

He therefore deceived the French into thinking that he would leave that area, near Leuwe, well alone and attack a weaker place. To breach the Leuwe sector his dragoons would need to be carrying fascines. Knowing that spies were everywhere and would report every move he made, Marlborough issued orders that no fascines would be carried; instead the dragoons would transport bales of hay, as if in preparation for feeding horses on a longer journey, possibly a wide flank attack. However, when the battle began Marlborough launched the attack straight forward, using bales of hay in the way that fascines were usually used, i.e. to fill ditches. It was expensive and wasteful and not as effective as using fascines, but it brought him victory.

A soldier who was destined to give Britain much trouble in future years had fought in the French army at Malplaquet when only a lad of thirteen. This was Marshal Saxe. Although he fought with the French and rose to be a Marshal of France he was really of German ancestry, and illegitimate at that. His father, Augustus of Saxony, was credited with 354 illegitimate children in all. Saxe had a variety of ideas which more conventional minds thought plainly ridiculous. One was marching to music, another was that men should be led rather than driven. Marlborough, of course, was a prime exponent of this latter idea. Martial music is, incidentally, a combination of the oriental drum and the European pipe, or pfeif. Another Germanic custom which came in at this time was that of firing three volleys over a soldier's grave.

But before we leave Marlborough and move on to the varied wars of the later eighteenth century, we should take a closer view of a battle from the viewpoint of a regiment which fought in it. The 5th Lancers, at that time entitled the Royal Irish Dragoons, have this account in their records:

> The Dutch, after routing the first French line, were driven back by the second, but some fresh squadrons under Marlborough himself checked the advance of the French. Marlborough then ordered up every squadron of the Right wing, except those of the British cavalry. The Duke was now in the thick of the fight, and being thrown from his horse, which escaped, was furiously attacked by some French dragoons and in imminent danger of capture. His aide-de-camp, Captain Molesworth, dismounted at once and gave his horse to the Duke, enabled him to escape and remained to face the enemy alone. The French, however, were so intent upon pursuing the Duke that Molesworth escaped with a few sabre cuts. He then recovered the Duke's horse and rejoined him. While Marlborough mounted, the equerry who was holding his stirrup had his head carried away by a round shot.

It seems remarkable that Marlborough could direct the battle and also take such a close and dangerous part in it. As soon as he was back in the saddle, he was ordering fresh attacks.

> Then the rest of the Allied horse rode against the French front and a fierce fight ensued. The famous French cavalry (the Maison du Roi) were cut to pieces and in spite of Villeroi's efforts, the whole of the French horse were driven in headlong flight off the field, leaving the infantry to their fate . . . The British Dragoons, amongst them being the Royal Irish Dragoons, pushed their way into the village of Autre Eglise and made a terrible slaughter of them [the French infantry.] The last two regiments, the Scots Dragoons and Irish Dragoons fell in with and captured the entire King's Regiment (Regiment du Roi) of whom, having killed many, the rest threw down their arms and begged quarter, which was generously granted.

The cavalry certainly earned its money in wartime. A colonel received nineteen shillings a day, a captain twelve shillings, a sergeant two shillings and sixpence, and a dragoon one shilling and fourpence. Once hostilities were over it was a very different matter, in Ireland, as we learn from a letter written by a cavalry surgeon:

> Cavalry corps in Ireland were extremely select, as from the very low establishment [the small numbers required]. It was in the power of the

Colonels of choosing among a number of young gentlemen of distinction who might wish to get a commission and who all could easily afford to add a hundred pounds a year to their pay. The warrants were also purchased at a high price, often by the sons of gentlemen for as much as five hundred guineas. The privates were always young men well recommended and whose connections were known. Indeed, the dragoon service was at that time extremely easy and pleasant, so much so that when a vacancy happened, several desirable recruits always offered, and the men selected in general got no more than one shilling bounty. Two thirds of the officers had general leave of absence for the greater part of the year. Many of the dragoons were often on furlough, and were sometimes allowed to take their horses with them to their parents' houses, and generally wore their own clothes while with their friends. The horses were a considerable time of the year at grass, but the whole corps assembled at headquarters once a year and were kept together for a couple of months to perfect themselves in the evolutions preparatory to it being relieved, after which most of the officers were again indulged in leave of absence, many of the men allowed to go on furlough, and several troops detailed to out quarters.

However, not many regiments were able to have as easy and pleasant a life as the above (which was written about the 8th Hussars, then the 8th Light Dragoons). The 7th Hussars did not enjoy home service in England during the eighteenth century. They were kept constantly moving from place to place to ensure the maintenance of law and order. There were very few barracks and most troops were billeted, a process disliked by the army almost as much as by the people on whom they were billeted. The records of the 7th state:

> 17th Dec 1740. The Tewkesbury troop was ordered to march immediately to Evesham to assist in putting down riots in that neighbourhood. These were corn riots which had been prevalent in several places during the year. The worst were at Newcastle-on-Tyne 7 to 25 June, where, owing to the militia which had been called out being unwisely disbanded, the mob broke windows, burnt public records and looted £1800. Some gentlemen armed themselves and fired upon the rioters. At Wisbech in the Isle of Ely similar scenes took place. Corn was seized and sold for 1d to 4d per bushel by the rioters. Next they levied £200 on the town. Eventually 500 men were raised who secured some 60 of the disorderly persons. At Norwich wheat was at 16s a comb. Dragoons were called out, and some rioters were arrested: the mob then broke open the gaol and released them. The dragoons fired on the mob, killing three men, two women and a boy, many others being dangerously wounded.
>
> There were also riots at Derby, Northampton, Wellingborough and Evesham.

Life in the cavalry seemed to be one of extremes. In wartime it varied between dashing charges, exciting, though murderous, pursuits, and the drudgery of flank

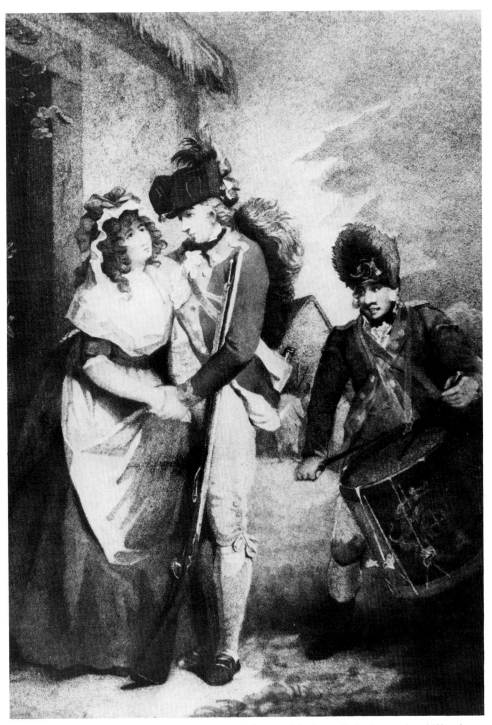

'The Billited Soldier's Departure.' Although the couple's farewell looks genuine, billeted soldiers were not generally popular.

Recruits: not perhaps the cream of the nation's youth, but it was amazing what a good troop sergeant could make of them.

protection; in peacetime it could be riot control, assisting the customs men, elegant manoeuvring, or self-indulgence in the form of drinking, gambling, hunting, or showing-off in the drawing-room. An expert in the last was Beau Brummell, who was commissioned in the 10th Hussars in 1795:

> He was endowed with a handsome person, and distinguished himself at Eton as the best scholar, the best boatman, and the best cricketer, and, more than all, he was supposed to possess the comprehensive excellences that are represented by the familiar name of good fellow . . . He made many friends

The recruit dislikes military life. He deserts, but is apprehended.

The 16th Lancers going to the review – always an impressive spectacle.

amongst the scions of good families . . . and his reputation reached a circle over which reigned the celebrated Duchess of Devonshire. At last the Prince of Wales sent for Brummell and was so much pleased with his manner that he gave him a commission in his own regiment, the 10th Hussars. Unluckily, Brummell, soon after joining his regiment, was thrown from his horse at a grand review at Brighton, when he broke his classical Roman nose. This misfortune, however, did not affect the fame of the Beau, and although his nasal organ had undergone a slight transformation, it was forgotten by his admirers, since the rest of his person remained intact.

In the zenith of his popularity he might be seen at the bay window of White's Club, surrounded by the lions of the day, laying down the law, and occasionally indulging in those witty remarks for which he was famous.

His gloves were made by two different artists, one being appointed to provide 'thumbs', the other the fingers and hands. His valet carrying the load of crushed handkerchiefs which the Beau had not succeeded in squeezing into the proper folds, and carelessly describing them as 'our failures', is an old well-worn legend. Once, being approached by the father of a young man who had lost money at cards while in his company, he merely replied, 'Why, sir, I did all I could for your son. I once gave him my arm all the way from White's to Brooks's.' [A distance of about fifty yards.] Being asked why he had not entered the lists of matrimony he explained how one attempt had been frustrated: 'What could I do, my dear fellow, when I actually saw Lady Mary eat cabbage.' It is said he never could master the names of the men of his troop, indeed he could only recognise his own troop by one old soldier who had a bottle nose, and was always placed in the front rank. Unfortunately for Mr Brummell, one day, his troop, being the junior, was broken up and mixed with the others. Coming on parade late, after the colonel, and when the regiment was formed up, he rode rapidly to where he expected to find his troop, but, being thoroughly puzzled, he galloped up and down, until he came opposite his blue nose, when he placed himself in front of it. 'How now,' vociferated the colonel. 'You are with the wrong troop.' 'No, no,' said Brummell, turning round in the saddle, 'I know better than that. A pretty thing, indeed, if I did not know my own men.'

After three years with the regiment Brummell resigned on the grounds that it had been ordered to Manchester, which he considered foreign service. However, eventually he ran through all his money, and died at Calais at the age of sixty, 'his body having outlived his mind', it was unkindly reported of him. One feels that Brummell might have been the original subject of the cherished remark: 'There was once a cavalry officer who was so stupid his brother officers noticed it.' Brummell was at least harmless; rich fanatics such as Cardigan caused endless misery to others, as well as damage to the army.

The 7th Hussars acquired an officer even more bizarre than Brummell in 1816. This was John Mytton, who stayed with the regiment for three years, spending most of his time in racing and gambling. His father had died when he was two and he had been spoilt by his mother. He was sent first to Westminster, where his extravagance

'A new hunter, Tally ho! Tally ho!' John Mytton, formerly 7th Hussars, riding a bear in his drawing room. The bear soon bit him, inflicting a severe wound. Mytton was notorious for madcap adventures and wild extravagance.

was notorious, before he was expelled. He then went to Harrow but was expelled from there, too. He was put down for both Oxford and Cambridge. He despatched three pipes of port (approximately 2,000 bottles) to await his arrival at Cambridge but never turned up to drink them. He was remarkably generous; he once borrowed £10,000 and lent £9,000 to a 'friend' who promptly bolted. He was a brilliant athlete, rider, oarsman and cricketer, but mad enough to go duck shooting stark naked in January and to ride a bear in his drawing room (it bit him). Eventually having squandered £2,000,000, he lived in poverty at Calais, but then came back to England and died in Fleet prison. He was never quarrelsome or offensive, although many people found his escapades somewhat trying.

7

A Mixture of Wars

Although the signatories of the Treaty of Utrecht, which brought the War of the Spanish Succession to an end, were by no means universally satisfied with its terms, the subsequent peace lasted for twenty-six years. The principal reason for this unusually long period of repose was that both Walpole, the British Prime Minister, and Fleury, his French counterpart, considered that co-operation was preferable to conflict. However, this happy state of affairs came to an end in 1739 in what was entitled 'The War of Jenkins' Ear'. In the Treaty of Utrecht there had been a clause allowing one British ship to trade with Spanish possessions in South America. One ship was thenceforward always to be found in port but it was constantly emptied and refilled by other ships from outside the harbour. The Spaniards, incensed, started searching British ships on the high seas, and there were naval battles. Captain Jenkins swore that his ear had been cut off by the Spaniards in one such fight and produced it in a bottle in Parliament. Current opinion held that he had probably lost it in an English pillory, but the sight of the plausible captain's ear caused Parliament to boil with indignation and declare war on Spain. Walpole gloomily remarked as he witnessed the general rejoicing: 'They are ringing the church bells now but soon they will be wringing their hands.'

While this was was getting into its stride it was eclipsed by another which became known as 'The War of the Austrian Succession'. The *casus belli* was the plight of Maria Theresa. On her father's death she succeeded to a vast empire. Part of this (Silesia) was promptly grabbed by Frederick the Great of Prussia; meanwhile the Elector of Bavaria tried to claim Austria itself. England thereupon decided to help Maria Theresa, and France gave its support to her opponents. That support encompassed sending two French armies to Germany. Walpole had now been succeeded by Carteret and that gifted politician, who could speak fluent German, managed to buy off Prussia and unite the rest of the German states against France. The next move was clearly to evict the French from Germany. An army was assembled under Lord Stair and, accompanied by George II himself, set off to accomplish this task.

Stair managed to put this army into a hopeless position at Dettingen (1743), lacking food and supplies, but the French kindly behaved with even greater folly by abandoning a strong position for a vulnerable one. This was the last occasion on which a British monarch personally led his troops in action. Unfortunately his horse was so scared by the noise of the muskets that it ran away with him at the beginning of the battle. He thereupon dismounted and rejoined the conflict on foot, saying he could trust his legs not to run away with him. His courage was exemplary and he appeared to be enjoying himself as he moved among the soldiers encouraging them with remarks like, 'Steady my boys, give them fire, they will soon run.'

There were nine British cavalry regiments in the field: the Horse Guards, Life Guards, 6th Dragoons and Royal Dragoons, 7th Dragoon Guards, King's Dragoon Guards, 4th Dragoons, 7th Dragoons, and Scots Greys. As the historian of the 7th Dragoons wrote:

> It was altogether a curious battle, for on the right of the British line a French attack had been repelled with ease. The enemy, indeed, did not appear to care seriously to face the volleys of the British infantry. A strange episode, however, took place, and it was this.
>
> Dashing between the opposing lines of infantry and en route receiving the fire of both friend and foe, the French Black Musketeers charged from what was their station on the right of the French line and hurled their squadrons on the Royal Dragoons who were posted on the British right. It was a mad enterprise at best. The chance now offered to the Allies was at once perceived by Marshal Neipperg, the Austrian commander. He ordered the British cavalry to make a frontal attack on the advancing Black Musketeers, while his own threw themselves on the flank of the Frenchmen. The French were thus caught between the two and cut to pieces. This achieved, the victorious cavalry turned its attention to the French infantry, whom it took in the flank.
>
> Declining to make a stand, the enemy fled, and this, as far as the left and centre of the French army, was the end of the battle. On the British left all was not yet over. There the cavalry, though they had repulsed the French after so much strenuous fighting, had not yet done with their opponents, and pressed them again as hard as ever.
>
> At this juncture, the Royal Dragoons, having disposed of the French infantry, who by this time had bolted, caught the remains of the French cavalry in the flank, pressed thus as they were also in front. An utter rout followed and the entire French army was speedily in headlong flight towards the two bridges at Seligenstadt, and also to seek any fords they could discover. Many plunged into the river haphazard and were drowned. There was no pursuit; there should no doubt have been. Stair proposed it and the King refused to permit it.

It was a brisk and bloody battle which the British were lucky to have won. Ironically, Britain and France were not yet formally at war, nor was the declaration made until several months afterwards.

However, after war was formally declared the French set to work in earnest and assembled an army of 80,000; this, commanded by Saxe, was victorious nearly everywhere it went. In 1745 it encountered the British at Fontenoy. The British would have won this battle if the charge by the infantry had not been checked by the Irish Brigade fighting in the French army. The British cavalry had little to do in the battle but plenty afterwards for it was called upon to protect the retreating army until it found shelter in the town of Aeth, which was well fortified.

George II doted on the army but did little of value for it in his long reign (thirty-three years – he lived till the age of seventy-seven). He believed that the more fanciful the dress the more recruits would be attracted. He therefore ordered that stockings should be replaced by long white gaiters, which were called 'spatter dashes'. Both the gaiters and the name were soon shortened – the latter to 'spats'. Hair had to be powdered and worn in a pigtail. Coats were given very wide facings. Hats were to be turned up on three sides, which was elegant but made for poor protection from the weather. Nothing was done to restrict the excessive consumption of alcohol. One of the cheapest drinks, and thus drunk widely by the poorer clases, was gin. An average of two gallons of gin per head of the population per annum was consumed at this time.

Officer of the 13th Dragoons, 1742.

Officer of the 2nd (R. N. Brit.) Dragoons, c. 1750. The huge fur head-dress is said to commemorate a victory over French Grenadiers.

The war of the Austrian Succession came to an end in 1748, with outstanding issues unresolved. Maria Theresa was, however, confirmed in her possession of Austria even though she had to surrender Silesia to the Prussians. The quarrel between Britain and Spain over searching ships on the high seas did not even get a mention, although it had triggered off a long and frustrating war. Nobody appeared to regard the 1748 peace treaty as anything more than a truce, although it was one which lasted for nine years in Europe. But out in the colonies matters were very different. Britain and France were engaged in a constant struggle in North America and India. From the latter country a new chapter in the development of British cavalry would be written.

Officer of the 14th Light Dragoons, 1776.

'The Relief, 1781.' The Guard is presenting arms in the form which continued with little change for over a century.

The conflict was bewildering for both sides in the distant territories. Owing to the slowness of communications, men could suddenly find, when letters came in, that they had been at war for months with the people they were proposing to dine with that evening. Even more disconcerting was to be locked in a life-and-death struggle, gain a victory and a possession with appalling losses, and then to learn that in a peace treaty signed several months previously the hard-won prize had already been allotted to one side or the other.

While Britain and France were engaged in a struggle for colonies, Austria and Prussia were as bitterly entangled in Europe. Maria Theresa had no intention of letting Frederick keep Silesia, and joined with France and Russia in an effort to make him disgorge it. This, inevitably, drove Britain into an alliance with Prussia.

The war began disastrously: in fact there was so much fear that Britain might herself be invaded that Hanoverian and Hessian troops were brought in to protect these shores. The French, it had been learned, had a force of 50,000 men waiting to be transported across the Channel in flat-bottomed boats. The tide began to turn in 1758 when William Pitt set himself the task of organizing victory. He put an army in the field in Europe with the intention of avenging the defeat of the Duke of Cumberland by the French at Hastenbeck. It won a striking victory at Minden in July 1759, although the manner of that victory reflected little credit on the commanders. Owing to a misunderstood order the British infantry advanced before it was expected to do so. It came up to the French cavalry and took such a toll with accurate musketry fire that the French could never get to close quarters and kill their tormentors. At that point the British cavalry should have come in and completed the rout of the French cavalry, but the British commander, Lord George Sackville, was too idle and stupid to realize that this was his supreme opportunity. In consequence the victory was completed by German infantry and British gunners. It was a poor day for the cavalry through no fault of their own, but their turn was soon to come. The following year there was a spirited battle at Emsdorff. Here the 15th Hussars went at the French with such skill and ferocity that they chased them for twenty miles.

It was July 1760 and in the same month there was an even more remarkable victory at Warburg. Here it was realized that the French commander, Broglie, had mishandled his troops and left 20,000 in an exposed position. It was a golden opportunity for the British, if only it could be taken, but only the cavalry could cover the distance in the time and the cavalry numbered a mere 7,000. However, they were led by the Marquis of Granby, who had had the misfortune to have to sit idly by while Sackville missed his chances at Minden. Granby made sure there would be no mistake this time. He went into action at such a pace that his wig fell off.[1] This gave us the expression 'going at it bald-headed', thus indicating a headlong carefree approach. Granby was extremely popular with his men and was unusual in that he was greatly concerned for their welfare when they left the army. After the war he helped many of his more responsible soldiers to get inns and they repaid the kindness by naming them 'The Marquis of Granby'. To this day, there are still many inns of that name throughout the country.

[1] Also said to have happened elsewhere.

Although Saxe commanded French armies, this did not prevent his ideas being copied by his rivals in other countries. This, of course, is a regular feature of warfare. Britain invented the tank; the Germans exploited it. The British then learnt from the Germans. At the Battle of Alam el Halfa in 1942 German tanks were lured on to British anti-tank guns which were used exactly as the Afrika Korps would have used them. The following year the Battle of Mareth was won by hook tactics of the type which Rommel had perfected.

Saxe was essentially a soldier's general. Although a great cavalry commander and strategist, he had little time for the popular attitude to the cavalry: magnificent horses, ample rations, elegance, and respect for tradition. He specified that his cavalry mounts should be hardy, mobile and lean. He considered that armour had been discarded prematurely, that most musketry fire was so inaccurate that it was less of a hazard than enemy swordsmen; if armoured horsemen confronted unarmoured opponents in a sword fight there could be only one result. But he insisted on breech-loading carbines for all ranks (the pistol was discarded), and the lance was reintroduced. Lances were fifteen feet long and bore a large pennant which, when flapped in front of enemy horses, would create almost as much havoc as the lance itself. In battle the cavalry always stayed together, even though this meant beginning at a trot and only breaking into a gallop later. Hussars were discarded: their work was taken over by dragoons. Dragoons carried a lance which was used as a pike when they were dismounted. They carried swords, and had to take on the duties of escorts, skirmishers, reconnaissance and message-carrying. Not all of Saxe's ideas were accepted but some, such as the lance, proved very popular in the British army. Saxe's theories were felt to have been proved right when in 1741, at Mollwitz, Austrian cavalry defeated a superior force of Prussian cavalry by vigorous sword-play. Later in this book we shall find British cavalry doing precisely the same.

Another development which attracted attention at the time, and became a standard cavalry practice, was to change formation on the move, rather than to form up while stationary and maintain that same formation throughout a battle. Obviously if changing formation on the move went wrong it could lead to an appalling disaster, but if properly executed would have enormous advantage in speed and surprise. This innovation was made by Seydlitz, an outstanding Prussian cavalry commander.

As the eighteenth century drew to its close it was apparent that there was much brilliant thinking being applied to making the best use of cavalry and that the day of mounted troops was far from over. But nobody suspected that before the end of the century Britain would be engaged in a long struggle which, with two short breaks, would extend over twenty-two years, and in which cavalry would be used more widely and decisively than ever before.

8

The Never-Ending War

One hundred and eighty years later it is almost impossible to imagine what our ancestors must have experienced under the threat of conquest by Napoleon, or even what it must have been like to be at war for over two decades. For many years they were fully aware that invasion was no remote possibility, but a danger which could materialize rapidly through a miscalculation on sea or land. If it occurred it could end in total disaster and humiliation; at best it would be bloody, devastating and costly. In order to put the cavalry battles of that time into their correct setting, the main events of the long-running conflict are first summarized.

The war, which subsequently seemed never-ending, began on 8 February 1793. For four years the majority of British people had been horrified by the savagery of events across the Channel, but felt that eventually reason would reassert itself and civilization reappear. However, when France's Revolutionary armies overran Belgium, and the French government announced its intention of making Antwerp into a great naval arsenal, disgust was replaced by apprehension. Pitt had withdrawn the British ambassador from Paris when Louis XVI and Marie-Antoinette were executed, and had begun preparations for war. On hearing the news about Antwerp from the Continent, he sent a strong protest to the French. To his surprise the French promptly declared war. The leaders of the Revolution were under the impression that if they declared war on Britain the British people would rise at once and kill their leaders. However, as the French quickly realized, the British reaction to the call for revolution was quite different from what had been anticipated. Nevertheless, the early stages of the war were very difficult for Britain which had only 30,000 troops to put against Revolutionary France whose victorious armies numbered over 500,000. Pitt, aware that most European countries were terrified by this new threat, set about making a coalition to fight against the French. Initially it seemed that the coalition would be needed for land forces only, for the British navy was already twice as strong as the French. However, by a combination of impressive land victories and adroit diplomacy, France soon managed to persuade the navies of Holland and Spain to come in on her side. In 1797 Austria was so heavily defeated by French armies that she dropped out of Pitt's coalition. The war spread, and soon there was fighting in northern Europe, in Syria and in Egypt.

By 1798 Napoleon decided that the only way to bring the war to a quick end was by invading England. He assembled an invasion force of some 50,000 men and kept it

'*His Majesty reviewing the Volunteers on the 4th of June, 1799.*' *There were sixteen years of war ahead of them, against the French in Europe.*

'*Showing the Difference between the Man and the Officer.*' *Cartoonists invariably failed to treat the Army with proper respect.*

Pope Pius VI blessing officers of the 12th Light Dragoons, 1793. The 12th had been sent to Italy to help defend that country against Revolutionary France.

The attack on Sir Ralph Abercrombie by the French dragoons at the battle of Alexandria, 1801. Abercrombie was fatally wounded but the battle was won.

Benevente, 1808. The 10th and 18th Hussars defeat the French Cavalry of the Guard, capturing its commander, General Léfèbvre.

on the French coast waiting for a suitable opportunity to cross the Channel. The opportunity never came for British sea-power, though greatly extended, was too strong for Napoleon to risk such a venture. The war dragged on, but both sides became so exhausted that a peace treaty was signed in 1802. The ink was scarcely dry before Napoleon was on the move again. Once more an invasion force was assembled near Calais, this time 120,000 strong. Thousands of boats were made ready to transport them, perhaps under cover of a fog, or at some time when the British fleet had been temporarily distracted by events elsewhere and had relaxed its vigilance in the Channel. The invasion force stayed in position, training and waiting, for over two years. One effect was a huge expansion in the English militia, from which, later, many recruits to the regular army were supplied: the cavalry benefited considerably from the yeomanry.

The Battle of Trafalgar in 1805 put an end to Napoleon's invasion plans for the foreseeable future, for it confirmed that Britain was truly mistress of the seas. However, Napoleon remained as active as ever on land. Not surprisingly, some of the countries he had conquered earlier were now proving distinctly restive under French yoke. This only made Napoleon more vigorous and repressive than ever. The Prussians were crushed at Jena in 1806 and the Russians at Eylau and Friedland the following year. In 1808 he invaded and overran Portugal which had been unwilling to cut off its trade with England. He also deposed the King of Spain and installed his own brother Joseph on the Spanish throne. The Spaniards were furious at this arbitrary behaviour and rose in rebellion. Patriots in Madrid were crushed with much ferocity but at Baylen a French general, Dupont, outnumbered and outfought, was forced to surrender an army of 15,000.

Wellington then landed with British troops in Portugal and, at Vimiero, defeated a French army under Junot. However, Wellington was recalled and censured for not capturing Lisbon, and while he was back in England Sir John Moore was given command of the armies in Spain. Meanwhile Napoleon, furious at the reverses the French had suffered in Spain and Portugal, took and commanded a huge army (250,000 strong) which captured Madrid and overran northern and central Spain. At this point he planned to advance to Lisbon and Cadiz, but Sir John Moore with a very small army, a mere 25,000, attacked the French line of communication. Napoleon promptly despatched 100,000 men to deal with Moore but the latter retreated with such skill that he drew the French into the extremely inhospitable territory of north-west Spain. Moore reached Corunna, where an English fleet was waiting to embark the remnants of his army, but in a final attack on the French (commanded here by Marshal Soult) the gallant Moore was killed. By the time the troops reached England Wellington was back in favour once more and Moore's veterans soon found themselves en route for the country they had so recently left.

Wellington proceeded to win victories at Oporto and Talavera (1809) but was then starved of the troops he needed to achieve further victories. At this point Napoleon decided to settle the Spanish question once and for all. He sent 70,000 troops to Masséna, a very able general, with the instruction that he was to use them to drive the British into the sea. Wellington, suspecting that a threat like that must be in the offing, had constructed a series of fortifications in three lines across the peninsula at

The Duke of Wellington, many of whose victories were won by his cavalry.

A caricature of Lieutenant-Colonel Michael Barne, 7th Hussars, a commander of dash and tenacity.

A Galloper from 7th Hussars, 1814. A caricature, but to the French commanders 'gallopers' were objects of admiration and despair. Such was their speed they could penetrate almost anywhere with impunity, could cross lines of march and hang on flanks, thus obtaining much useful information. If the enemy attempted a chase, the better mounted British officer easily outstripped his pursuer and vanished, only to appear again on some distant hill whence, safe, he calmly renewed his operations, note-book in hand.

the end of which Lisbon lies. These were known as the 'Lines of Torres Vedras'. He retreated slowly in front of Masséna's army, occasionally hitting back, and always devastating the countryside so that the French army could obtain no supplies from it. At Torres Vedras Masséna was stopped. He spent a frustrating four months trying to force a way through the lines, begging for reinforcements from the French troops in Spain. There were none to be spared and eventually Masséna had to retreat from Portugal, having lost a third of his army. As he made his painful way back over the bleak countryside, Wellington pressed hard on his heels, perpetually adding to his torments. In the early days of the Revolution French armies had been able to rely for supplies on plundering the countryside: now this policy contributed to their undoing for their supply train was totally inadequate.

However, Masséna was not finished. Yet his dismissal, if he could not defeat Wellington, could not be long delayed. In the meantime, in March 1811, another encouraging victory had been won by the Allies. This was at Barossa, near Cadiz. (The Spanish call it Cerro de Puerco, which means the Pig's Neck.) The reason for the battle was that Marshal Soult was blockading Cadiz from the land side, and could not easily be dislodged. In consequence an allied force was landed at Tarifa, further south, and marched, not without difficulty, to the Barossa ridge, a mile and a half from the coast, near Cadiz. The Spanish commander had omitted to make a reconnaissance and was unaware that the French had troops concealed on either side of this important tactical position. In consequence the battle went very badly for the Allies in the opening stages, but they recovered when Sir Thomas Graham, asked for instructions, replied with the single word 'Fight!' This stirring victory has been long forgotten, but there is a constant reminder of it in that the training area immediately behind the Royal Military Academy Sandhurst is named Barossa, which it resembles. For the last 150 years officer-cadets and many others have fought in practice over the Barossa ridges by night and day, in scorching heat and winter snow, mostly quite unaware of the origin of the name.

Two months later Wellington began besieging the frontier fortress of Almeida. Masséna set off with an army to relieve it but was intercepted by Wellington at Fuentes d'Onoro (1811) and beaten. This was a British cavalry victory if ever there was one, as we shall see later. In the same month, Wellington's second-in-command, Lord Beresford, was besieging Badajoz, another frontier fortress which was still in French hands, when he was attacked by Soult. The critical battle took place at Albuera and was won by courage rather than skill. The cost in British lives was high. Heavy casualties were also the price of capturing Ciudad Rodrigo, another frontier fortress.

The crowning battle was at Salamanca on 22 July, 1812. Having captured the town Wellington found himself threatened with superior numbers under a skilful French general named Marmont. However, at a critical point in the battle, Wellington realized that Marmont had opened up a gap in his own army. Into that gap Wellington hurled his cavalry. Marmont was wounded but Major-General Gaspard Le Marchant, the first Commandant of the Royal Military College (then at High Wycombe but later to move to Sandhurst) was killed in the last stages of the battle. It was Wellington's most brilliant victory and was described as 'defeating 40,000 men in forty minutes'.

But the war was not over. The French had strong forces in Spain, and Napoleon's brother was still established as their king. Wellington took Madrid but had not sufficient reserves to hold it. He was now a long way from his base in Portugal and when he had advanced as far as Burgos he realized he had no option but to retreat and shorten his lines. His men did not approve of retreating and showed their feelings with drunkenness and indiscipline but tactically it was undoubtedly a wise move to make.

Wellington re-entered Spain in 1813, with a well-equipped army ready to clinch the final victory. His strategy was to cut the communications between France and the French armies in Spain. King Joseph Bonaparte tried to prevent him but the result was

The Charge of the Polish Lancers at Albuera, 1811.

*Sir William Beresford's encounter with a Polish Lancer, at the battle of Albuera, 1811.
Beresford was immensely strong. Although he was the illegitimate son of the Marquess of
Waterford, he rose rapidly in the Army and became one of Wellington's most valued
commanders.*

Norman Ramsay at Fuentes de Onoro, 1811. In this hard-won victory in the Peninsular War Ramsay of the Royal Horse Artillery, flanked by Royal Dragoons and 14th Light Dragoons, burst through the middle of the French position. Ramsay was later killed at the battle of Waterloo.

the Battle of Vittoria on 21 June 1813, when Bonaparte was not merely defeated but lost his baggage, and all his artillery as well. (See 14/20th Hussars, Chapter 5.)

Napoleon, defeated on many fronts, abdicated in April 1814. Wellington was at this time successfully invading France, and had reached Toulouse. The critical campaign had therefore been in the Peninsula and we have followed this to its conclusion in order to put the cavalry battles into their strategic and tactical frameworks. We shall now look more closely into the battles at unit level. The Napoleonic Wars were not yet quite over but the final stages will need a chapter of their own.

Although the 10th Hussars did not arrive in the Peninsula till 1808, one of their captains, Henry Francis Mellish, was ADC to Sir Ronald Ferguson, one of Wellington's generals. It was reported one day that Mellish had been taken prisoner but when Wellington heard of it he said, 'They'll not keep him long.' Sure enough, the next day he was seen riding into the British camp on a donkey. Everyone laughed at his mount and said it was not worth £5. He retorted, 'I'll soon make it £35.' He then rode towards the enemy lines, had it shot from under him, and returned to claim £35 from the government for the loss of his mount in battle. After the war, the versatile Mellish was watching a race when one of the riders was thrown. He grabbed the loose horse, mounted it, and came in second. He was well-known as a successful cattle-breeder, carrying off all the chief prizes at the shows. Possessed of abilities as a painter and a musician, and happily married to an accomplished woman, his future seemed full of promise, but he died at the early age of thirty-five.

But there was nothing very glittering about the 10th Hussars when they joined Sir John Moore in 1808. 'The weather was extremely cold, snow lay on the ground, the roads were covered with ice, and many men had to dismount and lead their horses.' The 10th were then brigaded with the 15th under Lord Paget. The 15th went into action against a force of French dragoons. 'They charged, broke them up, and pursued them for some distance. Twenty killed, two lieutenant colonels, eleven officers, and 154 men prisoners was the result of this victorious action.'

Many of these brief brisk actions were recorded in the diary of General Slade. For example, 'Colonel Leigh, forming his small force into two lines, rode briskly forward, one squadron leading and the other supporting, till he gained the top of the hill. Here the men were commanded to reign up for the purpose of refreshing the horses after the ascent and they did so under smart fire from the French. But the horses had no sooner recovered their wind than the word "Charge" was given and in a few minutes the French were overwhelmed. Many were killed, many more wounded and upwards of ninety prisoners taken.'

But the losses were not all on one side. As Moore fell back,

> Soult with an army consisting of 70,000 strong, including 10,000 cavalry, now vigorously pressed the pursuit. Rain and snow rendered the roads almost impassable, but, in spite of everything, every position was disputed, every opportunity taken to stand and fight.
>
> The many delays were owing in the first instance to the depth of the snow, and also from the frequent interruptions we met with from carriages being overturned, artillery waggons burning, etc. In the 10th alone Captain Darby and seventeen private soldiers died of fatigue, while sixty horses were destroyed to prevent them from falling into the hands of the enemy.

They were the first of many. Thousands of horses were shot on the seashore when the army embarked. The 10th, which had left England with over 600 horses, returned with only thirty.

Sir Charles Napier described the opening stages of the battle of Fuentes d'Onoro as follows:

> The French with one shock charge drove in all the cavalry out-guards, and cutting off Captain Ramsay's battery, came sweeping in upon the reserves of horse and upon the Seventh Division. But their leading squadrons, approaching in a disorderly manner, were partially checked by the British, and, at the same time, a great commotion was observed in their main body. Men and horses then closed with confusion and tumult towards one point, a thick dust arose, and loud cries, and the sparkling of blades, and the flashing of pistols, indicated some extraordinary occurrence. Suddenly the multitude became violently agitated, an English shout pealed high and clear, the mass was rent asunder, and Norman Ramsay burst forth at the head of his battery,

his horses, breathing fire, stretched like greyhounds along the plain, the guns bounding behind them as things of no weight, and the mounted gunners followed in full career. Captain Brotherton of the 14th Dragoons seeing this, rode forth with a squadron and overturned the head of the pursuing troops, and General Stewart, joining in the charge, took the French General Lamotte, fighting hand to hand.

The French had the advantage of numbers in this battle, having 5,000 cavalry to the British 1200 and 40,000 infantry to 32,000. Captain Brotherton recorded other details:

> We had a very fine fellow, Captain Knipe, killed through his gallent *obstinacy* if I may so call it. We had the night before been discussing the best method for cavalry to attack batteries in the open field. He maintained, contrary to us all, that they ought to be charged in front, instead of the usual way of gaining their flanks and thereby avoiding their fire. Poor fellow, the experiment the next day, in support of his argument, was fatal to him. He had the opportunity of charging one of the enemy's batteries, which he did by attacking it immediately in front, and got through the discharge of round shot with little loss, but the enemy, having most rapidly reloaded with grape, let fly at his party at a close and murderous distance, almost entirely destroying it; he himself receiving a grape shot passing through his body. The shot went through his lungs. I was with the poor fellow the next morning, as long as he survived. He could speak distinctly and was most composed and resigned, and even argued the point over again. His chief anxiety, however, was to be permitted to write a line to his mother and he expired in the very act of attempting it.
>
> Captain Badcock, commanding a squadron of the 14th Light Dragoons, was sitting on a horse at the head of his squadron when he took for Spaniards running away some cavalry rapidly approaching him in line and remained perfectly steady, intending to charge those who appeared to be following the supposed Spaniards, the moment the latter had passed him. He was, however, not very agreeably surprised by being undeceived by a cut across the face from the French officers (for the supposed Spaniards were French). Badcock, however, who was an excellent officer, contrived, notwithstanding his surprise, to drive the enemy back in gallant style with the loss, however, of two of his teeth, but he never thought of the wound till he had completed his duty and then even never left the field for one moment.
>
> Colonel Hervey escaped losing his right leg by having put a thick book (Quenedo's *Works* which he had taken from a private house the day before) into his sabretache. An eight pound shot entering the sabretache went through the horse and just appeared on the other side of his body without coming through the skin and it was evident that the thick book prevented it from going through and taking off Colonel Hervey's leg. Poor fellow, he had already lost his right arm, and his leg, from the blow, immediately swelled to an immense size but he would not leave the field but had himself

placed under a tree where he remained during the remainder of the battle.

I had a charger shot under me, and got on a troop horse which was also shot under me, through the head by the pistol of a French officer, so closely that my own face was singed. The animal fell, and a sergeant behind me dismounted and gave me his horse, and I thought no more of the animal that was shot through the head, supposing that he never rose again, but on rejoining the main body of the regiment I found that the poor animal had arisen by an effort, gone back to where the regiment was formed, placed himself in the ranks of his own squadron and then fell down dead. This fact, almost incredible, can be vouched for by any officer or private belonging to the 14th Light Dragoons at the time.

A more conventional cavalry encounter was experienced by the 13th Dragoons at Badajoz:

The opposing forces were now some two hundred yards apart. The 13th moved regularly forward with the usual words of command: walk, trot, canter and charge, and with a loud cheer the men met the enemy. The enemy cheered likewise, and the two lines crashed into one another. The 13th penetrated the enemy and then wheeled round. The enemy did the same, though not so speedily and a second charge took place. Man to man with the sabre they went to work, and the 13th used their weapons with great effect. Meanwhile the right squadron of the enemy wheeled to the left, and came upon the left flank of the left squadron of the 13th (Captain Doherty's) and appeared likely to be troublesome, but they were beaten off. However, in a short space of time the left and centre columns were put to flight and then, very speedily, the right was induced to follow their example.

There were good times and bad times. 'In Serradilla there was no forage; the country round about was equally destitute. Hence each man took out his horse every morning and led him round the ditches and the roots of the trees – wherever in fact a blade of grass was to be found. The ground beneath the chestnut trees was also hunted carefully, and all stray roots secured and given to the luckless animals. In fact, the whole, or nearly the whole of the time of the men was given, and given willingly to save the horses.'

Salamanca was, of course, a triumph for the cavalry. An eye-witness account of this battle was given by Lt William Grattan whose regiment, the 88th (Connaught Rangers) was in the thick of this and many other battles:

The peals of musketry along the centre still continued without intermission; the smoke was so thick that nothing to our left was distinguishable; some men of the 5th Division got intermingled with ours. The dry grass was set on fire by the numerous cartridge-papers that strewed the field of battle; the air was scorching; and the smoke, rolling onward in huge volumes, nearly suffocated us. A loud cheering was heard in our rear; the brigade half turned round, supposing themselves about to be attacked by the French cavalry.

Wallace called out to his men to mind the tellings-off for square. A few seconds passed, the trampling of horses was heard, the smoke cleared away, and the heavy brigade of Le Marchant was seen coming forward in line at a canter. 'Open right and left' was an order quickly obeyed; the line opened, the cavalry passed through the intervals, and, forming rapidly in our front, prepared for their work.

The French column, which a moment before held so imposing an attitude, became startled at this unexpected sight. A victorious and highly-excited infantry pressing close upon them, a splendid brigade of three regiments of cavalry ready to burst through their ill-arranged and beaten column, while no appearance of succour was at hand to protect them, was enough to appal the boldest intrepidity. The plain was filled with the vast multitude; retreat was impossible; and the troopers came still pouring in to join their comrades, already prepared for the attack. Hastily, yet with much regularity, all things considered, they attempted to get into square; but Le Marchant's brigade galloped forward before the evolution was half completed. The column hesitated, wavered, tottered, and then stood still! The motion of the countless bayonets as they clashed together might be likened to a forest about to be assailed by a tempest, whose first warnings announce the ravage it is about to inflict. Thomières' division vomited forth a dreadful volley of fire as the horsemen thundered across the flat! Le Marchant was killed, and fell downright in the midst of the French bayonets; but his brigade pierced through the vast mass, killing or trampling down all before them. The conflict was severe, and the troopers fell thick and fast; but their long heavy swords cut through bone as well as flesh. The groans of the dying, the cries of the wounded, the roar of the cannon, and the piteous moans of the mangled horses, as they ran away affrighted from the terrible scene, or lay with shattered limbs, unable to move, in the midst of the burning grass, was enough to unman men not placed as we were; but upon us it had a different effect, and our cheers were heard far from the spot where this fearful scene was acting.

Such as got away from the sabres of the horsemen sought safety amongst the ranks of our infantry, and scrambling under the horses, ran to us for protection – like men who, having escaped the first shock of a wreck, will cling to any broken spar, no matter how little to be depended upon. Hundreds of beings, frightfully disfigured, in whom the human face and form were almost obliterated – black with dust, worn down with fatigue, and covered with sabre-cuts and blood – threw themselves amongst us for safety. Not a man was bayoneted – not one even molested or plundered; and the invincible old 3rd Division on this day surpassed themselves, for they not only defeated their terrible enemies in a fair stand-up fight, but actually covered their retreat, and protected them at a moment when, without such aid, their total annihilation was certain. Under similar circumstances would the French have acted so? I fear not. The men who murdered Ponsonby at Waterloo, when he was alone and unprotected, would have shown but little courtesy to the 3rd Division, placed in a similar way.

Nine pieces of artillery, two eagles, and five thousand prisoners were captured at this point; still the battle raged with unabated fury on our left, immediately in front of the 5th Division. Leith fell wounded as he led on his men, but his division carried the point in dispute, and drove the enemy before them up the hill.

In the spring of 1814 it seemed at last that a new era had dawned. Napoleon, the tyrant of Europe, the man whose name had struck fear into the stoutest heart, had been beaten, had tried to commit suicide, and had been exiled to the small island of Elba. France was a monarchy once more. All the countries of Europe began to disarm. There was still a war which Napoleon had caused between Britain and America but that, too, was soon settled. The world had been reborn – or so it seemed.

Battle of Toulouse, 1814. Everyone thought it was the end of the Napoleonic Wars but Waterloo was still to come.

9
Waterloo

The ease with which Napoleon escaped from Elba and once more raised an army was as unexpected as it was alarming. The European powers were too concerned with their own recovery from the war to take much notice of the incompetence of the restored monarch of France, Louis XVIII. Nobody appeared to realize that the defeated French armies were profoundly displeased with their King and his entourage. When Napoleon landed in France again the response of the French was overwhelming. Nobody opposed him, the army came over to his side, and Louis XVIII fled to Flanders. Napoleon thereupon declared that he was Emperor again, that he would be liberal rather than autocratic, and that he had no wish for war if the other European powers would accept his presence.

This approach was a little too plausible for the nations which had spent the best part of twenty years defeating Napoleon; their reaction was to have no nonsense, declare war, defeat him, and send him into exile once more. Unfortunately for them they had overlooked how quickly Napoleon could think and move, and in consequence he advanced rapidly into Belgium, and defeated a Prussian army at Ligny. However, this still left a combined force of British, Germans and Dutch commanded by Wellington. As his army consisted of 72,000 battle-hardened troops, with which to confront a mixed army of 67,000, of which 20,000 were Dutch and Belgian conscripts with no wish to fight, Napoleon looked forward eagerly to the encounter which Wellington was offering him on the hill of St Jean, near the small village of Waterloo. The position covered the road to Brussels and Wellington's army was deployed with the infantry in the centre and the cavalry on the wings, and in reserve. Ahead of Wellington's position were two farms, one at La Haye Sainte, the other at Hougoumont; the former held by British, the latter by Hanoverians.

The attack opened with an attempt to capture La Haye Sainte, but it was repulsed. Napoleon then launched a heavy attack on the left, but this was held and driven off by the infantry under Picton and the 'Union Brigade' of dragoons, Royals, Scots Greys, and Inniskillings. Next he sent 15,000 French cavalry in a series of desperate charges into the British centre. In between the charges French artillery raked the British line mercilessly. La Haye fell, and many Dutch, Belgians and Germans fled from the field in the face of the powerful French attacks, but the British squares still held fast. At a critical point Napoleon was greatly disturbed to see new troops appearing on the Allied side. These were Prussians who had been defeated at Ligny but whose wily old

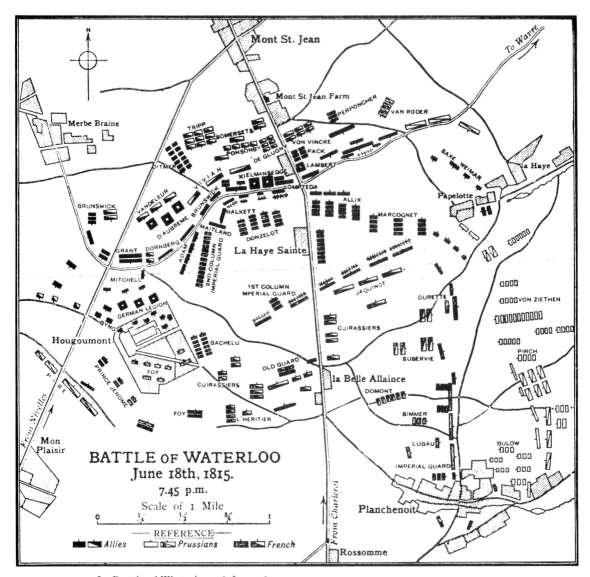

3 Battle of Waterloo, 18 June 1815.

general, Blücher, had rallied and regrouped. He had promised Wellington they would be at Waterloo and they were. Napoleon held them off with his reserves, which made a last desperate effort to break through the English line. For this he used 5,000 men of his 'Old Guard' but they met their match in the English guards, and when they were forced back the last reserve of the British cavalry turned the French defeat into a rout.

So much for the bare details. It had been a desperate battle, touch and go to the last minutes. This is how it seemed to some of the survivors. Lt William Cartwright, 10th Hussars, wrote to his father:

My dear Father – Although I have seen many battles in my life [he was only eighteen] I assure you they were a complete farce to this one. Bony, against us, fought like a tiger: we fought like Englishmen, and thanks to God, repelled him with great loss. Our cavalry behaved so finely that everyone when they saw us were quite thunderstruck. Poor Gunning is killed, as also Bouverie. I only wonder we were not all killed. Thank God I have been lucky enough to escape. I commanded a troop on this occasion. We charged four or five times our numbers – the men in armour – but we made a pretty hole in them; there are not above six officers left with the regiment. We are within three leagues of Brussels.

Three days later he had time to send a more detailed account:

Our proceedings commenced on the 16th, which day about 4 o'clock a.m. we were routed out and marched to Nivelle. It was just about 7 p.m. when we reached that place but as the scene of action was two leagues on we trotted on and got into the field of action just before dusk. We bivouacked there the whole night, and next morning the skirmishing again commenced. This lasted till about 10 o'clock from about 4 in the morning, when the Duke, our noble commander, having heard that Blücher, who was on our left, had been repulsed, he determined to retreat in order to communicate with this old gentleman. Accordingly the infantry went to the rear, and the Hussars – for they are always more employed than any other cavalry – were to cover the retreat. The Hussars General, Sir Hussey Vivian, appointed our regiment and the 7th to this unpleasant task, for such it is. We showed front to the enemy for two or three hours after the army had retreated, till at last the enemy brought up a very large force of Cuirassiers who are all in armour. We were then forced to retreat and, of course, the fellows followed us up. We fought and retired, and so on, till at length we came up to our infantry, who were in position. We then took our post and a great deal of cannonading ensued. We bivouacked on top of the position this night (17th) and a pretty rainy one it was. I was never so wet and miserable in my life. The next morning of course we expected an attack but 9 o'clock passed, and nothing new, so nothing till 11 when our picquet was driven in. Of course we all turned out immediately, and took our place in our position, which I assure you was rather formidable. The enemy then brought on very heavy columns, both of infantry and cavalry. All of ours awaited the attack which was conducted by Napoleon himself and with great vigour; they made attacks every moment, bringing on fresh troops every time, but our fellows, fighting more like lions than men, managed to keep them down. Of course, numbers will tell at last, and our fight began to waver, this was on the main road. We then moved from the left, which was our former place in the position, to the right, and supported the infantry in some style. We were kept under the heaviest fire that ever was heard, both of musketry and cannon, for some time (about 7 p.m.). However, the Prussians at length made their appearance on the left and began with the enemy. This gave us double spirit and we went on like tigers – we actually went up to the mouth of the cannon. While we were thus engaged the enemy heard the Prussians on the left; this they did not seem to like and we of course pushed on the more. However, our Commander, Sir Hussey Vivian, ordered us to form in column right in front: this brought me, as I was commanding the right troop, in front. We then went on, and the enemy formed square – we did not mind this but deployed steadily as if we were at a field day. It was just here that poor Gunning was killed. We then moved on and came to the charge. The squares of course made a desperate resistance, but our valour extinguished their squares. Their cavalry then came down with *Lancers, armour* etc, enough to frighten us, but we charged them, though twice our number, and quite panic struck them: some ran off, others were tumbling off their horses, others attempted to defend themselves and so on. We however gave a pretty fair account of them. After this they brought on more cavalry but we played them the same trick, We took an immense number of prisoners, cannon etc and flatter ourselves we were the means of saving the day.

We intend to be in Paris in a fortnight. Nobody knows where Bony is. They say we are to have another battle at Laon, where he is making a stand. The rascals killed all the prisoners they took. We are not working on their principle. I must now conclude as I am going to put on a clean shirt for the first time since we began.

Captain Charles Wood was not so lucky. He was wounded early on:

I got hit just as the Duke moved to the attack and bled like a pig. I took up my stirrups into the hunting seat and made the best of my way back to Waterloo. With the assistance of a dragoon I afterwards got into Brussels and found a lodging in the Rue Royale. Arnold will come home with me. He was shot through the lungs. They tell me he must not eat meat for six months. He says 'Wait till I get to Northampton with five hunters next November . . .' Bob Manners was struck in the shoulder by a lance and did not find it out till next day.

You should have seen us the night before the fight. Every one wet through. We had a shower that came down like a wall. It made the ground up to the horses fetlocks. I see the English papers say 'The Light Dragoons could make no impression on the French Cuirassiers.' Now our regiment actually rode over them. Give me the boys that will go at a swinging gallop for the last seventy yards, applying both spurs when you come within six yards. Then if you don't go over them I am much mistaken. I have found the ball which went through my thigh into the pad of my saddle, very high. I think it hit the bone, which drove it upwards.

Two paintings of the charge of the Scots Greys, one by Lady Butler, the other by Stanley Berkeley, give a vivid impression of the vigour and thrust of the battle. A less imaginative but no less forceful picture is given by Fortescue in his *History of the British Army*:

. . . Before the French columns reached the summit, Uxbridge had ordered the Union Brigade farther to the left, over against the line of Donzelot's and Marcognet's attack, and had himself taken post with the Household Brigade immediately to west of the Brussels road. As Travers's cuirassiers came up the slope he directed the King's Dragoon Guards and First Life Guards against their front, with the Second Life Guards in echelon to their left, and held the Blues in reserve. Travers's left being somewhat in advance was first checked, but the right, pushing on, came upon the deep cutting in the Chain road immediately to west of the cross-ways. Scrambling down one side and up the other, they were met, before they could re-form their ranks, by the remainder of the King's Dragoon Guards and First Life Guards. Thus caught at a disadvantage, the cuirassiers were broken and repulsed. Some turned straight back and galloped down the hill, pursued by the two British regiments; others inclined to their right, with the Second Life Guards at their heels, plunged into the Brussels road, and galloped down it as far as the barricade before La Haye Sainte, where, being stopped, they wheeled to their left and fled through the open space between the Chain road and the gravel-pit.

Simultaneously the Union Brigade swooped down upon the heads of the French infantry columns, the Royals on the right assailing Bourgeois's brigade, the Inniskillings falling upon Donzelot and the Greys upon Marcognet. They were barely one thousand sabres altogether, but their approach was hidden from the French by the hollows of the reverse slope of the ridge, and their onslaught was as furious as it was sudden. For a moment the French masses seethed madly as the unhappy men, tightly crowded together, strove to defend themselves with musket and bayonet; and then they dissolved into a mere pack of fugitives, flying down the slope towards their own position, with the sabres of the British dragoons playing havoc among them. As it chanced, some of Travers's cuirassiers were driven headlong into the broken ranks of the French infantry, increasing their confusion; and the Second Life Guards joining the right of the Inniskillings, the two regiments combined in the impartial chase of horse and foot.

Seldom in all military history has there been seen a more terrific smashing of formed infantry by cavalry. It is small wonder that the British troopers became drunk and maddened by their success. Their horses were good and fairly fresh, for there had been no weight crushing down their backs all night, as in the case of the French; the ground was in their favour; the men could not only sit in the saddle but could ride; and from ten to fifteen thousand French were retreating or flying before them. Quiot's troops, left in isolation at La Haye Sainte, abandoned the attack. Durutte on the extreme east, after driving the Nassauers from Papelotte and nearly reaching the crest of the ridge, found his right flank assailed by the Twelfth Light Dragoons, who drove him back in great confusion upon his reserves. It seemed as if the British cavalry would sweep all before them; and no sound of voice or trumpet could make the men stop.

The Household and Union Brigades galloped on over the plain and up the acclivity of La Belle Alliance, until the former came under the fire of

Bachelu's division, which had been slightly advanced to cover d'Erlon's flank during his attack, and were received with a storm of bullets which overthrew many men and scores of horses. Then, seeing a compact body of cuirassiers advancing against them, they wheeled about and retreated, the Blues, which were less out of hand than the rest, striving to cover the retreat. Farther to the left the Greys, with some of the Royals and Inniskillings, dashed into the midst of two divisional batteries, half-way up the ridge, cut down gunners, drivers and horses, upset the guns into a ravine, and then swinging sharply to their left assailed Napoleon's great battery of eighty pieces. The Emperor ordered two regiments of Delort's cuirassiers to attack them; but, before these could move, the 3rd and 4th Lancers of Jacquinot's division fell upon the left flank of the British and bade fair to annihilate them. In no kind of order, and with horses blown and exhausted, the remnants of the Union Brigade could make little resistance nor even attempt to fly. Sir William Ponsonby was borne down and killed, and indeed few of them would have escaped, had not the Twelfth and Sixteenth Light Dragoons of Vandeleur's brigade come to their rescue, charged the French lancers in turn, and given their comrades some respite. Thus tardily and with difficulty the remnants of the two brigades crawled back to their places behind La Haye Sainte. Of two thousand troopers and horses that had charged, over one thousand horses and from seven to eight hundred men were killed, wounded and missing.

Milhaud's cuirassiers pushed on and cut up a battalion of Hanoverians, but they themselves now fell to another English cavalry charge. This English force was then caught by French lancers, who in turn were dispersed by the 12th and 16th cavalry regiments.

Napoleon was now looking for the opportunity to make one of those lightning thrusts which had so often brought him victory in the past. Wellington guessed his purpose and deployed the infantry in squares separated by artillery. The French opened the next phase with a relentless cannonade on to these dispositions, then handed over the battle to the cavalry. From then on it was a desperate battle of attrition; the centres of the squares were clogged with dead and wounded, while outside lay a mounting wall of men and horses as all the remaining French cavalry was destroyed. In some of their desperate charges the outlying British guns were captured, but there was no French infantry to hold them. Now was the moment when Napoleon desperately needed a reserve to press an attack right into the squares, but that reserve had been used up earlier in the battle.

And so the French cavalry fell back, so depleted and exhausted they were unable to cover the retreat. Waterloo was a resounding triumph for the British because few losing armies have fought with more tenacity and courage than the French on that day.

It was said that during the battle the Gordon Highlanders, who were what is described as 'fighting mad', grabbed the stirrup leathers of the Greys and with them were carried forth in a series of long bounds into the enemy lines. Sergeant Ewart of the Greys captured a French eagle. As he charged forward and took it he was attacked by its bearer but he cut the man down with a blow across the head. Then a French

Men of the 14th Light Dragoons who later became 14th Hussars, 1815.

Genappe, 1815, was a skirmish the day before Waterloo in which French lancers were beaten off by Life Guards and 7th Hussars.

The 28th (1st Gloucester) Regiment receiving French cavalry at Waterloo, 1815.

lancer attacked him but Ewart slashed him across the face. Finally a French infantry man lunged at him with a bayonet only to receive a split head for his trouble. Ewart then rode back with the eagle.

Waterloo was noted for a certain nonchalance of comment. When a cannon ball sliced off most of the Earl of Uxbridge's leg as he rode alongside Wellington, he remarked: 'By God, I've lost my leg!' Wellington, preoccupied, gave him a quick glance. 'By God, you have, Sir,' he replied. The remainder of the leg was amputated on the battlefield and the butcher's saw used for the operation was later presented to the RMA Sandhurst Museum.

Lord Fitzroy Somerset, who would later become Lord Raglan and command the Crimean Expeditionary Force, was badly wounded in the arm; an immediate amputation was necessary. He was conscious at the time. As the remains of the arm were being removed from the room where this gruesome operation had taken place, he suddenly roused himself and said: 'Bring that back. I have a ring on the finger which I must remove before you throw the arm away.' People were accustomed to enduring considerable pain at that time; teeth were drawn without anaesthetics of any kind: for a serious operation the patient might be given a good swig of brandy, if he was lucky and if he could swallow.

Two different interpretations of the charge of the Scots Greys at Waterloo.

It seems unlikely that the Duke of Wellington said that Waterloo was won on the playing fields of Eton, not least because Eton had no playing fields in the modern sense at that time. But he undoubtedly did say: 'It was a damned nice thing ['nice' meaning close and all too finely balanced], the nearest thing you ever saw in your life.'

Comrades in arms (1815). Left to right: Sir Thomas Graham (Lord Lyndock), Lord Hill, Sir Thomas Picton, Marquis of Anglesea.

10

Cavalry in the Nineteenth Century

In the first half of the nineteenth century it seemed as if the world had had enough of full-scale war for the time being, and there was no major conflict between 1815 and the Crimean War in 1854. There were, however, minor wars between Russia and Persia, Russia and Turkey, and in India. Every country had, naturally enough, cut down its military expenditure after the defeat of Napoleon but few countries had wielded the Treasury axe as vigorously as Britain. Two army economies – the disbandment of the Wagon Train and the Staff Corps – were later proved to have been unmitigated follies. The effects of that were to be felt in the Crimean War.

The centre of cavalry development in the nineteenth century was undoubtedly India. As so often happens when the end of an era is in sight, the products of that age shine with unsurpassed excellence. Within a hundred years the machine-gun would have brought an end to this most spectacular element of warfare. The names would indeed be preserved, 'horse' artillery would reach its target by parachute and transport aircraft, hussars and dragoons alike would grind along in tanks, and the old reconnaissance duties of light horse would be performed by armoured car or helicopter, but the day of the horse in war was soon to be over – and will remain so, at least while world oil reserves last.

India produced first-class cavalry because it was used by both sides in terrain in which there was no room for mistakes. The speed of local cavalry – notably the Mahrattas – had an enlivening effect on the British units sent to confront them. The Mahrattas could appear from nowhere, fight furiously and, if defeated, disappear faster than any pursuer. Some spirited actions were seen in the Mahratta Wars. At the turn of the century the Mahrattas, who in many ways resembled the Mongols of old, both in their fighting methods and their depredations, were mainly officered by Frenchmen who were anxious that this mobile force should give the greatest possible trouble to the British in India. The Mahrattas were not only expert cavalrymen but also accurate and well-equipped gunners and formidable infantrymen. However, on 23 September 1803, at Assaye, they came up against Arthur Wellesley, later to become Duke of Wellington and conqueror of Napoleon.

Wellesley, with an army of 7,000, was outnumbered by seven to one. By the time the battle ended, Wellesley would have lost a quarter of this total. However, two factors were crucial in his defeat of the Mahrattas. First was his eye for ground, which constantly brought the enemy to a position as unfavourable for them as it was satisfactory for him; and second was his desperate charge at their hundred guns. Wellesley proved in this battle the old adage that in certain circumstances 'audacity is the best strategy'. When Wellesley gave the order to advance in the face of overwhelming odds, the Chief Officer of the Nizam of Hyderabad, who stood beside him, suddenly shouted 'God is great!' After the battle Wellesley, somewhat surprised at the remark, asked him what he had meant. The Chief Officer replied, 'I meant that you were mad.'

Wellesley had nearly 4,000 casualties at Assaye but the Mahrattas left all their guns behind and sustained casualties equal to Wellesley's entire original force.

Farther north a memorable campaign was being won by General Gerard Lake. Lake was an infantry officer, a Guardsman, but he showed a grasp of cavalry warfare far superior to many who served in that arm. He was a pioneer of horse artillery, which was an idea he had acquired from his studies of Frederick the Great. Lake won the battle of Delhi in September 1803, captured Agra in October, and won the battle of Laswari in November. He then came up against Holkar, who fought in traditional Mahratta fashion, with an all-cavalry army. He was said to have 60,000 light horse and 130 guns under his command. Initially it seemed as if the Mahrattas would carry all before them. Holkar defeated a force under Colonel Monson, then besieged and captured Delhi; he then set off southwards on a deep raid.

Lake went off after him. For seventeen days the Mahrattas remained thirty or forty miles ahead of their pursuers. On 16 November 1804 Lake halted thirty-six miles behind Holkar. That night he put in a forced night march and caught the Mahrattas just before dawn. After a short, desperate battle the pursuit continued for ten miles. This made a total distance covered in twenty-four hours of seventy miles – twenty-four the previous day, thirty-six during the night, and ten miles at dawn. This, in the Indian climate, was almost incredible. They had already completed 350 miles in fifteen days. Lake lost two men killed and two wounded in defeating 60,000 with a force of 3,500. It was a fine tribute to the value of speed and surprise. Six months later Lake caught another force of Mahrattas after a similar forced night march. Although a satisfactory peace resulted and Holkar was eventually driven deep into the Punjab, Lake's subsequent reputation was dimmed by his inability to capture the fortress of Bhurtpore. After four assaults, each involving heavy losses, Lake had been forced to lift the siege.

In 1806 there occurred a minor event which is nevertheless proudly remembered by all cavalry. A revolt and massacre – caused by new regulations – occurred in a local infantry battalion at Vellore, near Madras. Colonel Rollo Gillespie heard of the mutiny and set off to quell it with a single cavalry regiment, the 19th Light Dragoons (now part of the 15/19th Hussars). It was a typical cavalry dash, with the commanding officer leading and performing feats of astonishing gallantry on arrival. Gillespie, described by many as 'the bravest man in the British Army', subsequently became a general and was killed in 1814 storming the hill fort of Kalanga.

But while, in India, it was possible for a cavalry regiment to obtain plenty of exercise, training and fighting, the position at home was by no means as happy. Eight cavalry regiments had been disbanded soon after the Naploeonic Wars, leaving twenty-four. Of these, only half saw any overseas service before the middle of the century. Even worse was the fact that a regiment was often scattered over the country in small detachments, so that if necessary a unit could be brought into action quickly against civil unrest. This meant that if ever the regiment should be called to go into action, many of the NCOs and men would hardly know or be known to their officers.

However, the requirement to aid the Civil Power brought about one advantageous move. This was the acceptance of the idea of peacetime yeomanry regiments. Yeomanry regiments had existed from 1794, when invasion appeared to be an unpleasant possibility. They would, over the years, prove an invaluable recruiting ground for the regular cavalry, but in the early nineteenth century it was their close-knit, loyal and reliable quality which was most remarked on. Some were raised from a single estate; others were a form of gentlemanly riding club in which everyone from commanding officer to trooper came from land-owning gentry or their tenantry,

A nineteenth-century recruiting poster which caused some derisive comment.

Suffolk Yeomanry, reputed to be 'the backbone of England'.

West Essex Yeomanry, 1846 – lacking in experience but not in courage and endurance.

and the troopers were 'gentleman rankers'. Each man supplied his own horse and equipment. He received a grant of one pound ten shillings, but this of course left him well out of pocket on the year's outlay. If he was called up for duty, he received pay roughly equivalent to the regulars. The system was highly individualistic, and at times slightly chaotic, as members could resign at any time except when actually on service. However, when in the field, a yeomanry unit usually had enough experience of handling, managing and caring for horses to make it entirely adequate for its duties. Periodically, in a wave of ill-advised economy, the government would abolish a number of yeomanry regiments altogether; some time later, in a mood of near panic, it would try to reconstitute them or raise fresh ones. During riots the yeomanry were supposed to preserve good order and good temper in a shower of abuse, stones and unsalubrious missiles – and almost invariably managed to do so. Working-class people tended to dislike and distrust the yeomanry as instruments of their oppressors – even though many of the yeomanry were in favour of reform – and the yeomanry also had the uncomfortable knowledge that even in Parliament there were those who regarded them with a jaundiced eye. In spite of this they managed a variety of duties with cheerful efficiency. They were used not only for riots but also for a multiplicity of other tasks including the quenching of fires.

Both the yeomanry and the regular cavalry had a disastrous setback to their reputation as a result of the so-called 'Peterloo massacre'. In August 1819 a crowd of over 30,000 had assembled at St Peter's Fields, Manchester, to listen to an inflammatory orator named Hunt. On this occasion Hunt appears to have behaved with moderation. However, the magistrates decided to arrest him, using the Manchester and Salford Yeomanry for the purpose. This unit was unfortunately untrained and ill-disciplined and it became clear to Hunt and his followers that, though they had no intention of resisting arrest, the yeomanry had become confused, their horses were out of control, and order was being lost. Although the unit managed to make the arrests, the troopers became swallowed up in the crowd, swords were drawn, and fighting broke out. To extricate them, the 14th Hussars, on standby duty, were used and as a result about eleven people (the exact number is not known) were killed and many more injured. It was a sorry episode in every way and it underlined the vital need for control and discipline in such circumstances.

More serious riots occurred in other cities in 1831, on the eve of the Reform Bill, Bristol was in the hands of a mob for three days before being put in order by the 14th Light Dragoons. Here, as elsewhere, a firmer initial stand would have prevented subsequent bloodshed.

British cavalry was at its best in India, and a notable episode was the taking of Bhurtpore in 1826. It will be recalled that Lake had failed to take it earlier in the century. By 1826 it had become a focal point for opposition to the British and was also believed by many of its occupants and their supporters to be impregnable. Much against his will Lord Amherst, the Governor-General, decided that this standing threat to the establishment of law and order must be reduced. A cavalry force comprising the 16th Lancers, 11th Light Dragoons, 3rd, 4th, 6th, 8th, 9th and 10th Bengal Light Cavalry, plus four regiments of horse artillery, were despatched to capture the town. It was a formidable task, which was accomplished within a month.

This, incidentally, was the first time for approximately 200 years that a British unit had used a lance (or spear) in action, and was the first occasion ever for it to be used by a regiment in the modern sense. The lance, however, differed considerably from its medieval counterpart; it was much shorter and, of course, lighter. The standard length was nine feet, and it weighed just under four pounds. At this time it was made of ash, though later in the century this was replaced by bamboo. The point and butt were both of steel. The butt rested in a leather socket by the rider's heel.

However, the lance did not arrive in the British army without the controversy which normally surrounds a novel weapon. From the outset it was obvious that the lance was difficult to use and would demand long training. Even then, the dexterity which would enable a lancer to pick up a tent peg might not necessarily equip him for battle. Still worse was the fact that precise aiming of a lance point demanded a check in speed – and the loss of the effect of the charge. Although the charge at speed occurred very rarely, it did not stop cavalry men talking as if it were a *sine qua non* and universally used.

As the cavalry of India was the most active of all mounted regiments in the early nineteenth century, it is now appropriate to take a close look at its constituent parts. There were, of course, 'English' regiments, which contained Scots, Welsh and Irish and were all white. There were also Indian regiments with white officers. In general, these were of two kinds, regular and irregular. The term 'irregular' suggests an illegal, freebooting, undisciplined troop, but this was not so, except on rare occasions. in fact the irregular cavalry in India were roughly equivalent to the yeomanry in Britain. Regulars in India were provided with everything; irregulars provided their own horses and equipment, and virtually everything except ammunition. For this the irregular received a small monthly payment. He was, like his yeomanry counterpart in Britain, able to undertake a life of adventure with very few restrictions. In India, however, native princes who employed irregulars usually allowed their pay to fall into arrears, through incompetence or financial instability. In consequence, irregulars whose pay was months in arrears were inclined to attend to their own needs by private plundering or intimidation. This had given irregulars – or Silladars as they were known – a bad reputation in the past. However, the British irregular regiments soon enjoyed a high reputation and universal respect because their financial arrangements ensured that pay was regular and that, whatever happened, no irregular left the regiment at any time without a good cash sum in his pocket.

Although there were variations between different regiments, another advantage which the irregulars enjoyed was that all but the most senior officer posts were open to Indians. The Indians therefore approved of irregular regiments because they were independent and almost totally Indian; the government liked them because they were much cheaper to maintain than regular units in which everything was provided. In the Indian Mutiny eight of the eighteen irregular units remained loyal but all ten cavalry regiments threw in their lot with the rebels. There was a lesson to be learnt here but it was a long time before it was widely appreciated.

The names justly famous in irregular cavalry were James Skinner and William Gardner. Skinner was the son of a Scottish soldier and an Indian girl. Portraits show him to have been dark-skinned, stocky, and in appearance like an English yeoman farmer. Gardner, the son of an Irish officer who had married an American, was a tall, impressive figure. Their careers were equally dissimilar. Skinner, debarred from civil or military service with the East India Company by virtue of his native birth, joined a Mahratta regiment under French command, and was given a commission in it. However, when the Mahrattas were decisively defeated by Lake, and Skinner's regiment was disbanded, he and some 900 others decided it would be better to join the British and serve them than not to soldier on at all. That was in 1803. Lake asked them to choose a commander and, unanimously, they chose Skinner. Thus was born Skinner's Horse.

Soon the name – and appearance – of Skinner's Horse were widely known and acclaimed. Skinner was a strict disciplinarian, but while everyone in the regiment knew that misdoings would be duly and severely punished, they knew equally well that good service would be recognized and rewarded. His sowars (troopers) were probably the proudest men in India and they were also the most spectacular. They had red turbans and cummerbunds with silver edging, white trousers and long yellow jackets. Officers wore blue coats faced with silver, red and gold cummerbunds, and dragoon helmets with white cockades. So popular was his regiment that he had no difficulty in increasing its strength to 1,700. After the Holkar campaign, in which Skinner's Horse particularly distinguished itself, the regiment went up to 3,000 and was divided into three sections of 1,000 each. Another unit which had a famed but short life was the Rohilla Horse. This unit was attached to Skinner's.

To return to Gardner. More favoured in birth and background than Skinner, Gardner had begun his military life by being bought a commission as an ensign (today's second lieutenant). At the age of twenty-three he resigned from the army and entered the service of Holkar. Nobody appeared to think it extraordinary that a man should spend eleven years in an army and then become a mercenary in another, which might fight against his former comrades. However, neither Holkar nor Amrit Rao, whose service he entered later, completely trusted Gardner's loyalties – quite rightly. Eventually he went to Lake, who gave him a command. A few years later he was ordered to raise a regiment. This, Gardner's Horse, soon became as famous as Skinner's. The sowars wore green coats trimmed with silver lace, and red trousers. Gardner's reputation drew the cream of India's horsemen and fighters. But not for nothing were such regiments known by the name of their commanding officers. Brave, resourceful, and skilful though the sowars were, every man in their regiments knew that Skinner or Gardner was so completely superior in every military way that service under him was a privilege indeed.

There were, of course, others. There was the Poona Horse, Hodson's Horse, the Gujarat Irregular Horse and the Scinde Irregulars. Nowadays such names sound so archaic that many wonder whether they ever existed. Such doubts would be quickly cleared away if sceptics could be privileged to travel back in time and stand in the path of one of Gardner's squadrons, or the Rohillas, or the Poona Horse, as they rode in for the kill.

However, the colourful activities of the irregulars must not obscure the many other cavalry activities in India. In the First Afghan War, 1838, the 16th Lancers took part in the invasion. The hardships of this march (cavalry, although on horseback, are

The 16th Lancers and Skinner's Horse driving the Jats into Bharatpur, 1825.

The 3rd Light Dragoons at Chillienwallah, 1849.

A soldier of the 13th Light Dragoons fires from the saddle, 1845.

referred to as 'marching') were enormous. Throughout the day the temperature could vary from cold to blazingly hot, rations and forage were severely limited, and water was scarce. The 16th lost thirty men in a quicksand, and many more from snipers and disease. Fortunately resistance was minimal, but the campaign went down in history as one of the most exhausting the regiment had known; a hundred encounters against impossible odds would have been preferable to the slow drain of exhaustion, disease and heat.

Another remarkable cavalry commander of this era was John Jacob. Jacob went out to India at the age of sixteen and stayed there all his life. Jacob was a professional to his fingertips, utterly fearless, but also a man of great culture. He had the Scinde Horse at the Battle of Miani in February 1843 and again at Hyderabad in March 1843. On both occasions the speed and control of the final charges proved decisive.

Before we look at the wars of the second half of the nineteenth century we should perhaps take stock of the dress, capability, weapons and philosophy of the cavalry at that stage in its evolution.

During the eighteenth and nineteenth centuries, in all countries, cavalry dress became more elaborate and expensive. There is a limit to the finery you can heap on an infantryman, for he has to march and will sometimes have to negotiate muddy places. His uniform must retain some vestige of practicality – although there have been periods in history when even that has declined. But the cavalryman need have no such limitations. The only restraint on the extravagant finery of cavalry uniform was the depth of the commanding officer's purse. And, in many instances, that seemed long enough to met all fanciful requirements.

The function of cavalry had always been known to be limited and dependent – although this never prevented enthusiastic cavalrymen from seeing other arms as dependent on them. In action cavalry gains can only be held if there is infantry to follow them up. Holding ground has sometimes been achieved by cavalry dismounting and performing as infantry but it does not lessen their dependence on that arm. Out of action the cavalry is particularly reliant on the services for supply and maintenance. Nowadays it is a matter of fuel, ammunition, maintenance and spares; in the past it was forage, farriers and veterinary surgeons. A member of a modern mechanized cavalry regiment may be astonished at the number and variety of ills which can make his metal steed unroadworthy, but the cavalryman of the past could parade an equally impressive list of horse ailments. It is said that when Richard III set out on the Third Crusade he took 50,000 horseshoes with him; he probably needed them all, and his veterinary requirements must have been on an equal scale.

But with all its vulnerability and its varieties the cavalry had a quality which was grudgingly, though universally, accepted by the other arms. The cavalry had style and dash. Almost anyone could be a foot-soldier but it was by no means everyone who could be a cavalryman. It has always been an unquestioned assumption that the aristocracy, whatever its other failings, had unlimited courage. The tradition went straight to the army officer and nowhere was it more clearly demonstrated than in the cavalry. The Charge of the Light Brigade may have been the wonder of the world but it was certainly not the wonder of the cavalry. Given the order any alternative action was unthinkable. And, as an action, it was by no means unique. The only remarkable

Officer of the 10th (The Prince of Wales's Own) Royal Regiment of Hussars. The satchel, on long straps, was called the sabretache and was used for carrying despatches (officially).

Elegance and beauty in a mounted officer, though greatly prized, were not always discernible.

Officer of the 17th Lancers. The badge of skull and crossbones over the words 'or glory' have caused them to be known as 'The Death or Glory Boys'.

6th Dragoon Guards, Officer (Carabiniers) 1844. Officers wore sashes which were often coloured red so as not to show bloodstains if used as bandages.

feature of the Charge of the Light Brigade in the eyes of many troopers was the excessive zeal with which it had been written up.

Psychologically there is doubtless an explanation for 'cavalry dash'. Any driver, however incompetent, who gets into a car and puts his foot on the accelerator feels a certain sense of being better than his normal self. An extra, and often misplaced, confidence seems to animate him. He will try to race an obviously more powerful car from the traffic lights; he will cut in and try manoeuvring for which his vehicle is scarcely suitable. Challenged, he will yell abuse at strangers to whom he would politely apologize if he brushed against them on the footpath. In short, he will be anything but his normal self. There are, perhaps, a few exceptional drivers, who never behave selfishly or obstreperously, but one never seems to come across them.

This is not to criticize the cavalry. Their function is to demolish the opposition, not to assist it. It does, however, suggest an explanation for certain activities which have made the cavalry unpopular in the past. One was riding over growing crops; another was a certain arrogance which was characteristic of many hunts in the nineteenth century. With it, of course, went a way of life. It was a short life and a merry one as often as not, reckless over the fences, reckless over the gaming tables, as quick to snatch the opportunity of eloping with an attractive woman as to react to an insult which may not even have been intended.

But, with all the speed, mobility, and prestige the cavalryman possessed, he was still greatly circumscribed. He had his spear or lance but, if it missed, his failure was obvious. He had his carbine, but very few men can fire straight from a moving horse. He had his sword, but the range of a sword is limited. Of his weapons the last was one of the most effective. A cavalryman acquires such dexterity with his sword that he can cut, parry, thrust, and cut again before anyone else has taken much note of what is happening. Swordmanship is a fine art and many of its greatest practitioners have been in the cavalry.

When summarily dismounted many a cavalryman has given a remarkably good account of himself with his sword. In the Sudan in the 1880s and 1890s British cavalrymen found themselves confronted with some of the bravest fighters the world has ever known. These were the Dervishes. The Dervishes – themselves superb horsemen – also knew how to destroy their opponents. Some of their foot-soldiers would lie on the ground, preferably concealed in grass or scrub, as the opponent rode through – at whatever pace. Then, with superb timing, they hamstrung the horse, bringing it and its rider down on top of them. From then on it was a hand-to-hand combat with the horseman, as like as not, partly disabled from shock. But on many occasions he would draw his sword and give as good as he got.

In this period there were desperate encounters when the swordsman was confronted with several opponents and a variety of weapons. Thus fell – after a titanic struggle – Colonel Fred Burnaby in the Battle of Abu Klea in 1885. Burnaby in fact was in the Grenadier Guards, which is scarcely a cavalry regiment but he was on horseback in this battle. Another occasion when a man fought to the end when unhorsed (though in this case through his own fault) was the death of the Prince Imperial in 1879. Ambushed by Zulus he put up a tremendous fight and sustained eighteen wounds before he fell.

An enormous advantage of the cavalry has always been its ability to exploit surprise. Surprise, like deception, is one of the great winning factors in warfare. A cavalry troop far from its parent unit can burst upon the enemy, brush aside pickets and sentries, and spread desolation and dismay. For this very reason a well-organized army will use its cavalry as a counter to surprise raids, and will have an elaborate system of screening, of which we shall say more later.

In spite of the variations in clothing, style and equipment which are the natural outcome of different people and different periods, many items have been standard in cavalry regiments whatever the country or period. The first was a sword. Whole books have been written on the sword but all that needs to be said of the cavalry sword, for the time being, is that it needed to be of a certain length, weight and sturdiness. It was required to slash its way to victory. Only by a slashing stroke inflicting a wound with the edge can a cavalryman be reasonably sure of retaining possession of his weapon. If he jabs at an opponent it is as likely as not that his point will stick and the sword be wrenched out of his hand as the enemy falls or turns away. In general, light cavalry favoured the curved sword and heavy cavalry the straight. The heavy dragoon's sword was about three inches longer and broader, about 39 inches instead of the 36 inches of the hussar and about $1\frac{1}{2}$ inches instead of $1\frac{1}{4}$ inches in width. But, of course, there was infinite variation close to these figures. In England there were periodic orders that all officers would be armed with the same weapon as their troopers; but they were widely disobeyed. A popular weapon, although its use was theoretically limited to the highest ranks, was the scimitar. This was usually thirty-two inches long and had a sharp point. The blade was slightly curved. It was an elegant weapon and was frequently adopted by cavalry officers who chose to ignore the fact that it virtually symbolized Generals and Field Marshals.

The problem with the sword was the same as the problem of armour and other weapons: should it be heavy enough to deal with all obstacles or should it be light and easy to handle? The same decision had to be taken over armour, which during the Middle Ages had become heavier and heavier. The problem of armour was solved when firearms were invented, for no armour was invulnerable to firearms. In consequence armour was almost totally discarded. However the debate over strength and weight for armour has emerged in a different form in the late twentieth century for tank design posed the question, should a tank be light, manoeuvrable, and fast, but vulnerable; or should it be heavier, slower, more thickly armoured and scarcely affected by any but the heaviest anti-tank weapons but nevertheless an easier target to hit? The sword, of course, had no effect at all on medieval armour and was subsequently designed only to cut thick cloth or leather jerkins. However, on certain occasions later, cavalry swords were confronted with chain mail and this produced disturbing results. In the nineteenth century some swords were found to be so badly made that they bent or broke easily. There is, of course, a knack to breaking an opponent's sword but many nineteenth-century swords bent through bad workmanship not through good swordplay by an enemy.

A general commonsense rule – which, needless to say, was at times disregarded – was that the sword should be attached to the saddle and not the man. Other commonsense rules were that uniform, though tight enough to look smart, should not be so tight that it hampered a man's freedom of movement. An important article of clothing was the long overcoat or cloak. The sleeveless cloak, although more picturesque, was undoubtedly less practical. The overcoat was protection not only against the weather but also against sword cuts. The reader may test the efficiency of this for himself by slashing at a thick curtain; he will be lucky to inflict much damage on it.

The most vulnerable points of the cavalryman were his head, his shoulders, his hands and his legs.

The head was best protected by a metal helmet but if this was too heavy it became very irksome to the wearer. There was an infinite variety of other forms of headgear, with plumes, with tufts, with flaps, with peaks, and so on. Headgear could easily be lost in action so a chinstrap was necessary. The top of the shoulder was particularly vulnerable, so here a man wore a covering of chain mail sufficient to protect that area. It is still to be seen in ceremonial dress today and is a good example of how what was once a purely utilitarian matter is now a feature of picturesque adornment. Hands, also extremely vulnerable, were protected by heavy gauntlets, some of which extended almost to the elbow. Many personal reminiscences of cavalry skirmishes recall that the writer had his wrist or lower arm slashed. To prevent this, some gauntlets included steel stiffeners. Jackboots were another practical article of clothing, although later they came to be almost symbolical of foppishness or tyranny. They kept the legs dry in wet weather and in a fight prevented the owner receiving a dangerous cut from a blow which had been only partially parried. They had a useful secondary function in protecting the legs when the squadron was hustled together and close-packed.

A substitute for the jackboot, which was supposed to give greater freedom, was the leather-covered overall. Titles of military dress are frequently puzzling because they often date from a different use. Overall in the army signifies tight-fitting trousers, elsewhere it would be a loose garment, probably covering the entire body. The original 'overalls' in the cavalry were cotton trousers which buttoned up on the outside of trousers as an additional protection.

Weight, of course, should be kept to the minimum. It might be thought that as a man was on horseback he could carry a full complement of equipment. This would be to confuse the function of the cavalry with that of the packhorse. Unfortunately both horse and foot were frequently overloaded with marginally useless equipment and lost speed and mobility in consequence.

Within the cavalry itself there were numerous modifications of the basic pattern. The light dragoon who might often fight dismounted would have a close-fitting cap rather than a helmet, lighter boots, and an efficient firearm. There have been many occasions when cavalry has been unable to be used as such because the roughness of the country made it unsuitable for horses; at such times it has had to wait chafing at its inability to perform, or fight dismounted. The effect of leaving a mettlesome and perhaps arrogant force outside a battle which they can see being fought near them is sometimes a strain on discipline. Forced inaction also causes men to make irrational decisions and there have been all too many occasions of frustrated cavalry units volunteering for action which could only result in their own extermination – and did. But it is not the cavalry alone which is prone to this fault of petty vanity.

Cavalry's worst enemy is perhaps its own impetuousness. Success – leading to exhaustion and disorder – leaves it highly vulnerable. If attacked after a success it is frequently routed. A competent commander will therefore always keep some part of his force in reserve – to complete or resist an attack. This policy was a key factor in many of Oliver Cromwell's successes.

The history of cavalry emphasizes over and over again that there can be no half-measures with this arm. Either it is well-mounted on horses which are properly shod, fed and cared for, and thus has great potential, or it is a shambling mess, ill-mounted on sorry nags. Equally, it is a force of well-disciplined, intelligent men who can carry out orders and fend for themselves if cut off, or it is a rabble on horseback. Supremely important is whether or not it has the right commander. If he is a man who knows his officers, his men, his horses, his tactics, and his assets and limitations, it will be a happy and successful regiment. If, alas, he is a man whose position has been attained by money and influence and not by merit, his deficiencies will soon be obvious to all. In the second half of the nineteenth century we encounter some commanders who belong to the latter category.

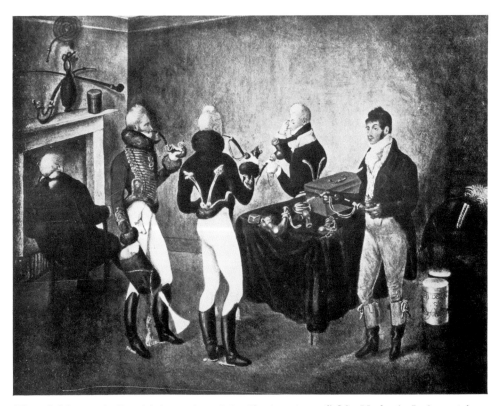

The 7th Hussars in Ipswich barracks, 1808 – 'buying pipes off Mr Hudson'. Left to right: Earl of Uxbridge, Lord Paget, H.R.H. Duke of Cambridge (afterwards King of Hanover), Hon. Berkeley Paget, Mr Hudson. The regiment bought 500 pipes, mainly meerschaums, which were very expensive.

11

The Crimean War and its Aftermath

The fate of the cavalry was sealed in 1823 when Captain John Norton of the 34th Regiment (later the King's Own Border Regiment) invented the cylindro-conoidal shot. Nevertheless, the cavalry had already had some previous experience of its fate being sealed; it had been sealed by the longbow, and the crossbow, by the phalanx and the pike, by the musket and the caltrap. Like Charles II, the cavalry took an unconscionable time in dying, but unlike that gallant though unreliable monarch made no apologies for it. Its fate would be sealed once or twice more before horsed cavalry regiments disappeared from the battlefield, but it was the machine-gun which was to administer the *coup de grâce*.

However, by the mid-nineteenth century a most unpleasant weapon – from the cavalry point of view – was appearing on many battlefields. This was the Minié rifle, which took its name from its French inventor, Captain Minié. For a century or more there had been experimental guns which showed ominous possibilities for the future – there had even been a prototype machine-gun in 1718 (invented by an Englishman). However, the principal concern was not so much rapidity of fire as accuracy. Muskets such as the famous 'Brown Bess' were reasonably reliable and could fire five shots a minute, but their lack of accuracy dictated that musketry must be at short range and in volleys. However, once it was realized that a spinning bullet was infinitely more accurate, rifles clearly had fresh possibilities. The Minié was still a muzzle-loader but it had a rifled barrel with three grooves which would twist the bullet one inch in seventy-two inches. The bullet was seven-tenths of an inch in diameter and the weapon had a range of 1,000 yards. Although it was not especially accurate, it was considerably more so than its predecessor. Its range and stopping-power would take the heart of any cavalry charge before it could get under way. At the same time – the early 1850s – artillery weapons were making rapid progress. Krupps made a breech-loading cannon in 1851, the famous six-pounder, which would see service as far afield as Africa. Britain then produced a superior version with a rifled barrel. The stage was now set for what might be described as the first of the modern wars – in the Crimea.

The Crimean War is mainly remembered for one futile but heroic cavalry action – the Charge of the Light Brigade. It took some twenty minutes. The whole war lasted over two years and included several other cavalry actions and a number of interesting set-piece battles. There was also an extensive period of gruelling trench warfare, which gave a foretaste of what was to happen later in 1914–18.

The Allied war aim was to capture the town and port of Sebastopol and, to do so, they sent an army to attack it from the north side. Years of neglect and official parsimony had reduced the British Army to a sorry state, and the French was little better. Owing to the vast distances involved and complete lack of experience among the administrators, the campaign began in chaos which took a year to eliminate. On arrival the Allied armies were stricken with cholera and it is astonishing that they were able to fight at all. The opening battle, at the Alma river on 20 September 1854, was won by heroic actions by British infantry. Confusion and blunders abounded on both sides. A British cavalry division was present, consisting of the ill-fated Light Brigade under the Earl of Cardigan and the more successful Heavy Brigade under General Scarlett. However, the British cavalry was not committed till the battle was nearly over. Rather more surprising was the fact that the Russian cavalry was not committed at all. When the British infantry finally forced the Russian foot out of their positions, 3,000 Russian horsemen sat idly by and watched it happen. Still more surprising was the fact that when the Russians were retreating in disorder Raglan did not order the Allied cavalry to pursue. Various explanations have been offered for this omission but the most likely was that Raglan considered that his cavalry was so inexperienced that if he let them pursue he would be lucky to see them for days. If this was his reasoning – and his conduct of the battle gives little cause to suggest that logic affected his acts and decisions – it was presumably vindicated by the chaos which occurred in what was known as the flank march. Three days after the Alma battle the Allied armies set off to march right round Sebastopol on the inland side so that they could then attack the town from the south. The explanation for this strange decision was that the north of Sebastopol was thought to be heavily protected. This does not seem to have been true, but owing to Raglan's dilatoriness the southern side was well fortified when the Allies eventually made an effort to attack it. However, the moment of truth for cavalry training had come on the march itself. Near a point called Mackenzie's Farm (named after as Scotsman who had settled in the area thirty years before), the leading Allied troops blundered into the rear of a Russian division which was marching north-east to Baské-Serai. The cavalry, which should have been ahead of the Allied army on reconnaissance, had drifted off down a side road from which it had to be recalled. However, if Allied cavalry was hopelessly at fault, so was the Russian. On the alert being raised, the Allied cavalry returned promptly and attacked the Russian rearguard, capturing some baggage. As an example of utter incompetence by the cavalry on both sides this episode was unmatchable.

The next large battle, on 25 October 1854, was wholly a cavalry action. It became known as the Battle of Balaclava but was in fact three separate actions: one was the Charge of the Heavy Brigade, another was the Thin Red Line, the third was the Charge of the Light Brigade.

Soon after dawn on 25 October a Russian army commanded by General Liprandi moved towards Balaclava where the Allies had a vital harbour. Liprandi's force

The Earl of Cardigan, K.C.B. Eccentric and obstinate, but remarkably brave.

The Charge of the Heavy Brigade at Balaclava, 1854.

The Charge of the Heavy Brigade as C. E. Stewart, the artist, thought it must have looked to the Russians.

Lord Cardigan leading the Charge of the Light Brigade, Balaclava, 1854.

consisted of 25,000 infantry, thirty-four squadrons of horse and seventy-eight guns. A warning of the impending attack had been given by a Turkish spy, but no one had seen fit to act on this interesting information. The cavalry, which should have had a screen of pickets and videttes out in the path of the Russians, apparently had nothing of the sort. (This deficiency was remedied later in the war when, with desperate over-compensation, the cavalry was watching for attacks from points from which attacks were impossible.)

The Russians reached the Turkish redoubts and slaughtered those who tried to resist them; the remainder fled. Four squadrons of Russian cavalry now moved forwards towards Balaclava. There was nothing between them and their vital objective other than a force of 550 members of the 93rd Regiment, which was later to merge with the 91st to become the Argyll and Sutherland Highlanders. On this day they were in no shape to be heroes for most of them were sick – and being sick in the Crimea could mean anything from malaria to cholera and dysentery. The sudden unannounced appearance of the Russians gave the 93rd no time to take up the square formation they would normally adopt when facing cavalry and Sir Colin Campbell, their commander, merely had time to draw them up in two lines and steady them. The first volley was fired as the Russians came into range, the second as they were much

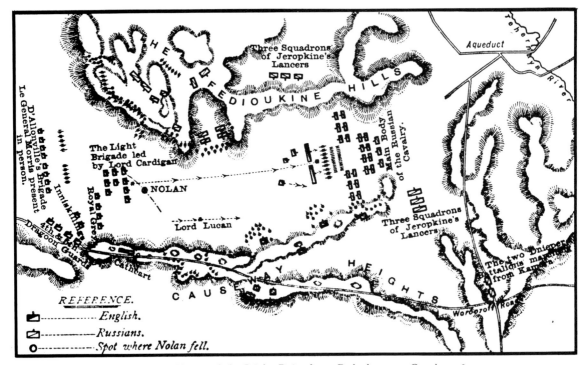

4 *Plan of the Charge of the Light Brigade at Balaclava, 25 October 1854.*

closer. Presumably the Russians were in very open formation for no one was killed; however, their commander gave the order to wheel left and they moved out of range. It has been said that the Russian cavalry was merely testing the strength of the defences and once the 93rd exposed themselves their object was achieved. Interesting though this possibility is, it seems unlikely that the Russians would have allotted four squadrons for such a task. Reconnaissance was certainly part of their activity, but if the 93rd had not presented such a resolute face, that reconnaissance would have taken them into Balaclava itself, with disastrous results for the Allies.

Meanwhile the remainder of the Russian cavalry, amounting to 3,000, although none of the allies knew it at the time, were coming over Causeway Heights. Even Temple Godman (see below), who fought them, believed they numbered less than 2,000. General the Hon. J. Scarlett, confronting the Russians, had a mere six squadrons (a total of 800) to oppose them. The Heavy Brigade consisted of the 1st Dragoons (now part of the Blues and Royals), the 2nd Dragoons (later the Scots Greys, now with the Carabiniers, the Scots Dragoon Guards), the 6th Inniskillings (now joined with the 5th Dragoon Guards who were also in the charge), and the 4th Dragoons (who are now the 4/7th Dragoon Guards), plus one troop of Divisional Horse Artillery. Having reached the top of the hill, the Russian cavalry paused for a moment, uncertain which way to go. Their indecision was noted by Scarlett and without hesitating a moment he wheeled his left column into line and led the charge himself. Scarlett, incidentally, was sixty-five but he fought like a tiger in the action, and received five wounds. Fortunately for Scarlett the Russians had closed up so much in their advance that there was no reserve to send in when the Heavy Brigade was exhausted. Instead, the whole Russian force, bemused and bewildered, began to fall back.

A vivid account of the action came in a letter from Temple Godman, a captain in the 5th Dragoon Guards, who wrote home with conscientious regularity:

> At this time a large mass of cavalry came over the hill in front of our camp and would in a few minutes have been in our lines, and have cut down the few men left, when we got the order to advance. The Greys and Inniskillings went in first, then we came in support of the Greys. The enemy front must have been composed of three regiments and a very strong column in the rear, in all about 1,500 or 2,000, while we were not more than 800. However, the charge sounded and at them went the first line, Scarlett and his ADC well in front. The enemy seemed quite astonished and drew into a walk and then a halt. As soon as they met, all I saw was swords in the air in every direction, the pistols going off and everyone hacking away right and left. In a moment the Greys were surrounded and hemmed completely in. There they were, fighting back to back, in the middle, the great bearskin caps high above the enemy. This was the work of a moment. As soon as we saw it the 5th advanced and in they charged yelling and shouting as loud as they could split; the row was tremendous and for about five minutes neither would give way, and their column was so deep we could not cut through it. At length they turned, and well they might, and the whole ran as hard as they could pelt back up the hill, our men after them, all broken up, and cutting them down right and left. We pursued about 300 yards and then called off with much difficulty, the gunners then opened up on them and gave them a fierce peppering. It took some time to get the men to fall in again, they were all mixed up together of course. The enemy being gone, and we all right, we had time to look around. The ground was covered with dead and dying men and horses. I am happy to say our brigade lost but seven men dead, but had a considerable number of wounded, some mortally. The ground was strewn with swords, broken and whole, trumpets, helmets, carbines, while a quantity of men were scattered all along as far as we pursued. There must have been some forty or fifty of the enemy dead besides wounded. The Russians seemed very steady and well-disciplined but our men wrought havoc among them with their long straight swords.

This letter was to Godman's father. Godman sent another letter to his brother a week later. It included a few gory details omitted from the earlier account – presumably because he thought his brother had a stronger stomach than his parents:

> We had time to look about. There were over forty lying dead and in pools of blood from the most fearful cuts. We lost a corporal, quite hacked to pieces and one man was shot. Another must die; his lungs came through his back.
>   I had one or two shaves during the day, my coat sleeve was cut through and my wrist bruised but not cut as I had on some very thick jerseys.

It is interesting to compare this account with Richard Atkyns's experiences at Roundway Down. Between them they give the essentials of a cavalry fight. Atkyns, on a fast nimble horse, was desperately trying to engage his notable opponent but had, if anything, the worst of the encounter. Godman, with a rare eye for detail of historical interest, mentions the types of injury sustained in a cavalry mêlée. It is clear from his account that numbers of swords and other weapons were lost almost immediately in the fight. He himself was nearly caught by a lance thrust. Had the lance found its target, its owner would of course have lost it.

The Russians took the charge at the halt, but once the initial shock had been absorbed, the battle became simply a matter of swordplay on horseback. Woe betide the man who had lost his sword for any reason: he would be hard put to survive.

Although the charge of the Heavy Brigade was a fine performance there was a lot of luck in it. The Russians, having been thrown back, should have been harried by a pursuing charge from the Light Brigade. The culprit here was clearly the Earl of Cardigan, who watched the Heavies but failed to follow up their success. It has been suggested that he was waiting for orders which did not come and therefore became so frustrated and bad-tempered that he was incapable of interpreting correctly the orders his own brigade received shortly afterwards. This seems highly unlikely. Cardigan knew very well what a unit of light cavalry should do in a situation such as had occurred on Causeway Heights and his failure to take appropriate action was more likely due to lethargy and slow-wittedness rather than to blind obedience to orders. Apart from the famous charge, Cardigan was not renowned for his respect for the wishes of higher authority.

The Charge of the Light Brigade, which took place an hour later, has unfortunately created the impression in the minds of many that cavalry merely performed desperate and futile charges. This delusion has been fostered by poets and literary men who have no idea of the function of armies. Tennyson's famous *Charge of the Light Brigade* is full of inaccuracies. They were not 600, but 673; there were cannon in front but not at the left and right; and Lord Cardigan did not say 'Forward, the Light Brigade'. And so on. However, it is a spirited poem and commemorates a very gallant occasion. The reason for this ill-fated charge was that Raglan, up on the Heights, had noted that the Russians were preparing to drag away the Turkish guns which they had overrun earlier in the day. He therefore told Airey, the Quartermaster General, who functioned as his Chief of Staff, to write down a message. Raglan had seen and heard enough of verbal orders being misunderstood in this and other campaigns, so he dictated to Airey the following message: 'Lord Raglan wishes the cavalry to advance rapidly to the front, and try to prevent the enemy carrying away the guns. Troop of Horse Artillery may accompany. French cavalry is on your left. Immediate.'

At least, that is the message written on a page torn from Airey's notebook and sent to Lord Lucan, commander of the Cavalry Division, which included both Heavy and Light Brigades. The message was handed to the ADC, Captain Nolan, a superb horseman, the author of a book on cavalry tactics, and as placid a character as you would expect from his Irish father and Italian mother. Nolan rode down a near precipice and found Lord Lucan. Lucan regarded Nolan as a cocky young upstart and

Nolan regarded Lucan as an over-promoted ninny. Nolan handed over the message as if it were an ultimatum. Lucan read it, and burst out angrily: 'Attack, sir, attack . . . what guns?' (The word 'sir', in military and naval circles, is used as a conventional address and may be preceded or followed by highly disrespectful comment.) Nolan, who should have realized that from 800 feet farther up the hills Raglan could see guns invisible to Lucan in the valley, merely swept out his arm towards the Russians and said, 'There my Lord is the enemy, there are the guns.'

Lucan then rode up to Cardigan, who was his brother-in-law. The two detested each other but that did not affect the present issue. Cardigan was amazed at the order (incidentally no 'order' had in fact been issued, it was only a 'wish'), but never for a moment contemplated disobeying. He gave orders for the squadrons to form up and dress the lines, then spoke the vital words, 'The brigade will advance. Walk. March. Trot.' At no time was the Charge ever sounded. As they set off, with Cardigan leading on his chestnut, Ronald, Nolan suddenly spurred his horse forward and rode obliquely across Cardigan's front. Hardly had he covered a few yards when a Russian shell dropped near him and blew half his chest away. He gave a last scream, described by Cardigan as 'screaming like a demmed woman', and died. Perhaps, at the last moment, he had suddenly realized that Cardigan was now on a death ride for the wrong guns and that Raglan had really meant him to go for the other guns; if he now altered the direction of the charge by twenty degrees, and went for the other guns, that would have made the whole enterprise practical though still dangerous. However, he died, and there was Cardigan leading his brigade steadily up the valley, over a mile long, losing men all the way. The order of battle was 13th Light Dragoons and 17th Lancers, then the 11th Hussars, then the 4th Light Dragoons and 8th Hussars. As they swept up the valley the Russian fire became more concentrated, and as the brigade came over the last few yards the guns fired a final salvo which seemed as if it would blow them all away. Miraculously Cardigan was untouched and was first in among the Russian gunners, slashing away with his sabre. Not only did the brigade reach the Russian guns, but they also rode right into and through them. That was it. There was no means of holding the position. Cardigan turned his horse and followed the remnants of his brigade as it made its way back up the valley.

Heavy though casualties were before, they were even worse now, for Cossack and other riflemen took a steady toll on the brigade as it returned up the valley. The world may have been astonished and impressed by this example of selfless bravery, but the Russian riflemen saw no reason to let anyone survive it. Casualties would have been even higher if the French 4th Chasseurs d'Afrique, commanded by General d'Allonville, had not charged a Russian battery on the Fedioukine hills.

Of the 673 in the charge, 195 were present to answer the roll that night: 113 had been killed, 134 were wounded, a total of 442. The fate of the remainder is shown by the casualties to the horses, of which 475 were killed. Unhorsed and surrounded in hopeless circumstances, men were easily taken prisoner. Cardigan displayed little interest in the fate of his unfortunate command but he addressed a comment to one of the survivors: 'It was a demmed stupid thing,' he said. 'Oh we'd do it again,' said the man. That seemed to be the end of the matter, so Cardigan rode back to his yacht, had a bath, drank a bottle of champagne and went to bed. Subsequently he found plenty to say about the occasion.

It was, of course, a feat of amazing courage. Such is human resilience that even the Charge of the Light Brigade is not unique in military history: there have been other equally gallant forlorn hopes. But, of its kind, it was a great inspiration to other forces in the war and in other wars later.

One of those who rode in the charge was Sergeant-Major G. Loy Smith of the 11th Hussars. Smith had joined the regiment in India in 1836. He retired in 1858. His straight-forward, matter-of-fact narrative of the events of that day spares the reader none of the gruesome details but nothing is written for dramatic effect. Traditional versions of the charge imply that all the damage was caused by the Russian guns as the Light Brigade charged up the valley. Smith makes it clear that Russian Lancers and infantry killed and wounded many of the Light Brigade on the way back.

Shortly after we took up a position on the left rear of our encampment with our backs to Balaclava, facing the opening at the top of the valley, through which it was thought the Russian Cavalry would come, so as to prevent them getting in our rear. We were out of sight of the enemy, but expected every moment to see them. Lord Cardigan now gave the order to 'Draw swords'; the French Artillery fired down the valley over our heads, occasionally we heard a bullet from the Russian Infantry that had occupied the Redoubts. Our Heavy Cavalry was in our rear behind our encampment. The Cossacks that had pursued the retreating Turks now came boldly on (for we had retired without being covered by skirmishers), galloping into our encampment and wounding the spare horses that had been left tied up in the lines; the tents at this time were all lying on the ground, the ropes having been let loose soon after the battle commenced by the guard left in the encampment, the object being to prevent the enemy so readily seeing the situation of it. Had this body of Russian Cavalry, consisting of the 11th and 12th Hussars, with several squadrons of Cossacks, come on a little further, they would have been brought face to face with us on immediately crowning the hill, but just as we were expecting them, we saw the head of their column crown the heights of No. 4 Redoubt; they then steadily descended the hill, and halted not far from our encampment. Our Heavy Cavalry now advanced and charged into them. We then expected to be ordered to sweep down on their right flank; had we done so at the proper moment, I feel that few of them would have escaped being either killed or made prisoners, but much to our chagrin we were held as spectators of this unequal combat, for nearly ten minutes we could distinctly hear the din and shouts of our people, being about five or six hundred yards off. Our excitement became very great, and I am of opinion, nothing but the strict discipline under which we were held, prevented our breaking loose to assist our comrades of the Heavies, but to our relief and joy we saw this mass of Russian Cavalry retreat over the Causeway Heights, the same way that they came. Had we received the order, in all probability the charge down the North Valley would not have taken place. We shortly after this took up a position facing directly down the North Valley; we could distinctly see the Russian position. The 11th was on the left of the first line, the 13th on the right, and the 17th in the centre, the 4th and 8th formed the second line. We had not been long in this position when Lord Cardigan received the order from Lord Lucan to attack the battery of guns which were placed across the valley, immediately in our front, about a mile off. There was likewise a battery on the Fedioukine Hills on our left, and the enemy had possession of the Redoubts Nos. 2, 3, and 4 on our right, where the batteries and battalions of infantry and riflemen were posted. This army in position numbered about 24,000, and we, the Light Brigade, not quite 700. The trumpets now sounded the advance. The 13th and 17th moved off, and we, the 11th, were ordered to support them. As soon as they, the first line, had advanced about 100 yards, we moved off, soon breaking into a gallop, but did not actually cover the 17th the whole way down, consequently we swept down the valley, much nearer the Fedioukine Hills than any other regiment. As we moved off the Russians opened fire from all their batteries, the round shot passed through us, and the shells burst over and amongst us, causing great havoc. The first man of my troop that was struck was Private Young, a cannon ball taking off his right arm, I being close on his right rear, fancied I felt the wind from it as it passed me, I afterwards found I was bespattered with his flesh. To such a nicety were the enemy's guns elevated for our destruction, that before we had advanced many hundred yards Pte. Turner's left arm was also struck off close to the shoulder, and Pte. Ward was struck full in the chest, a shell too burst over us, a piece of which struck Cornet Houghton in the forehead, and mortally wounded him. When Pte. Young lost his arm, he coolly fell back, and asked me what he was to do, I replied: 'Turn your horse about and get to the rear as fast as you can.' I had scarcely done speaking to him when Pte. Turner fell back, calling out to me for help, I told him, too, to go to the rear. I then galloped on after the regiment; happening at this moment to look at the rear, I saw the Chasseurs d'Afrique charging up the Fedioukine Hills, at the battery that was taking us in the flank. We now came under a terrific fire, for the infantry in and about the Redoubts kept up a continual fusillade as we came opposite to them; but the men hung well together, keeping their line and closing in, as their comrades fell wounded or killed. Many riderless horses were now galloping along with us, forcing their way up into the ranks, and keeping their places as though their masters had been on their backs, many of these horses belonged to the first line, for we now frequently met with their lifeless bodies. I was particularly struck with one of the 17th Lancers, lying on his face with his arms stretched out, and a short distance from his right hand was his lance with the pole broken. As we neared the battery, a square of infantry that had been placed in advance of the left of the guns gave us a volley in flank, the very air hissed as the shower of bullets passed through us. Many men were now killed or wounded. I, at this moment, felt that something had touched my left wrist; on looking down I saw that a bullet, which must have passed close in front of my body, had blackened and cut the lace on my cuff. Private Glanister had his lower jaw shattered by a bullet entering on the right side, and a bullet passed through the back of Pte. Humphries' neck just missing the spinal column. At this time we were at a sweeping gallop, in another moment we passed the guns, our right flank brushing them. When about a hundred yards in rear Colonel Douglas halted us. During the advance Lieut. Trevelyan and Cornet Houghton had fallen out, being wounded, the latter mortally. Regt.-Serjt.-Major Bull, Trumpeters Smith and Keates had their horses killed or wounded, so that the only leader in front of the right squadron was Troop.-Serjt-Major Trevan; Serjt.-Major Joseph and I were the only two now left as Serrafiles.[1] It now became my particular duty (the Regt.-Serjt.-Major's horse having been wounded) to note every word of command the Colonel should give, as I now considered the Regt.-Serjt.-Major's duty devolved on me. After halting, the word was 'Close in on the centre', so that the squadron interval was filled up. During the advance, which had not taken many minutes, we had lost, as near as I could calculate, about 50 men, so that we had about 80 left. I am sure we had quite this number from what I witnessed afterwards.

During the advance the 11th, 4th, and 8th were in eschelon; the fact of our right flank brushing the guns, brought the 4th directly in front, so that they drove right into them, where those of the 13th and 17th that had not yet retreated were still fighting. We were now but a short distance directly in front of the same Russian Hussars and Cossacks that our Heavy Cavalry had charged in the South Valley. Lord Paget at this moment galloped up to our right flank. Colonel Douglas seeing him, called out, 'What are we to do now, Lord Paget?' He replied, 'Where is Lord Cardigan?' and galloped away. Colonel Douglas, seeing that there was no time to lose, having no order to retire, and expecting every moment that we should be charged by this body of Cavalry in our front, called out, 'Give them another charge men, Hurrah.' At this moment I particularly noticed the gallant bearing of Lieut. Dunn; he was a fine young fellow, standing 6ft. 3 inches, and mounted on a powerful horse, and wielding a terrific sword, many inches longer than the regulation; his heroic conduct throughout the affair, inspired all round him with courage; he saved the life of Serjt. Bentley, when surrounded by Russians, by cutting them down right and left; so conspicuous was his gallantry, that Colonel Douglas justly recommended him for the Victoria Cross, which he received at the hands of her Majesty (strange to say he was the only Cavalry Officer on whom this honour was conferred). Waving our swords over our heads, on we galloped, expecting the next minute to be amongst them, but to our surprise, when not more than 20 yards off, they wheeled about and galloped away in front of us, we, shouting and feeling rather amused, for they were 20 to one, there not being at this time more than about 80 of us, the Eleventh, left. We now lost all hold of the other part of the Brigade, for we saw nothing more of them till we returned to the ground we charged from. The 4th, after sabring the gunners, retired with the remnants of other regiments. After galloping a short distance, on looking round, I saw one of the guns some distance to our right being taken away; it was a large brass gun, with carriage painted green,

---

[1] Riding immediately behind the formation.

drawn by six horses, there were only three men, and driver with it. Feeling that it had escaped from the battery, and knowing that the 4th Light Dragoons had possession, I at once formed the resolution to retake it, so seeing three men riding independently in the rear, they having just been crushed out, I called to them to follow me, saying, 'Let us take this gun.' I at once galloped off, supposing they were following me, when within a short distance of it I saw a Hussar Officer and three Cossacks, who had detached themselves from the main body for its protection, and were coming rapidly between me and my regiment. I was now considerably to the right rear of it, about three or four hundred yards, and within fifty yards of the gun; on looking round I found I was alone, that the three men had not followed me as I had expected. Feeling it would be madness to attempt the capture single handed, I instantly halted, turned about and galloped off in the direction of my regiment. The first Cossack and the officer might have engaged me on my track, but hesitated, calling out to the other two, who were a little distance in their rear. This hesitation enabled me to rejoin my comrades. If there had been any other troops, either of ours or the Russians, any distance in rear of the guns at this time, I should have seen them, for I went beyond the left flank of the battery. All this space was perfectly clear at the time. As I galloped up to the regiment, I noticed one of the 17th Lancers in our right squadron; his was the only flag that waved either with us or the cavalry we were pursuing, the Cossacks having no lance flags. I afterwards learnt there was one of the 13th Light Dragoons there as well. His name was Nicholson, beyond these and one or two stragglers that joined us on our way back, we were not in any way mixed up at any time with any other part of the Brigade. We were now nearing the extreme end of the valley, about a mile and a half from our position, still pursuing this body of Cavalry. In their confusion I saw one of their leading Cossacks fall from the bridge into the Aqueduct, there being no parapet. Near the bridge was a moderately steep hill which formed the end of the valley, up which they rode a short distance, their rear being at the foot, close to us. They now halted, but remained for a few moments with their backs to us, looking over their shoulders. Seeing there were so few of us, and without supports, they turned about, and we sat face to face, our horses' heads close to theirs. As we looked up at them they had all the appearance of a vast assemblage in the gallery of a theatre, the stillness and suspense during these moments was terrible; at last it was broken by their officers calling out to their men to follow them, and break through us, which they themselves attempted to do by driving their horses at our front rank, but their men failed to display the same courage as their leaders, and our men showed a firm front, keeping close together, and bringing their swords down to the right front guard, kept them at bay . . .

It is evident that the 11th was the last regiment, and I was the last man that returned up the valley. I then formed up with about half a dozen dismounted men in the rear. Colonel Douglas now came round, and ordered me to march the dismounted men down to the encampment, mount them on any spare horses I could find, and bring them back. On arriving at the encampment I found that all the horses left there had been wounded by the

Cossacks, who after pursuing the Turks, had ridden into our encampment. Of the 4 horses of my troop left in, belonging to men in hospital, one was missing, the other three had received severe sword cuts, one across the head, another across the back, the other a terrific gash on the near quarter, a foot in length and several inches deep. If we had retired with skirmishers this brutality might have been prevented, also the lives of numbers of the Turks saved. So being unable to procure horses I decided on remaining. Going to my tent, which was lying on the ground, as were they all, I found near it my comrade, the orderly-room clerk; he shook hands with me, saying, 'How glad I am you have escaped, George.' I told him I had lost my horse, and how fearfully the regiment had been cut up, he then said – 'What is this on your busby and jacket,' on picking it off I found it to be small pieces of flesh that had flown over me when Private Young's arm had been shot off. I now sat down, and the feelings that came over me are not easy to describe, I was moved to tears when I thought of the havoc I had witnessed, and that I had lost my beautiful horse; she was a light bay, nearly thoroughbred, I became her master three years before.

It was now about twelve noon, and I had eaten nothing since the day before, so my comrade made me some tea, which was very acceptable. We then strolled together over the ground in front of our encampment, where the affray of which I have before spoken, between the Heavy Cavalry and the enemy, took place. Close to my tent lay one of the 12th Russian Hussars dead, and not far off several others; there was also a young fair-haired Russian officer badly wounded, with five or six of his men also wounded, sitting huddled together, for as yet our people had had no time to attend to the prisoners.

These belonged to the 11th and 12th Hussars. As dusk drew on the remnant of the 11th returned to the camp. I then assembled the men of my troop and called the roll: one-half were missing – 6 being killed, 10 wounded, and 2 were made prisoners; 3 of the 10 lost their right arms, and one his left, he died three days after, another his left leg, he died at Scutari; of the two prisoners one died in Russia of his wounds, the other returned, having lost a leg. Twenty-four horses were killed, and five wounded, two so severely that they had to be destroyed the following day. Captain Cook was wounded, and had his horse killed, Cornet Houghton was mortally wounded. Thus ended a day of disasters, which might have been avoided if our commander had had more forethought and discretion. It had been expected, and was well known that the Russians were preparing to attack us, for only two nights before we stood to our horses the whole night in the plain, about half way between Canrobert's Hill and our encampment, still no preparation was made. Had a few battalions of English or French Infantry been posted in the Redoubts to support the Turks, and more of our Artillery brought into action, the day would have ended very differently. General Liprandi might well ask our prisoners 'If we were drunk'. In retiring after Canrobert's Hill was taken, we were not covered by skirmishers; had we been, numbers of our Allies, the Turks, would have been saved. Then, when we retired through our encampment we left it without any protection; this encouraged the Cossack skirmishers to gallop into it and mutilate our spare horses that were fastened up to the picket ropes. Again, when the body of cavalry that we were sent to prevent getting in rear of our encampment passed over the hills in front of it, and became engaged with the Heavy Cavalry we were held as spectators of the fight, instead of being hurled on their right flank. They were the troops we were intended to encounter should they invade the neighbourhood of our encampment. Again, only one of the troops of Horse Artillery were brought into action, and they not again during the day, after they retired from between the Redoubts, the first thing in the morning. And who, I ask, was answerable for all this? The same man who ordered Lord Cardigan to charge with 670 men an army in position, and then left them to their fate – it was not unlike leaving the forlorn hope, after storming a town, to fight their way out again, instead of pushing on the supports. We cut their army completely in two, taking their principal battery, driving their cavalry far to the rear. What more could 670 men do? A glorious affair might have been made of it, had our infantry been pushed along the Causeway Heights with the Heavy Cavalry, and the French Infantry with the Chasseurs d'Afrique along the Fedioukine Hills. The enemy were so panic-stricken, that I feel convinced the greater part of this army of 24,000 men would have been annihilated or taken prisoners, they having only two small bridges to retreat over, the Tractir and the Aqueduct. Never, I should say, was such an opportunity lost.

As soon as it was dark, we retired about a quarter of a mile, and took up a position nearer the Chersonese. About midnight we again retired, and took up a position on the hillside about a mile to the rear of our original position – the order was, 'No fires to be lit, no noise to be made'; this was indeed a sorry night, scarcely any had had more than a little biscuit and a dram of rum since the day before, it was spent by us standing in groups talking over the sad misadventures of the day.

In the rest of the Crimean War the cavalry had a frustrating time. The only occasions on which they could perform cavalry duties were when they were required to chase off marauding Cossacks. However, the Cossacks usually galloped off before the British could get to grips with them. Worst of all was being required to use their horses as pack mules and struggle through muddy roads up to the lines.

Once the siege of Sebastopol settled down there was no more scope for cavalry charges, but still plenty of work for them to do. Temple Godman managed the almost incredible feat of keeping alive the three horses he had taken out with him. He wrote in a letter to his father:

The cavalry are encamped about 4 or 5 miles from the town and we are harassed night and day with picquets and patrols. We cannot have much to do with the siege, unless in the case of a sortie, or in clearing the steets when they get in . . . We are just ordered to be ready to turn out, some Cossacks or someone are coming so I must finish as the post may be gone on my return. In great haste.

Then:

> My last letter ended rather abruptly as we got the order to turn out the
> Brigade, but though we remained saddled all day we were not called to go
> out. It was merely that our patrol had been driven in by a large body of
> Cossacks. These gentlemen keep us well employed, though often two or
> three hundred together they never dare attack even a picquet of thirty men
> of ours. I am longing to have a go at them and I hope to get a chance before
> long.

Godman had an eye for unusual, though often more macabre, details:

> I regret extremely that we were not at the Alma, if we had been we must have
> taken all their guns and lots of prisoners and cut them to pieces. Though the
> Light Cavalry were there they will get a medal for doing nothing. The
> Cavalry may say what they like about the affair but they were hardly under
> fire. I would have given anything to have been there. I saw a horse in camp
> today which had a bullet through his ear which first passed through the
> body of the adjutant of the 23rd.

Although cavalry officers almost invariably came from rich families, where they
had been waited on and enjoyed the best that money could buy, they seemed to be able
to rough it when the occasion demanded – as we saw in the Peninsular War. Godman
wrote:

> I can't bear to hear of our servants being so fastidious, it really is too bad,
> and here are plenty of the sons of the highest men in England living on
> biscuits and salt pork, and so far from complaining are glad to get it. When
> we landed we had a lump of pork to carry, about three times the size of one's
> fist, not the better for being carried about, and some ships biscuits. This was
> all we had for three days. Yesterday we got some very skinny mutton and
> tomorrow pork again, no bread here. Our mess when cooked, for we put
> three or four fellows rations together, put me in mind of what Keeper
> collects in buckets for the dogs, however it agrees very well with me.

Temple Godman was twenty-four at the time of the Balaclava battles. He was a
'regular', having been bought a commission at the age of nineteen after leaving Eton.
His first rank was cornet; and his father had paid £840 for it. When the Crimean War
broke out in 1854 Godman was a lieutenant. In 1856 he was a captain and could sell, if
he wished, for £3,225. He was lucky. Many of his contemporaries who had bought in
for similar sums were now buried in the Crimea as a result of bullets or cholera. Unlike
many cavalry officers he had had some pre-war experience of training and manoeuvres.

Following the Crimean War there were several isolated actions which deserve
mention. In 1857 an expedition was sent to Persia. This was said to be one of the

contributory causes of the Indian Mutiny, for it drained India of some of its best units. However, it afforded an opportunity for the 3rd Bombay Light Cavalry to distinguish itself by breaking a Persian square 500 strong.

The efficiency of cavalry over the years had been shown to be related to many different factors. The quality of generalship, leadership, national temperament, and horsemanship contributed principally to success – or failure – but there were seldom occasions when well-trained units were defeated by badly-trained ones, numbers and equipment being equal.

The 'book' for cavalry training in Britain in the second half of the nineteenth century was *Cavalry Regulations* which came out in revised editions, each lengthier than the last. It was comprehensive and thorough but open to the criticism that many of the manoeuvres were so complicated that they were difficult to execute on a peacetime parade-ground and, in the face of the enemy, would be dangerous if not impossible.

However there were certain principles of cavalry training which experience had shown to be essential. Both horses and men had to be fit; this meant daily exercise for all. Squadrons were required to perform every type of manoeuvre, maintaining formation even among obstacles, and at varying pace, occasionally letting a defensive one fall back, wheeling into line, then back into column; the variants of these moves ran into dozens. Usually at the end of the morning's work the regiment would form up for the charge it was every cavalryman's dream to execute in battle: 'Walk, trot, gallop, charge.'

Part of manoeuvres was devoted to clearing the ground after a successful charge. This would enable the second line to come in either as support or for pursuit. At close quarters there were twenty sabre positions to be executed. Each of these had to be learnt and practised to perfection. When one considers that the regiment had to be ultra smart in every detail of dress and equipment it is obvious that the trooper was rarely idle. When the lance was introduced this added a whole new dimension to training for this, too, had a number of possible positions, including a parry.

By the end of the nineteenth century every possible type and breed of horse had had its turn as a cavalry mount. Some of the earlier breeds are now extinct, others have a less exalted use as draught-horses. Over the years careful breeding produced horses which, as far as possible, were suited to requirements. Obviously, heavy cavalry required the ability to carry weight and smash through opposition, while light cavalry required speed and manoeuvrability. However, both required stamina. Stamina involved not merely the shock of battle, but survival in bad weather, on poor and insufficient rations, on rough sea voyages (when they were tied closely together to keep them on their feet) and on long marches with little rest.

The best horses in the world for cavalry work were the English thoroughbreds. They were, of course, Arab in distant origin and the nineteenth-century stock was bred from horses imported at the beginnning of the sixteenth century. At the time of the Crimean War such a horse was fifteen hands in height, weighed roughly 1000 lbs and could carry up to 200 lbs. English thoroughbreds had an amiable disposition – the occasional awkward customer was quickly discarded – but they did not take too kindly to rapid changes of climate, and transporting them by sea was one of the obviously difficult logistical problems to be faced. Landing in the Crimea was managed by putting them in slings and lowering them into boats. Mortality rates in the Crimea were appallingly high for horses as well as man, but in the former case it was mainly through lack of forage. A horse on active service needed eighteen pounds of hay and eight of corn daily. It needed at least five gallons of water a day and would drink much more in a hot climate. It needed shoeing, it would go lame, it could develop a variety of diseases. But sad though many cavalry men were when horses were replaced by mechanical vehicles there were many who would nod approval at the remark, 'A tank may be noisy and smelly but at least it doesn't get taken ill in the middle of the night.'

12
Small Wars in Large Countries

The Crimean War had revealed so many deficiencies and inefficiencies in British army organization that a programme of reforms was clearly essential. It fell to the Gladstone government of 1868–74 to take the necessary steps and the Secretary of State for War in that government, Edward Cardwell, thus found himself with an exceptionally difficult task. He was, as he proved, the man for it. Though mild in manner he was doggedly determined; in consequence he was able to wear down the opponents of many of his proposals. Most of the reforms he made do not concern us here, but one in particular does. That was the abolition of the purchase of commissions.[1] The reform cost the country £7,000,000 in compensation but it was undoubtedly worth it. For too long rich nincompoops had abused their positions and mishandled the men under them. Many senior officers had found the purchase system absurd and dangerous. In 1707 Marlborough had written to the then Earl of Cadogan, who requested a commission for his son in a regiment serving under Marlborough's command in Spain. Marlborough wrote: 'I have so just a sense of the father's good service that I am always glad to embrace any opportunity of showing it to his family, but your Lordship tells me that he [the candidate] is not above five years old. Thus giving him command in the army would be decidedly contrary to the rules the Queen has prescribed to herself in that matter; beside that the enquiry this Parliament is making of the officers absent from their commands in Spain makes it yet the more difficult.' Such was the decision of the great Duke in 1707. Cardwell's reforms seem to us nowadays so sensible and so necessary that it is difficult to appreciate the difficulties he encountered in pushing them through.

Small wars continued during the latter half of the century and culminated in one in South Africa that involved troops from all over the world. The 1867 war in Abyssinia and the Ashanti War of 1873 gave little scope for cavalry, but the Afghan War of 1878 produced several spirited clashes. However, the Afghan War sounded an ominous note for future cavalry warfare, for in it the Gatling machine-gun was used for the first time. As the ones tested were not reliable, their potential was not fully appreciated at the time.

[1] See Chapter 3.

The 9th Lancers at Delhi, 1857, earning the title 'The Delhi Spearmen'.

Saving the Guns at Maiwand. During the 2nd Afghan War in 1880 a British force which contained two cavalry regiments was confronted by a force ten times as great. The battle was brisk, but much of the force was saved by the heroic stand by the last eleven men of the 66th Foot.

An eye-witness account of a cavalry action in 1878 came from Lt George Younghusband: 'Once an Afghan horde is set going in one of these mad charges, it takes a good deal to stop it. Consequently, when the infantry came up we found a very critical state of affairs: the guns run back by hand and firing reversed shrapnel: the cavalry unable to get home an effective charge owing to a deep nullah which ran between us and the enemy . . .' It was Younghusband's first battle and he was too busy and too interested to feel afraid, even though two men close by him were hit. '. . . we were into them in a wild melée: hitting, thrashing, cursing, kicking, throwing stones, clubbing rifles, firing pistols. The devil's own delight.' Then, looking around, Younghusband had his first sight of a regiment he would later command, The Guides. (At the time of this battle he was in the 17th Foot (Leicestershire Regiment).)

> Looking along to our right we saw a brave sight, the bravest possible – a body of cavalry charging. It was none other than the renowned cavalry of The Guides, which by a wonderful effort had crossed the seemingly impassable nullah and was now falling with dauntless fury on ten times their number of the enemy. They whirled past us and we, cheering like mad, dashed after them.

It is a splendid sight, such as no other perhaps equals, the wild charge of horsemen. Each man going for all he is worth, yelling to Allah, or other deity, to help him, yelling curses the most blood-curdling on his enemy; low bent so as almost to be lying along his horse's neck, and swish after swish, bringing his keen curved sword on to the head, or neck, or back, of a fleeing enemy.

No time here for quarter, given or taken. The pursued, when overtaken, stops, turns, fires point-blank at his pursuer, or goes down like a blade of corn. There were separate single combats, but here and there were little miniature battles where clumps of the enemy had got together and where clumps of The Guides were attacking them.

Younghusband described the procedure of giving battle at that period. Each squadron had two British officers, a captain and a subaltern. Before the battle began these two had been patrolling up and down the flank, looking for targets and provoking action against themselves:

The subaltern had as a charger a very sporting little bay Arab, full of blood, very quick and handy, and not to be daunted by anything. Like the war horse in the Bible, he had been sniffing the battle from afar, and had been stepping about on the very tips of his toes, with his head in the air, nostrils wide open, snorting again and again, and again and again, giving short excited squeals. His tail arched up and cocked to one side as only can a high-caste Arab. Every time the troop wheeled around he gave a hilarious dash round, as much as to say, 'Now we're off, anyhow . . .' He was the joy of his owner's life. Extraordinary good friends they were those two, horse and man who went to battle together, for the master used to sit by the hour by his horse to see him groomed and fed and always had a carrot or something sweet in his pocket for him.

In the battle 'an Afghan horseman, armed with a twelve-foot lance, came straight at the squadron . . . charging at full gallop, leaning well down on his horse's neck, yelling like a fiend'.

Now some people are fond of deprecating the lance: they say it is heavy, unwieldy and hampers a man. Quite so, but if you ever happen to be situated as were the British officers at that moment with no weapon of offence or defence but a poky little sword, perhaps you might take a different view.

Of course, theoretically the gallant swordsman with one turn of the wrist thrusts the lance aside, and with another deft turn spits the rash lancer through the waistcoat or other vulnerable part. In practice, however, if the lancer means business, he will have two feet of lance through you before your turn comes.

On this occasion, a sowar (trooper) had seen what was happening, had come up from behind and had ridden into the approaching Afghan at an angle. This had deflected the lance but caused all three to crash on to the ground. Nobody was badly hurt, although all were bruised and dazed. The Afghan lancer was taken prisoner much to his disappointment for he had planned to die in battle.

But there were many ways other than in battle in which men could die. The 10th Hussars crossing a ford in the Nabul river in the moonlight strayed slightly from their route: 'At a turn in the ford two mules, giving way to the stream, were taken off their legs and swept down. The Tenth leaders, following in the dim moonlight, left the ford, and those in the rear, doing the same, were carried away rapidly and silently in the dark and cloudy night. Not a sound was heard, and no one seemed to be aware of what was taking place.' They had been following the line of the column which had been gradually forced nearer the edge of the ford by the strength of the current. In a moment the whole squadron was in deep water. 'On account of the night march each man had a tunic on under his khaki; thirty rounds of ammunition were carried and the haversacks were well filled with the next day's rations so that although many amongst them were excellent swimmers they found it of no avail: the water was bitterly cold from the melting snows, and the poor fellows were quickly numbed. Forty-seven members of the regiment and fourteen horses were drowned: some of the bodies were recovered sixty miles down the river.'

Other wars with important cavalry actions were the Zulu War of 1879, where the 17th Lancers clinched the victory at Ulundi, the Egyptian campaign of 1882, when Drury-Lowe's cavalry brigade (7th Dragoons, Life Guards, and Royal Horse Guards) made a spirited charge at Kassassin, and the 1st Sudan War where the cavalry had their first experience of Dervish tactics.

The 2nd Sudan War, which was a continuation of the campaign which had been begun in 1881 but abandoned in 1885, was a triumph for Kitchener's organizing ability.

In the 1880s the Sudan, which is a million square miles in area, had an estimated population of 14,000,000. The northern half is desert country, the southern swamp, scrub and jungle. When in 1881 Mohammed Ahmed, the son of a boat builder, proclaimed himself 'The Mahdi' – The Expected One – he was received by the Sudanese as the true descendant of the prophet, who would launch a Holy War and cleanse the land. The overwhelming response to the Mahdi's call was the first demonstration the West had seen of the tremendous force and dedication which the Islamic religion instils in its followers. The West did not understand it and did not at first take this religious crusade seriously. In the 1980s, having seen the power of the Islamic religion in the Middle East, we understand these matters rather better.

When Britain had, very reluctantly, become responsible for the administration of Egypt after 1882, it fell to her also to endeavour to see that there was some degree of law and order not only in Egypt itself but also in the Sudan, which was at that time an Egyptian province. The Mahdi's army easily defeated the forces which were at first sent against him; General Gordon was therefore sent up river to Khartoum to arrange for the evacuation of the remaining British and Egyptian personnel in 1884, but was himself besieged in Khartoum, where he was killed in January 1885; a relief expedition had failed to reach him by two days only. Gladstone's Liberal government decided against sending an expedition to recover the lost province: it had plenty of other problems to deal with, not least in Ireland. However, Egyptian affairs and administration were rapidly being put in order by Sir Evelyn Baring and from that country two expeditions were sent to Suakim on the Red Sea, but without much effect.

The Mahdists controlled the Sudan and approached the borders of Egypt itself. By this time there were no illusions about the fighting power of the Dervishes even though the Mahdi himself was dead. Observers such as Andrew Haggard, elder brother of Rider Haggard, the novelist, gave an account of what he saw at El Teb in 1884. It was a form of warfare the British cavalry had not experienced before:

> The cavalry had as difficult a time as the infantry. They were very active in charging the enemy whenever possible but unfortunately it seems only too probable that they suffered themselves more than the enemy, who stepped behind bushes as they approached, or, lying down behind mounds, jumped up suddenly and slashed and cut at the horses' hocks. When the rider was down, they jumped upon him and speared him. About thirty of their number who were mounted even charged back at a squadron of the 19th Hussars which was charging under Colonel Barrow, and some three of them, after actually getting through Barrow's squadron unhurt, turned and pursued them.
>
> The enemy carried with them a short stick curved at one end. This stick was very heavy, and they were skilled at throwing it with precision, and it was the throwing of this weapon at the horses' legs which brought them down.
>
> Although on subsequent occasions we again tried cavalry against these Hadendowah Arabs it must be confessed they were never a success. They had all that was required – bravery, skill, discipline. It was no use to charge with cavalry an enemy who had all the agility of acrobats – who could jump about and bound from side to side like a rubber ball. I have myself, for fun, tried to ride down members of the Amarar tribe with whom we were friendly. The man I would pursue would only be armed with a long stick instead of a spear. I have ridden right on him, and only when actually under my horse's head would he spring to one side, striking me as I passed him with the point of his stick. And this is how our cavalry lost so many at El Teb without doing any harm to the enemy themselves.

The reconquest began in 1896. Kitchener's army was very small by modern standards: its initial strength was 18,000. It included four cavalry squadrons, which must have been the least impressive-looking of all cavalry in history for the expedition was extremely economically equipped. Nothing was ever considered unserviceable until it had dropped to pieces and ceased to exist. But there was nothing wrong with the army's fighting efficiency.

The key to the success of the campaign was Kitchener's methodical planning: a major part of it was the railway he constructed across the desert. It seems that there were only two wells in a one-hundred mile stretch. Both were discovered by a young

Cavalry uniform, 1891.

officer in the Royal Engineers who, like his fellow-officers, had had to take a course in dowsing, or water-divining. His name is not recorded.

There were two major battles, one at Atbara, the other at Omdurman, just in front of Khartoum. By summer 1898, when Kitchener was manoeuvring his army in position for the final battle, its strength had grown to 25,000; there were ten gunboats in support. The battlefield was an open plain with two ridges and several *khors* (dried-up watercourses): one of these last would play a significant part in the battle. The Dervishes, who were fanatically brave, numbered some 60,000, but their weapons were inferior. Nevertheless their courage came near to winning this battle. An eye-witness wrote of the scene:

> The Baggara cavalry on this occasion showed remarkable and reckless daring. They evidently intended to break through our lines and divert our fire, so as to give the Dervish infantry an opening. To carry this out was hopeless, for it meant riding to certain death, but they galloped forward in loose open order, their ranks presenting one long ridge of flashing swords. A continuous stream of bullets from our lines was emptying the saddles, but on they came till not a single horseman was left. One Baggara succeeded in getting within thirty yards of our lines before he fell. The whole of the Dervish cavalry had been annihilated. There was no instance in history of a more superb devotion to a cause or a greater contempt for death.

That was at the beginning of the battle, soon after 5.30 am on 2 September 1898. During the following hours the Dervishes came very close indeed to breaking into the British lines and if they had succeeded there would have been a scene of almost unimaginable carnage, perhaps even a British defeat. But the lines held. At 9 am it seemed as if victory might be within Kitchener's grasp, for a number of Dervishes were retreating to Omdurman itself, where they would be regrouped to join in the battle once more. Kitchener therefore ordered his cavalry to come forward and force these retreating Dervishes away from Omdurman and into the desert. The Egyptian Horse took the left; the 21st Lancers the right. As the 21st Lancers trotted forward

Arab horsemen outside Metamneh. The Dervish cavalry were no inconsiderable opponents.

Charge of the Light Brigade, Balaclava, 1854.

Lance-Sergeant Joseph Malone VC helping to rescue a wounded officer (under heavy fire) at Balaclava. Malone was commissioned later.

The Guides winning the Battle of Swat in the Frontier War of 1897–8. Two VCs were won (Adams and Maclean).

10th Hussars on patrol in India wearing the uniform of 1873–84.

The charge of the 21st Lancers at Omdurman, 1898.

5th Lancers at Elaandslaagte, South Africa, October 1899.

A bullock wagon crossing a drift in South Africa. During the Boer War transport was extremely vulnerable.

A Captain in the Life Guards, 1900. He looked very different on active service.

5th Lancers exercising in Long Valley, Aldershot, 1908.

Kettle Drummer in the 1st Life Guards, 1909. Originally these very expensive coats and banners were paid for by the officers.

21st Lancers at Omdurman, 1898.

they saw ahead of them a *khor* in which they estimated some 200 Dervishes might be concealed. The regiment numbered 320. As it reached the *khor* 2,000 Dervishes suddenly rose to their feet and opened fire. After that the 21st were amongst them. One of the attached officers riding with the 21st was Winston Churchill, from the 4th Hussars, who had requested to be allowed to accompany the 21st.

The charge succeeded in its purpose but the cost was high. Out of the 320, twenty-one were killed and forty-six wounded. One hundred and fourteen horses were killed. Winston Churchill later described the charge in the following words:[1]

> The intentions of our Colonel had no doubt been to move round the flank of the body of Dervishes he had now located, and who, concealed in a fold of the ground behind their rifle-men, were invisible to us, and then to attack them from a more advantageous quarter; but once the fire was opened and losses began to grow, he must have judged it inexpedient to prolong his procession across the open plain. The trumpet sounded 'Right wheel into line', and all the sixteen troops swung round towards the blue-black riflemen. Almost immediately the regiment broke into a gallop, and the 21st Lancers were committed to their first charge in war!
>
> I propose to describe exactly what happened to me: what I saw and what I felt. I recalled it to my mind so frequently after the event that the impression is as clear and vivid as it was a quarter of a century ago. The troop I commanded was, when we wheeled into line, the second from the

---

[1] Reproduced from *My Early Life* by Winston S. Churchill, with thanks to Hamlyn Publishers Ltd.

right of the regiment. I was riding a handy, sure-footed, grey Arab polo pony. Before we wheeled and began to gallop, the officers had been marching with drawn swords. On account of my shoulder I had always decided that if I were involved in hand-to-hand fighting, I must use a pistol and not a sword. I had purchased in London a Mauser automatic pistol, then the newest and the latest design. I had practised carefully with this during our march and journey up the river. This then was the weapon with which I determined to fight. I had first of all to return my sword into its scabbard, which is not the easiest thing to do at a gallop. I had then to draw my pistol from its wooden holster and bring it to full cock. This dual operation took an appreciable time, and until it was finished, apart from a few glances to my left to see what effect the fire was producing, I did not look up at the general scene.

Then I saw immediately before me, and now only half the length of a polo ground away, the row of crouching blue figures firing frantically, wreathed in white smoke. On my right and left my neighbouring troop leaders made a good line. Immediately behind was a long dancing row of lances crouched for the charge. We were going at a fast but steady gallop. There was too much trampling and rifle fire to hear any bullets. After this glance to the right and left and at my troop, I looked again towards the enemy. The scene appeared to be suddenly transformed. The blue-black men were still firing but behind them there now came into view a depression like a shallow sunken road. This was crowded and crammed with men rising up from the ground where they had hidden. Bright flags appeared as if by magic, and I saw arriving from nowhere Emirs on horseback among and around the mass of the enemy. The Dervishes appeared to be ten or twelve deep at the thickest, a great grey mass gleaming with steel, filling the dry watercourse. In the same twinkling of an eye I saw also that our right overlapped their left, that my troop would just strike the edge of their array, and that the troop on my right would charge into air. My subaltern comrade on the right, Wormald of the 7th Hussars, could see the situation too; and we both increased our speed to the very fastest gallop and curved inwards like the horns of the moon. One really had not time to be frightened or to think of anything else but these particularly necessary actions which I have described. They completely occupied mind and senses.

The collision was now very near. I saw immediately before me, not ten yards away, the two blue men who lay in my path. They were perhaps a couple of yards apart. I rode at the interval between them. They both fired. I passed through the smoke conscious that I was unhurt. The trooper immediately behind me was killed at this place and at this moment, whether by these shots or not I do not know. I checked my pony as the ground began to fall away beneath his feet. The clever animal dropped like a cat four or five feet down on to the sandy bed of the watercourse, and in this sandy bed I found myself surrounded by what seemed to be dozens of men. They were not thickly-packed enough at this point for me to experience any actual collision with them. Whereas Grenfell's troop next but one on my left was brought to a complete standstill and suffered very heavy losses, we seemed to push our way through as one has sometimes seen mounted policemen break up a crowd. In less time than it takes to relate, my pony had scrambled up the other side of the ditch. I looked round.

Once again I was on the hard, crisp desert, my horse at a trot. I had the impression of scattered Dervishes running to and fro in all directions. Straight before me a man threw himself on the ground. The reader must remember that I had been trained as a cavalry soldier to believe that if ever cavalry broke into a mass of infantry, the latter would be at their mercy. My first idea therefore was that the man was terrified. But simultaneously I saw the gleam of his curved sword as he drew it back for a ham-stringing cut. I had room and time enough to turn my pony out of his reach, and leaning over on the offside I fired two shots into him at about three yards. As I straightened myself in the saddle, I saw before me another figure with uplifted sword. I raised my pistol and fired. So close were we that the pistol itself actually struck him. Man and sword disappeared below and behind me. On my left, ten yards away, was an Arab horseman in a bright-coloured tunic and steel helmet, with chain-mail hangings. I fired at him. He turned aside. I pulled my horse into a walk and looked around again.

In one respect a cavalry charge is very like ordinary life. So long as you are all right, firmly in your saddle, your horse in hand, and well armed, lots of enemies will give you a wide berth. But as soon as you have lost a stirrup, have a rein cut, have dropped your weapon, are wounded, or your horse is wounded, then is the moment when from all quarters enemies rush upon you. Such was the fate of not a few of my comrades in the troops immediately on my left. Brought to an actual standstill in the enemy's mass, clutched at from every side, stabbed at and hacked by spear and sword, they were dragged from their horses and cut to pieces by the infuriated foe. But this I did not at the time see or understand. My impressions continued to be sanguine. I thought we were masters of the situation, riding the enemy down. I pulled my horse up and looked about me. There was a mass of Dervishes about forty or fifty yards away on my left. They were huddling and clumping themselves together, rallying for mutual protection. They seemed wild with excitement, dancing about on their feet, shaking their spears up and down. The whole scene seemed to flicker. I have an impression, but it is too fleeting to define, of brown-clad Lancers mixed up here and there with this surging mob. The scattered individuals in my immediate neighbourhood made no attempt to molest me. Where was my troop? Where were the other troops of the squadron? Within a hundred yards of me I could not see a single officer or man. I looked back at the Dervish mass. I saw two or three riflemen crouching and aiming their rifles at me from the fringe of it. Then for the first time that morning I experienced a sudden sensation of fear. I felt myself absolutely alone. I thought these riflemen would hit me and the rest devour me like wolves. What a fool I was to loiter like this in the midst of the enemy! I crouched over the saddle, spurred my horse into a gallop and drew clear of the melée. Two or three hundred yards away I found my troop already faced about and partly formed up.

The other three troops of the squadron were re-forming close by. Suddenly in the midst of the troop up sprung a Dervish. How he got there I do not know. He must have leaped out of some scrub or hole. All the troopers turned upon him thrusting with their lances: but he darted to and fro causing for the moment a frantic commotion. Wounded several times, he staggered towards me raising his spear. I shot him at less than a yard. He fell on the sand, and lay there dead. How easy to kill a man! But I did not worry about it. I found that I had fired the whole magazine of my Mauser pistol, so I put in a new clip of ten cartridges before thinking of anything else.

I was still prepossessed with the idea that we had inflicted great slaughter on the enemy and had scarcely suffered at all ourselves. Three or four men were missing from my troop. Six men and nine or ten horses were bleeding from spear-thrusts or sword cuts. We all expected to be ordered immediately to charge back again. The men were ready, though they all looked serious. Several asked to be allowed to throw away their lances and draw their swords. I asked my second sergeant if he had enjoyed himself. His answer was 'Well, I don't exactly say I enjoyed it, sir; but I think I'll get more used to it next time.' At this the whole troop laughed.

But now from the direction of the enemy there came a succession of grisly apparitions; horses spouting blood, struggling on three legs, men staggering on foot, men bleeding from terrible wounds, fish-hook spears stuck right through, arms and faces cut to pieces, bowels protruding, men gasping, crying, collapsing, expiring. Our first task was to succour these; and meanwhile the blood of our leaders cooled. They remembered for the first time that we had carbines. Everything was still in great confusion. But trumpets were sounded and orders shouted, and we all moved off at a trot towards the flank of the enemy. Arrived at a position from which we could enfilade and rake the watercourse, two squadrons were dismounted and in a few minutes with their fire at three hundred yards compelled the Dervishes to retreat. We therefore remained in possession of the field. Within twenty minutes of the time when we had first wheeled into line and begun our charge, we were halted and breakfasting in the very watercourse that had so very nearly proved our undoing. There one could see the futility of the much vaunted *Arme Blanche*. The Dervishes had carried off their wounded, and the corpses of thirty or forty enemy were all that could be counted on the ground. Among these lay the bodies of over twenty lancers, so hacked and mutilated as to be most unrecognizable. In all out of 310 officers and men the regiment had lost in the space of about two or three minutes five officers and sixty-five men killed and wounded, and 120 horses – nearly a quarter of its strength.

Such were my fortunes in this celebrated episode. It is very rarely that cavalry and infantry, while still both unshaken, are intermingled as the result of an actual collision. Either the infantry keep their heads and shoot the cavalry down, or they break into confusion and are cut down or speared as they run. But the two or three thousand Dervishes who faced the 21st Lancers in the watercourse at Omdurman were not in the least shaken by the stress of battle or afraid of cavalry. Their fire was not good enough to stop the charge, but they had no doubt faced horsemen many a time in the wars with Abyssinia. They were familiar with the ordeal of the charge. It was the kind of fighting they thoroughly understood. Moreover, the fight was with equal weapons, for the British too fought with sword and lance as in the days of old.

The term *Arme Blanche* which Churchill uses was the French phrase for cavalry armed with sword or lance – literally, the 'White Arm'. Already by 1898 there had been much discussion on whether swords and lances were obsolete. Those who wished to see them discarded in favour of the carbine or rifle did not want to see the end of the cavalry, but they felt that cavalry would be more mobile, better armed, and therefore better able to carry out the tasks of reconnaissance and harassing if it abandoned their traditional weapons for modern ones. Erskine Childers, author of *The Riddle of the Sands*, published a book in 1910 entitled *War and the Arme Blanche* supporting this argument. In the foreword Field Marshal Earl Roberts, VC, stated: 'I need not labour to say how entirely I agree with the author's main thesis.'

Roberts had, of course, been Commander-in-Chief in the Boer War of 1899–1902, at the end of a long and distinguished career, and it is to this war that we must now look for the next stage in the history of the British cavalry.

The causes of the Boer War go far back in history but may be briefly summarized. The 'Boers' were farmers of Dutch descent, some of whose ancestors had settled around the Cape as early as 1652. In the early days they had a series of small battles against the Hottentots, who resented these intruders into what they believed to be their own territory, but the Hottentots were pushed back. The Dutch were later joined by settlers from other countries, including France, Germany and Portugal. Towards the end of the eighteenth century the Cape settlers began to clash with the Xosa, a branch of the formidable Bantu, who were now moving south. During the Napoleonic Wars the Cape was occupied, to prevent a French seizure, such as had occurred during the American War of Independence. In 1813, by the Treaty of Paris, the Dutch government gave up its rights in the Cape in return for £6,000,000 compensation, paid by the British.

But in 1836 the Boers, exasperated by the reluctance of the British to deal firmly with the Bantu, whose raids were a constant danger, moved further inland in the Great Trek, eventually establishing themselves in the Orange Free State and the Transvaal. The relationship between British, Boers, and Bantu was never stable and occasionally erupted into serious conflicts, such as the Zulu War of 1879 and the First Boer War of 1881–2. In 1899 when Kruger, the Dutch President, was receiving heavy imports of arms from Germany, the British government belatedly began to reinforce the Cape garrison. Kruger promptly sent an ultimatum demanding that all the troops should be withdrawn and all troops approaching on the high seas be turned back, or war would be declared within two days. Hostilities thereupon began on 12 October.

The opening stages of the war were disastrous for Britain, for the Boers were immediately able to put 50,000 trained men in the field against 20,000 British. Later the Boers mustered 90,000, but to defeat them the British eventually required a force of 450,000. The operational area was equal to the size of France and Germany put together: there were few roads or bridges and no reliable maps.

One of the opening battles took place at Elandslaagte. It was one of the few British successes of that period. Major W. Wilcox, 3rd Hussars, an ex 5th Lancer, wrote of it:

> At Elandslaagte the Boers suddenly delivered a counter-attack when the British, thinking the battle was already won, had sounded 'Cease fire'.
>
> The Imperial Light Horse, on the right, again rushed to the charge but not before they had lost their gallant Colonel Scott Chisholme. He was binding up a wounded trooper when the counter-attack took place and was shot in the ankle. Waving his men on with his old regimental scarf, he called out 'My boys are doing well', and immediately after got a bullet through his lungs, while a third bullet pierced his brain. His gallant corps, however, leapt forward, the infantry rallied and once more the khaki-clad line advanced.
>
> . . . Now the opportunity for which they had waited had come. The Boers were streaming off their main position in a northerly direction, and with the 5th Lancer squadron under Captain Oakes on the right, and the 5th Dragoon Guards under Major Gore on the left, the cavalry extended and were let go. As they topped the rise which had concealed them, they found the Boers crossing their front at a distance of a few hundred yards. For over a mile did the two British squadrons ride through the enemy, spearing some forty of them. Then, rallying, the troopers wheeled about and galloped back again through the still streaming crowd of fugitives. Many Boers endeavoured to fire their Mausers from the saddle, but after the first onset of the cavalry, the Burghers were straining every nerve to gallop away from those terrible lance points.
>
> This charge created the greatest terror and resentment among the Boers, who vowed at the time they would destroy all Lancers they captured. On the other hand, an officer who rode with the squadron stated that in the return gallop he repeatedly saw Boers throw up their hands in token of surrender, and as the lance point was turned and the lancer passed, a rifle would be treacherously fired by the Boer at his generous enemy. A somewhat extraordinary occurrence was the act of Lance Corporal Kelly of the 5th Lancers, who speared two Boers riding on one pony with his lance.

Major Wilcox seemed surprised at the unsporting tactics of the Boers, being perhaps unaware of the long build-up of resentment against the British presence. British troops were often surprised and resentful when the enemy displayed a lack of sporting ethics. The expectation that other arms might display chivalrous characteristics seems to stem from the days of the Crusades when, it was said, the Saracens often behaved more decorously than the Crusaders.

Soon after the beginning of the war it became clear that the Boers had a better grasp of tactics than the British generals. In consequence, the second week of December 1899 became known as 'Black Week'. Gatacre was defeated at Stormberg, Methuen at Magersfontein, and Butler at Colenso. It was clear that the Boers were very formidable opponents indeed. They were expert mounted troops and could shoot straight from the back of a galloping horse. Furthermore they used smokeless powder.

The consequence of the Black Week was that Lord Roberts was now given the post of Commander-in-Chief, although he was sixty-eight. However, he soon showed he had lost none of his former tactical skill when he took over the Kimberley front in February. The Boers did not believe that the British would leave the railway, but Roberts did, in a move eastwards. On 15 February Sir John French, with a strong cavalry force, met Cronje's army just north of the Modder river. French launched the cavalry right at them, achieving shock and surprise. Kimberley was relieved.

The 9th Lancers were in South Africa at this time and their regimental history, as written by Captain F. H. Reynard, shows that they were happy to take the rough with the smooth:

At about 1 am on the 11th the final advance was made and by dawn the battle of Magersfontein was raging. It was an artillery and infantry engagement more particularly, and has been ably described by many writers.

Sergeant Ambrose of the regiment had his horse shot under him and when it fell pinned him to the ground so that he was unable to extricate himself. In this position he was incessantly fired at by Boers who eventually hit him in the arm. He was rescued late at night by some of the Guards Brigade, having suffered intensely from the heat. The casualties of the regiment were 2 men killed 9 wounded: 8 horses killed 16 wounded.

On the 6th some races were held, and Major Little won the Modder River Cup on his bay-waler horse 'Oceano', beating a large and varied field of quadrupeds.

On the 15th the officers played those of the 12th Lancers at hockey, and beat them by 4 goals to 2.

On the 25th the Cavalry Brigade played the Guards Brigade at hockey and beat them 4 to love.

On the 28th Lieutenant and Adjutant Bell had to go on the sick list with enteric fever.

Enteric. Of the Boer War it was said: 'The doctor killed more than the butcher,' for more people died of disease than by enemy action.

The cavalry division was composed of three brigades.

1st Brigade contained:
    The Carabiniers
    Scots Greys
    Inniskillings
    14th Hussars
    New South Wales Lancers
    G & T Batteries R.H.A.

2nd Brigade contained:
>Household Cavalry Composite Regiment
>10th Hussars
>12th Lancers
>Q & U Batteries R.H.A.

3rd Brigade contained:
>9th Lancers
>16th Lancers
>O & R Batteries R.H.A.

Before setting out, the division was addressed by Lord Roberts: 'The division is about to start on an expedition which it will remember all its life. A British cavalry force of this size has never been employed before, and it rests with the division to show that it can maintain the traditions of the British cavalry and relieve Kimberley at all costs.'

They justified his confidence. Conan Doyle described the action in these words: 'Disregarding the Boer fire completely, the cavalry swept in wave after wave over the low nek, and so round the base of the hills. The Boer riflemen must have seen a magnificent military spectacle as regiment after regiment, the 9th Lancers leading, all in very open order, swept across the plain at a gallop, and so passed over the nek.' But he went on to say: 'The war was a most cruel one for the cavalry, who were handicapped throughout by the nature of the country and the tactics of the enemy. They are certainly the branch of the service which had the least opportunity for distinction. The work of scouting and patrolling is the most dangerous duty which a soldier can undertake, and yet from its very nature can find no chronicler.'

Whether the war was worse for the cavalry than for the other arms is debatable; it was hard for everyone. The fact that much of the time was spent on a plateau which was 6,000 feet above sea level meant that nights were often bitterly cold; officers and men would curl up inside the legs of their horses as they lay on the ground, each helping to keep the other warm. Boer tactics were what might have been expected: in other words, they never did what was anticipated and this made them difficult to bring to battle. Had they made more use of wire, for example, at Klip Drift, the cavalry would have had an even more difficult time. The fact that the cavalry had successes in the Boer War, when modern weapons were used, appears to have had the unfortunate result of convincing the generals that horsed cavalry could still be used against entrenched positions. When the First World War began in 1914, some of those generals were in high positions.

The cavalry certainly had its triumphant moments. The history of the 9th Lancers records: 'Lieut Sadleir-Jackson distinguished himself by his promptitude in seizing a small kopje [hill] and driving off about forty of the Boers who were galloping for it. A small party of nine men of the "C" Squadron, under Captain Fiennes and Lt Lord F. Blackwood charged into the tail end of some flying Boers and every man got his lance home.'

Gradually the British clawed their way back from that disastrous December. The battle of Paardeburg in February 1900 led to Cronje surrendering with 4,000 men.

Boer War – a reconnaissance in force with General French's cavalry near Colesberg.

Boer War – taking the 4.7 naval gun across the Tugela.

Night attack on a Boer convoy by mounted infantry under Colonel Williams.

The fight at Brakenlaagte: Boers charging (1901). The Boers displayed astonishing skill at firing accurately from the back of a fast-moving horse.

Mishap to the Scots Greys at Klippan, 1902. The Scots Greys had their setbacks as well as their successes. A section on the flank of Hamilton's column was cut off and attacked by a large Boer force, and casualties were high.

Roberts entered Bloemfontein in March. Ladysmith was relieved on 28 February but there was no cavalry pursuit of the retreating Boers: Winston Churchill said that General Buller had issued orders to the cavalry to hold back. Buller's generalship had already provoked criticism, but this order must have helped to prolong the war. As it was the Boers were able to retreat in good order taking all their artillery with them.

These successes were followed by the capture of Pretoria in the following June. To the optimistic and the unimaginative the war must have seemed virtually over. In fact it had another eighteen hard months to run. Kitchener took over from Roberts in November 1900 and found that the Boers had turned defeat into an advantage. Instead of having to defend fixed points, they could harass the British communications at will. They blew up railways, derailed trains, ambushed convoys and attacked detachments. They could move freely everywhere and did so, until Kitchener methodically began to restrict them. His tactics, much criticized subsequently, were to establish small bullet-proof blockhouses within rifle shot of each other, to clear areas of all potential hostile forces and then to wire them off. Isolated farms which could give shelter to the Boer guerrillas were burnt, and the inhabitants put in large central camps. When disease broke out in these camps the Boers blamed the British for putting them there, but in fairness it must be explained that the country Boers had no idea of camp hygiene and many of their troubles were caused by this fact. The camps ruined what would otherwise have been a war lacking bitterness. British and Boers respected each other as fighters. Boers sent their wounded to British hospitals: they reserved their hard feelings for the Cape Dutch who refused to help them, and for the European countries which had sent sympathy for their cause but no help.

In the later stages there were desperate hunts to track down and capture the guerrilla leaders. This gave the cavalry plenty to do. Thus the 9th Lancers spent 12 July 1901 as follows: 'Scobell's column was at Elands Poort by dawn of the 12th. The day was spent hunting the enemy about and eventually a chain of small posts about 200 yards apart was formed. Scheepers, however, was not to be caught, and he made his escape with the bulk of his command through a long kloof [ravine] up the precipitous side of a hill. Lieut Theobald captured a Boer who was carrying despatches to

Haig at the time of the Boer War. Later he rose to the rank of Field Marshal.
His enthusiasm for cavalry was enormous and much criticized.

Scheepers. Lord D. Compton and Lieut Bell captured several Boers among whom was Lieut Limburgher.'

But the worst effect of the war was not on future Anglo-Boer relations, bad though that was, but on the views and careers of some of the commanders. In the *Historical Records of the 11th Hussars* by Captain G. T. Williams (published in 1908) appear the words: 'To cavalry the [Boer] war is especially interesting, vindicating yet again, as it does, the truth of Napoleon's oft repeated maxim as to the indispensability of that arm, when properly led and handled.' As that book contains many interesting facts and much sound comment, it is all the more surprising that this author makes such a deduction from a campaign which clearly foreshadowed the end of the mounted regiments.

He was not, of course, alone in his opinion. Haig, who had been in the Sudan campaign as well as the Boer War, would be a corps commander in the early days of the First World War and later become Commander-in-Chief. In 1907 he published a book entitled *Cavalry Studies: Strategical and Tactical*. It was mainly based on his experiences as Inspector General of Cavalry in India between 1903 and 1906. In it he wrote: 'It must be borne in mind that the days of small armies are past and it is a simple fact that *large Armies entail large numbers of cavalry.*' He continued: 'The Army, then, which assumes the strategical offensive, has, as a general rule, the best chance of employing the most effective manoeuvres but much depends on the quality and handling of the cavalry. Cavalry, then, sharing enormous defensive power conferred by the low trajectory rifle and rapidity of fire, plays a rôle in grand tactics of which the importance can hardly be over-estimated.'

In support of this thesis he quoted various authorities, one writing in 1868, another in 1882. He went on to say:

The rôle of the cavalry on the battlefield will always go on increasing because:

1 The extended nature of the modern battlefield means that there will be a greater choice of cover to favour the concealed approach of cavalry.

2 The increased range and killing power of modern guns, and the greater length of time during which the battle will last, will augment the moral exhaustion, will affect men's nerves more and produce greater demoralisation amongst the troops. These factors contribute to provoke panic, and to render troops (short-service soldiers nowadays) ripe for attacks by cavalry.

3 The longer the range and killing power of modern arms the more important will rapidity of movement become because it lessens the relative time of exposure to danger in favour of the Cavalry.

4 The introduction of the small-bore rifle, the bullet from which has little stopping power against a horse.

This took Haig to the following conclusion: 'The rôle of the Cavalry, far from having diminished, has increased in importance. It extends to both strategy and tactics; it alone is of use in the service of explorations and it is of capital importance in a general action.' It is clear that Haig had no conception of what a European battlefield would look like in the future. When he saw one it was as a field commander under the command of General Sir John French, who, in turn, was under Kitchener. At that point Haig demurred at using his infantry, let alone his cavalry, over exposed ground. He spoke of the Loos country: 'It is as flat as my hand.' But in August 1914 many of the higher appointments in the War Office were held by cavalry officers, all apparently sharing the conviction that the cavalry rôle in the future would be greater than ever before.

13

The Great War

Until a second, even larger, conflict broke out in 1939, the war of 1914–18 was known as 'The Great War'. Although the principal contestants had been expecting this event for several years, the outbreak itself seemed to take everyone by surprise. First the Archduke of Austria had been assassinated by an amateur revolutionary, then, reluctantly, as the ultimatums were unanswered, the European nations began to mobilize. Graf von Schlieffen, Chief of the German General Staff, had, seven years earlier, formulated a plan to knock out France with a right flank attack, pivoting the army on Metz, sweeping through Belgium, whose neutrality would obviously be violated in the process, encircling Paris from the north, and finally crushing the French armies against the Germans who had been left on the southern flank. Von Schlieffen died in 1913, so he never had the opportunity to see his master-plan be put into operation, and fail. The flank attack in the north was checked long before it could encircle Paris, and an entirely unexpected form of warfare came into being.

When the German armies were stopped the Allies dug in. Both sides then hastily extended their trenches from Switzerland to the Channel. At first the trenches were neither extensive nor complicated, but they rapidly became so. In the early stages these defensive lines could probably have been penetrated (if the right methods had been used) and the gaps exploited by cavalry. But soon, on the Western Front, all hope of a breakthrough which might be turned into a victory by a fast mobile group of horse was rapidly dispersed. Instead, this became a war of attrition, a war 'to bleed the Germans to death', a war of apparently unlimited infantry being flung in hopeless waves against barbed wire defences interspersed with machine-guns. It was a war of endless artillery battles and it was fought over land on which there was no cover except in the trenches and nothing underfoot except mud, shell-holes, and corpses. However, to the very end there were cavalry formations held in reserve for the hoped-for, but impossible, breakthrough. The cavalry story is best told through short excerpts from the various official histories (as will follow).

But the Western Front, although the largest and most devastated, was by no means the only theatre in which bitter fighting took place. And wherever cavalry might perhaps be used, cavalry was always present. In many areas – Africa, Macedonia, Italy, Mesopotamia – the cavalry which took part was not usually British, although there were notable exceptions. But an area in which British cavalry was extensively and effectively used was Palestine and Syria. A fuller account of that campaign will follow.

173

Astonishing though it may seem, large numbers of cavalry were employed in the First World War, and some spectacular charges took place. This is a typical action picture by Stanley L. Wood, whose eye for accurate detail was quite remarkable.

From Private to Field Marshal – the notable
cavalryman, Field Marshal Sir William Robertson,
G.C.B., G.C.M.G., K.C.V.O., D.S.O.

But the fact that there was, overall, little scope for cavalry action does not mean that horses did not play an enormous part in the war. They were used by the thousand for transport of every type, and casualties were, in consequence, enormous too.

The British Expeditionary Force (BEF) consisted of six infantry divisions and one cavalry division. The cavalry division contained four brigades each consisting of three regiments: in addition it included artillery, engineers, signals and medical units. This gave a strength of 9,000 (approximately half that of an infantry division) and 10,000 horses. It had twenty-four 13-pounder guns and twenty-four machine-guns. The Yeomanry became the second-line cavalry with a strength of fourteen brigades.

Although war was declared on 4 August 1914 first contact was not made with the Germans until 22 August. The cavalry division, with a 5th Independent Cavalry brigade, led the advancing British troops as they moved towards Mons. The Commander-in-Chief, Sir John French, had to issue a firm order to stop the cavalry trying to win the war on its own. It ran: 'In no circumstances does the C-in-C wish the cavalry division to be seriously engaged till he is ready to support it.'

However, at dawn on 22 August C Squadron of the 4th Dragoon Guards found a German picquet on the road near Soignies, opened fire, and drove it off. Soon afterwards another troop of the same squadron met a larger body of German cavalry and turned them back near Casteau. The 4th D.G. began to pursue but ran into heavy fire. (The Germans agree that this was the first continental exchange of fire in the war: there had, of course, already been battles at sea.) Soon other cavalry units, the Scots Greys and 16th Lancers, were in contact. In these early clashes the British cavalry was cheered to find itself superior to the German, both with rifle and sword. However, it reported large numbers of German infantry moving steadily westward. Then, after reporting the whereabouts of the enemy, the Cavalry Division was ordered to withdraw. To its surprise it was shadowed by a German airship as it made its way to billets some fourteen miles behind its earlier position.

During the following weeks, as the British and French armies retreated in the face of the huge numbers of oncoming Germans, the cavalry was largely employed in its traditional rôle of scouting, harassing, and liaison. On 28 August, the 5th Cavalry Brigade was at Moy, two miles from Cérizy, ready for the advancing Germans. The Scots Greys put out a troop with a machine-gun in a copse to the side of the road, but the troop was driven in by superior numbers. However, the rest of the squadron were in the village of La Guinguette and checked the enemy advance. Two German cavalry squadrons were put to flight. The 12th Lancers then advanced around the German eastern flank and the 20th Hussars along the west. This move caused the forward German units to retreat rapidly from the closing pincer. The 12th Lancers then made contact with some German cavalry, forced them to dismount, and stampeded their horses. They then charged into the remainder of the German cavalry (over fifty yards) and speared seventy of the German 2nd Guard Dragoon Regiment. The 12th Lancers had five killed and five wounded. This was known as the Battle of Moy and was mentioned in the official history: 'Though the action had been comparatively insignificant it had very effectively damped the ardour of the German cavalry.'

On 31 August, near Compiègne, the 3rd Hussars found themselves in a brisk battle with their counterparts in the German Army, the 3rd Hussars of the German 3rd Cavalry Corps. The British regiment had the better of the exchange.

The memory that most soldiers retained of those days was of a degree of exhaustion which they had not believed possible. The Army philosophy was that men would march as long as they could and then lie down: 'they would be too tired to march but not too tired to fire their rifles.' The cavalry became equally exhausted from the constant calls made on them. On numerous occasions units were told to leave their horses and go into the trenches as replacements. Unfortunately the cavalry proved so useful in these early battles that more was expected of it than it could possibly manage. Lt R. H. O'Brien, an infantry subaltern, recalls being told to draw his platoon to the ditch beside a road because the cavalry was about to mount an attack. Knowing that the Germans, with machine guns, were at the other end of the road, he waited for the inevitable result. The regiment galloped past, and was virtually wiped out. During the Second World War, when O'Brien was serving again, this time as a colonel, he met a retired general who, he discovered, had commanded the regiment he had seen slaughtered. O'Brien asked how, as commanding officer, he could have ordered such an attack knowing his regiment would be wiped out. 'I had to,' was the reply. 'Those were my orders. If I had refused to carry them out I should have been court-martialled but the regiment would have gone just the same.'

By 1915 it was obvious to all but the most obtuse that in this static warfare the only use for the cavalry would be as mounted infantry or as infantry replacements. Nevertheless the hope that proper cavalry action would once again, by some miracle, become possible, remained alive.

On 1 July 1916 the great Somme offensive was launched, following an eleven-day bombardment. At the end of the day, the official history records: 'More than 57,000 casualties had been suffered, and on two-thirds of the front the gallantry and devotion of the troops had proved of little avail: by evening there stood revealed the true character of the task which confronted General Rawlinson's Fourth Army.' However, there had been gains in some places along the fourteen mile front and the attack was continued. On 14 July 7th Division was told to advance on High Wood; the cavalry would cover the right flank:

> Thus at about 7 p.m. began the advance towards High Wood, which stood nearly three-quarters of a mile away to the north-east on a ridge beyond a slight dip of open ground.
>
> A machine-gun in Delville Wood opened up on the cavalry but was silenced by an airman; a little fire came from riflemen hidden in the crops near High Wood.
>
> The advanced squadron of the 7th Dragoon Guards and Deccan Horse had reached the high ground between Delville Wood and High Wood where they came under shell-fire from the direction of Flers, beyond the ridge. There was some sniping but an enemy barrage which was put down dropped in a valley behind the horsemen. The 7th Dragoon Guards charged some infantry and machine-gunners in the crops, killed a number with the lance and captured 32, whilst a German machine-gun near Longueval was silenced by the cavalry machine-guns before it had done much damage. At 9.30 p.m. when it had grown too dark for mounted action the squadrons took up a line from near Longueval to the southern corner of High Wood, a convenient bank beyond a rough road providing cover for the horses.

Attempts to bring the cavalry into other attacks were less successful. At Mametz in 1916 they were interspersed with tanks, but the tanks proved mechanically unreliable and the horses too vulnerable. In September, at Flers: 'A mounted patrol moved eastward round the village but was heavily shelled on turning north and had to withdraw: the remainder of the squadron dismounted and entered Gueudecourt on foot.'

During the battle of Arras in 1917 XVII Corps 'had insufficient resources to exploit its remarkable success on 9th April . . . for this purpose it would have been desirable to place a cavalry brigade, well forward at its disposal. As it was, while cavalry was massed south of the Scarpe, none was allotted to the XVII Corps until any possible opportunity for its effective use had passed.'

The year 1918 told much the same story: 'General Pétain withdrew the two cavalry corps into reserve, pointing out that the form which the battle had assumed precluded any possibility of employing cavalry corps in the fighting.' (July 1918)

As the advance continued, British troops often outran their supplies and had to rely on the French. 'What the troops missed most were the ordinary Expeditionary Force canteen supplies, particularly cigarettes and tobacco. It should be added that the local estaminets on the line of march of XXII Corps on 17th July dispensed a clear brown liquid which looked like beer and was treated as such by a whole brigade that had never heard of still champagne, with disastrous results.'

The last days of the war, October and November 1918, saw the cavalry once more able to resume its proper rôle. Instead of being used in small patrols, picking their way over former battlefields littered with débris and cut up by trenches, it was able to advance in squadron order. The Germans were in retreat and the cavalry was detailed to maintain contact. For this purpose an immaculate appearance was deemed essential and it is said that the appearance of troops of cavalry which looked like survivals from a different age had as great an effect in quelling any German feelings of further resistance as the heaviest artillery barrage could have done. At the end of a war in which a million cavalry horses had been held in readiness for that long-expected breakthrough, a war in which 250,000 horses died of disease or gunshot wounds, a war in which few regiments had had a chance to perform otherwise than as mounted infantry, this final demonstration of cavalry style was some consolation.

The fact that the war had been a battle of attrition by infantry and artillery did not mean that the cavalry had escaped unscathed. As one example, in the Battle of Arras the 3rd Cavalry Division had lost 41 officers and 553 other ranks; the 8th Cavalry Brigade lost 30 officers and 367 other ranks. Casualties among horses was higher. In the 2nd Cavalry division 274 horses died from exhaustion or had to be destroyed.

But in proportion to infantry casualties these losses were minute. One of the most appalling battles on the Western Front was at Bullecourt in May 1917, 'a battle in which, with occasional lulls, the fighting was intense for a fortnight, with extraordinary expenditure of ammunition and the most ghastly accompaniments. [The Official History: 1917] By the end the dead of both sides lay in clumps all over the battlefield, and in the bottom or under the parapets of the trenches many hundreds had been hastily covered with a little earth. One witness, after speaking of the nauseating stench, expresses his astonishment 'that any human beings could hold and fight under such conditions'. He adds that he never saw a battlefield, Ypres in 1917 not excepted, where the living and the unburied dead remained in close proximity for so long.' On the other hand, life behind the line was almost normal. Many regiments were involved in this blood-bath: Australians, Devons, Manchesters, Warwicks, to name but a few. The cavalry had no equivalent experience.

But while the Western Front produced little but frustration and casualties for the cavalry, the scene in the Middle East was very different. In spite of Allied efforts to persuade her not to do so, Turkey had joined Germany and Austria in October 1914. This led to the Allied attempt to seize the Dardanelles in 1915, which ended in costly failure. Basra, at the head of the Persian Gulf, was vital to Britain's oil supply, so this had been captured in November 1914. The Turks tried to recapture it in 1915, but failed. At that point Britain decided to push on from Basra to Kut-el-Amara and, if all went well, to Baghdad. General Townshend, making excellent use of his cavalry, reached Aziziya, which was halfway between Baghdad and Kut, and this campaign looked very promising indeed. However, after a drawn battle at Ctesiphon, the Turks received a large number of experienced reinforcements and put so much pressure on Townshend that he was forced to retreat to Kut (8 December, 1915). Four and a half months later his starving garrison was forced to surrender. This catastrophe completely obscured Townshend's earlier achievements when with smaller numbers he had defeated larger forces. The Turks rated him as one of the best generals of the war.

In December 1916 the Mesopotamian offensive was resumed, this time under General Maude. Maude gained a useful victory at Sannaiyat in February 1917 but failed to use his cavalry effectively to follow it up. The handling and use of the cavalry in this campaign left much to be desired. Nevertheless Maude was able to enter Baghdad on 11 March 1917. Clearly the Turks were not doing very well in this war but they were still a long way from being finally defeated. They were persuaded by the Germans that the loss of Baghdad was of no consequence, nor should they be concerned by the other defeats they had sustained from British forces. These included the repulse of a Turkish army of 20,000 which had tried to cross the Suez Canal and 'liberate' Egypt (then a British Protectorate), in February 1915, and an attack in the Western Desert in January 1916. For the latter the Turks had made arrangements with Sennussi Arabs from Libya who had co-operated with them previously against the Italians. The Turkish-led Sennussi force advanced towards Sollum, on the coast, but were then given a discouraging reception by British infantry. The Sennussi thereupon decided to retreat and regroup, but while doing so were charged by the Dorset Yeomanry. This charge was no inconsiderable feat, for it was made over open ground from a distance of fifty yards under heavy fire from an enemy who had been repulsed but not destroyed. The cost was high: out of a total strength of 84, five officers and twenty-seven troopers were killed, and twenty-six men were wounded; however, the result was the complete defeat of the invaders and the capture of their commander.

As the major part of this book has been concerned with the activities of regular cavalry regiments, it is very satisfactory to be able to describe a theatre where the Yeomanry were given an opportunity to display their mettle and did so superbly. Over the years the regular cavalry have always relied on the Yeomanry for recruiting and support and are fully conscious of their debt: however, in the eyes of the general public and the government, the Yeomanry have tended to be regarded as 'second-line' cavalry, available for reinforcements, or conversion into some other arm such as artillery or signals. In the Middle Eastern campaign there were no regular British cavalry regiments: the achievements were the Yeomanry's own.

In mid-1917 Turkish morale received a considerable boost from the knowledge that a special force, the Yilderim, had been formed and was being trained in Syria. Its commander was the renowned German General Falkenhayn and the recapture of Baghdad was to be the first of its many victories. At the end of the Yilderim's campaign it was confidently assumed Egypt would have been captured, British shipping be unable to use the Suez Canal, Mesopotamia and its oil supplies – as well as those of Persia – be in Turkish hands, and, for good measure, an invasion force be on its way to India.

Meanwhile the British public, naturally concerned at the colossal sacrifices in the trenches of France, was questioning why a large garrison should be maintained in Egypt, and even why the Mesopotamian campaign was necessary at all.

A somewhat sinister aspect of the situation in the Middle East was that, if Britain sustained any more defeats like Kut, many Moslems, in Egypt, Persia, and even India, might decide to follow Turkish requests and stir up widespread trouble. The Allied High Command now felt that the only way to settle the Turkish problem, once and for all, was to inflict a crushing defeat on a Turkish army and in the process capture Jerusalem. The loss of the prestigious Holy City would be a blow from which Turkish morale would be unlikely to recover: Jerusalem, although a symbolic Christian city, ranks closely behind Mecca on the list of places sacred to Islam.

Fortunately for the Allies, the Mesopotamian situation now seemed well under control. General Maude had pushed on from Baghdad driving the Turks in front of him, but he had died of cholera in November 1917. His successor, General Marshall, continued the successful campaign and defeated the Turks twice more. This was highly satisfactory, but it was not the heart of the Turkish problem.

The capture of Jerusalem would clearly be a formidable task, but the High Command had the foresight to appoint an appropriate man to undertake it. This was General Allenby. He took over in July 1917 after his predecessor (who was far from well) had twice failed to capture Gaza. The approach to Jerusalem was flanked by the two towns of Gaza and Beersheba: the former is on the coast and the latter twenty-five

The Palestine Campaign, 1917–18. British Horse Artillery and Australian Cavalry advancing over the Philistine Plain.

miles inland. Allenby was not merely an experienced general in the field, as his previous record on the Western Front showed, he was also extremely adept at obtaining the troops he needed from Higher Authority. In consequence he began to train a force of seven infantry divisions, and the Desert Mounted Corps. The Desert Mounted Corps, which is of particular interest to us, consisted of 20,000 horse, drawn from Australian, New Zealand, Indian, and British Yeomanry units. Its achievements were soon dramatic. Whereas in the temperate northern hemisphere horses carried 22 stones of weight, in Palestine the DMC horses carried 20 stones in temperatures ranging from freezing-point to 125° Fahrenheit. The DMC was the largest tactical force of cavalry ever to operate under one command and its feats, such as regular marches of sixty miles a day, seem almost incredible. Water was always scarce but one regiment, the Worcestershire Yeomanry, established a remarkable record of marching ninety miles without fresh supplies.

Allenby (later Field Marshal Viscount Edmund Allenby of Megiddo and Felixstowe) had joined the Inniskilling Dragoons in 1882 and had fought in the Zulu War and Boer War. He was a formidable personality, treated with great respect by both friends and enemies. He was popular with troops because they felt that under him they were likely to be on the winning side. The Germans, realizing that the Allies would feel humiliated by two defeats at Gaza, decided that the next Allied attack would be on a larger scale altogether. They therefore made extensive preparations to withstand it. Spies were operating efficiently on both sides and plans could hardly remain secret once dispositions were made. Numbers, at this point, seemed evenly matched, therefore if changes in deployment were made it was inevitable that enemy spotter aircraft would see what was happening and be able to forecast events. In order to conceal his intentions, Allenby directed that abandoned camps must still look as if they were in full use.

The plan of attack had been formulated by General Sir Philip Chetwode, Commander of 20 Corps, the previous May, and required very little modification. To approach Jerusalem it was necessary to capture Gaza and Beersheba, the former, as we noted, being on the coast, and particularly well defended. Beersheba must also be captured, but in view of the lack of water in the region it was assumed that this could not be taken before Gaza had fallen. Allenby's plan reversed this thinking and instead made Beersheba the first target and Gaza the second. But to cross the waterless area and capture Beersheba meant taking a tremendous risk: if it failed the Allied force would be in a worse position than it had been in the previous spring. And, although it was possible to make abandoned camps look as if they were still occupied, it was obvious that once large-scale movement began the Turks and Germans would realize that an attack was in the offing. The deception therefore had to be extended, to make it seem that the main attack would be on Gaza but there would also be a much smaller operation in the direction of Beersheba. But on the night of 31 October, the Desert Mounted Corps and 20 Corps, also cavalry, with infantry behind, made a dash across the desert and occupied the town. Before the Turks had recovered from the shock of losing Beersheba, they found another attack was being launched on to Gaza. It was heavy and it was successful, though costly. While the Gaza battle was in full spate Allenby now switched the direction of a proportion of his force and drove forward into the space between the two towns, right into the Turkish centre which had just been weakened by sending troops to reinforce Gaza on one side and to prevent the victors of Beersheba moving onward from that town.

On 7 November, four Allied divisions, including the 4th Cavalry Division, burst through the gap which recent moves had created in the Turkish lines. The Turks in Gaza, fearing they would be cut off and besieged, hastily evacuated the town, which was promptly taken over by the British. The Turkish army had now been split into two halves, one half north of Gaza, the other half west of Jerusalem. Nevertheless the Turks still had a substantial and resolute army and would only be crushed if Allenby could keep up the momentum of the attack. It would be, as the cavalry realized, a campaign in which charges at the right moment would be decisive. The Australian Light Horse had already given a dramatic demonstration of the power of a cavalry charge in this theatre when at Beersheba they had acted as the spearhead of the cavalry force. They had crashed through two lines of trenches, detaching a few of their members to dismount and clear them with bayonets as the remainder went on. The main body had then continued relentlessly forward, overrunning Turkish guns, slicing through transport and cutting down anyone who showed resistance. The result of it had been the capture of 1,500 Turks for the loss of thirty-two killed and thirty-two wounded.

The British Yeomanry would have indignantly, and rightly, disclaimed the need for an example; all they looked for was an opportunity to show that they could do better than their Allies. The chance was not long coming. At Huj, which is at the top of an equilateral triangle of which the base-line runs from Gaza to Beersheba, there was a strong enemy position on a ridge; it held artillery batteries, infantry, machine-guns, and adequate supplies. As the Desert column approached the ridge it was greeted with heavy and accurate artillery fire. An open plain stretched in front of the enemy position; an infantry attack over such open ground would be extremely costly and might well fail.

The Divisional Commander reconnoitred the position from an armoured car and decided it was unsuitable for a conventional infantry attack. He therefore called on the cavalry to take the ridge by storm if it were possible. A force of 158 horse was therefore made ready. It consisted of a squadron and a half from the Warwickshire Yeomanry and a similar number from the Worcestershire Yeomanry. There was no covering fire available, for there were no 18-pounders or machine-guns in the area.

The joint force trotted gently up to a point a thousand yards from the Turkish position. This took them into range of the enemy machine-guns, so they charged the infantry first and then turned towards the heavier guns. The charge was so swift, audacious and disciplined that eleven guns were captured and seventy prisoners taken. Many of the enemy gunners and infantrymen stood by their guns and were killed with the sword. On examination the casualties were seen to include a number of Germans and Austrians. However, the cost of this superb example of cavalry skill was high: the killed amounted to six officers and twenty-six troopers; a further forty were wounded. Over one hundred horses were killed.

Lt-Colonel R. M. P. Preston served throughout the campaign with the Horse Artillery and subsequently wrote a vivid description of the battle:

At about 3 p.m., as the right flank of the 60th Division was approaching Huj, it came suddenly under a devastating fire at close range from several concealed batteries of enemy artillery, which with two battalions of infantry, were covering the withdrawal of the Turkish VIIth Army headquarters. The Turks had in position a battery of field and one of mountain guns, with four machine-guns on a low hill between the two batteries, and three heavy howitzers behind.

As our cavalry appeared, thundering over the rise, the Turks sprang to their guns and swung them round, firing point-blank into the charging horsemen. The infantry, leaping on the limbers, blazed away with their rifles till they were cut down. There was no thought of surrender; every man stuck to his gun or rifle to the last. The leading troops of the cavalry dashed into the first enemy battery. The following troops, swinging to their right, took the three heavy howitzers almost in their stride, leaving the guns silent, the gun crews dead or dying, and galloped round the hill, to fall upon the mountain battery from the rear, and cut the Turkish gunners to pieces in a few minutes. The third wave, passing the first battery, where a fierce sabre v bayonet fight was going on between our cavalry and the enemy, raced up the slope at the machine-gun. Many saddles were emptied in that few yards, but the charge was irresistible. In a few minutes the enemy guns were silenced, their crews killed and the whole position was in our hands.

This was the first time our troops had 'got home' properly with the modern cavalry thrusting sword, and an examination of the enemy dead afterwards proved what a fine weapon it is.

Preston went on to discuss the problems faced by cavalry in modern warfare. At Beersheba, as we saw, the Australian Light Horse had charged with the squadrons in line and 150–200 yards behind each other. The leading squadron charged with the sword and galloped straight through the enemy position to attack any supports. The other squadrons did not carry swords but instead used rifle and bayonet. The second squadron also galloped through, then dismounted and attacked the enemy in the trenches from the rear with their bayonets. The third squadron dismounted before reaching the trenches and went in from the front with the bayonet. This last squadron also carried two machine-guns which were set up on the flanks to deal with any counter attack.

If the enemy was well furnished with artillery and machine-guns the best approach was to be in column of squadrons in line of troop columns. However, for this, the distance between the squadrons was shortened to 100 yards instead of 200, and the distances between troops was not *less* than 25 yards. This formation resulted in fewer casualties than any other form of deployment.

The charge at Huj had results which extended beyond the taking of ground and killing of enemy. One squadron of the Worcestershire Yeomanry spotted a Turkish ammunition depot with a number of enemy cavalry busy setting fire to it. Ignoring the Turkish cavalry, the squadron commander charged straight at the fires which they then managed to extinguish. The ammunition thus saved proved extremely useful later in the campaign when a number of enemy guns had been captured. Few activities

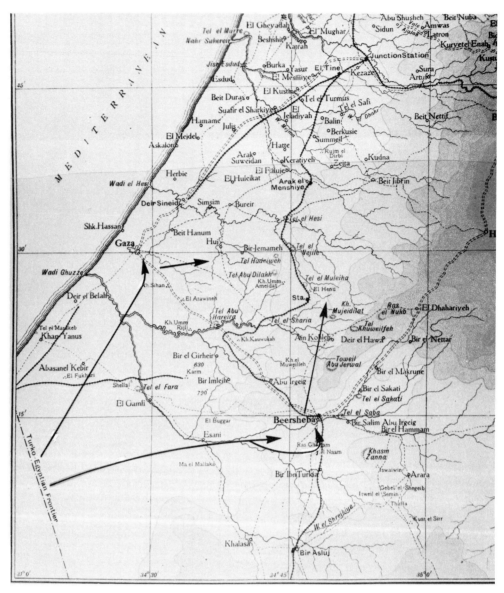

5 *Opening moves in the Palestine Campaign, 4 October 1917.*

have a more depressing effect on an enemy than to receive captured shells from captured guns on to his positions, when he himself is already running short of both. The Turks lost all their code books and telephone equipment at Huj and thereafter had to rely either on 'gallopers' or wireless for conveying messages. As the Turks seemed unaware that their code books were in Allied hands, they continued to use an unchanged code. This meant that the Allies knew what orders the Turks were receiving at the same time as the Turks themselves received them.

The campaign now moved forward onto the plains of Philistia, originally the home of the Philistines. In spite of attempts to cut off the retreating Turks, considerable numbers had managed to get away. Shortage of water, forage and supplies slowed down the Allies, as the Turks had destroyed most of the roads, bridges and culverts, as well as portions of the railway line. In addition the Turks broke up the water-lifting apparatus at all the wells, totally indifferent to the effect this would have on the local villages. The DMC spent most of its time in a far from successful search for water. Unfortunately the delays caused by the hunt for water enabled the Turks to establish strong defensive positions. Any chance of capturing Jerusalem by a swift cavalry raid had now vanished.

On 13 November the Allied attack was resumed, but after initial successes found itself held up on the slopes approaching El Mughar. The ground here was so bare and featureless that it would be inviting massacre for the infantry to attack. The only possible way to cross the long stretch of open ground was by a cavalry charge. This could be launched from the east of the position but at best would involve a two-mile gallop over open ground. The selected units, the Dorset Yeomanry and the Bucks Yeomanry, were then both advanced discreetly into the Wadi Jamus (a wadi is a dried-up watercourse) and then, on the order to attack, scrambled up the sides and took up the formation we described earlier. As soon as they appeared there was an outbreak of devastating fire from both sides; for the Allies the Berkshire Battery was particularly successful in dropping shells into Turkish positions on the ridge.

The Yeomanry trotted calmly for the first mile and a half, then shook out to a canter. One hundred yards from the top of the slope they received the order to charge and went like men and horses possessed. The leading squadron of the Bucks Yeomanry crashed through, spearing the enemy with their swords as they went. By the time they had pulled up, the second and third squadrons were at work with their bayonets in the trenches. The Dorsets had a slightly more difficult time, for the ground in front of them was much rougher and took the speed out of their charge. In fact, their leading squadron dismounted and went in with the bayonet. The other two squadrons passed them and went in with swords. It was interesting, and significant, that the losses among the dismounted squadron were heavier and that most of the killing had been done with the sword before the dismounted squadron arrived. The charge was not quite the end of the matter, for there were Turkish machine-gunners in the nearby village and these now began making the ridge very unhealthy. Two squadrons of the Berkshire Yeomanry were sent to deal with them; they went up at a gallop, dismounted, fought their way into the village on foot, and took 400 prisoners. A further 1100 prisoners were captured around the position, and 600 Turkish dead were counted. Allied casualties amounted to 129 men and 265 horses.

Meanwhile further encouraging advances were reported from farther north. On the 15th the Anzac Mounted Division had occupied Ramleh and on the 16th the New Zealand Mounted Brigade had taken Jaffa. (Jaffa, formerly Joppa and later Yafo, is a port from which oranges were shipped. It is now a suburb of Tel-Aviv. During this account we shall continue to call it by the name used during the war.) The Turks were not interested in defending either of those two towns for they were intent on reaching the strong defensive position of Khurbet Hadrah which was on the north bank of the

Auja river. This they did, without further engagement, and dug in. Here the Anzacs were ordered to wait pending reinforcements while the difficult but essential task of capturing Jerusalem was completed. There was a road from Jerusalem to Jaffa which, for the first part, ran through a deep and narrow valley which then broadens out, from Amwas onwards, into the vale of Ajalon. Immediately to the east of Amwas the plain is crossed by a ridge, at one end of which is Sidun and the other Abu Shusheh. This had been of great tactical importance since biblical times. Sidun, although sounding much like it, is not to be confused with Sidon (now Saydn) often mentioned in the Bible in connection with Tyre (now Sur), both of which are in Lebanon.

The Turks had deployed 4,000 troops and numerous guns on the ridge, most of the force being grouped around Abu Shusheh. There was also a large force of Turks, well armed with machine-guns, further south; this was to discourage any outflanking manoeuvres the Allies might have thought of making. The ridge rose steeply from the plain and held a number of caves in which the Turks had thoughtfully placed machine-guns. Because of the difficulties of using an infantry approach over the open plain, it was decided that the cavalry should be used. They had been very successful in a not dissimilar attack at El Mughar and might be expected to repeat their feat. In fact the ridge was steeper and rougher than El Mughar and was not really suitable for cavalry at all.

The charge was entrusted to the Buckinghamshire and Berkshire Yeomanry, with the Dorset Yeomanry in reserve. The Bucks Yeomanry led in column of squadrons in line of troop columns and soon came under very heavy fire from rifles and machine-guns. Their commander, Colonel Cripps, decided that further progress needed support if his entire regiment was not to be annihilated, and took advantage of some 'dead' ground and requested that support. 'Dead' ground is ground on which one cannot be seen and fired upon (except from howitzers or mortars): it may be a convenient hollow or the near side of a rock. Artillery fire from the Allied side was increased and the Dorset Yeomanry now began a flanking movement in the south, working round to the rear of the enemy's position. As they did so, the Turkish machine-gunners traversed and ranged on them. This gave the Bucks Yeomanry a respite and they quickly emerged from their cover and raced forward. Although their appearance led to a further burst of frontal fire, the Bucks Yeomanry surged through it with minimal loss to reach the foot of the ridge. There they tackled the steep and slippery slope, reached the summit and crashed through the Turks. Two squadrons of the Berkshire Yeomanry now came hard on the left of the ridge at the same moment. The Dorsets, their diversion having succeeded, raced on to the machine-gunners to the south of the position. These, not expecting to be in action so soon, were either cut down by sabres or hastily surrendered. A total of 400 Turks was found to have been killed by the sword. It was a classic example of co-ordination and mutual support and was surprisingly light in casualties. The total casualties in all three regiments was only 37. However, the battle looked like being the end of cavalry actions for the time being, for the Turks were now firmly established in the narrow rocky valley which extended as far as Jerusalem. Furthermore, the cavalry, having covered 170 miles since the campaign began less than three weeks before, desperately needed a rest. The horses had performed magnificently, but the experience of feeding on a mere $9\frac{1}{2}$ lbs of grain a day, combined with watering once in every thirty-six hours, had been an unprecedented strain. Some horses had only been watered at 72-hour intervals, incredible though this may seem in those conditions. Most of the horses were walers. Walers were Australian horses imported from New South Wales. Their origin was rather unusual for they were bred from English racehorses which had failed to come up to the hopes of their owners and backers. Though acquired cheaply, they were ideal saddle horses for up-country stations in Australia – hard, compact and full of courage and endurance. The Australians believed that a well-bred horse could always carry weight longer than its bigger, heavier contemporary: in Palestine the walers also took much less time to recuperate after campaigns than other horses did.

But not even walers could function properly in the country in which they now found themselves: it was suitable for donkeys and goats only. However, the DMC had to get through it, and get through it they did. 52 Infantry Division then managed to capture the hill of Nebi Samwil. This is where the prophet Samuel was said to be buried, and is also the nearest point to Jerusalem that Richard Coeur de Lion, in the twelfth century, reached.

The first stage of the campaign having been successfully completed, the Allies dug in both at Nahr el Auja and Nebi Samwil. At the same time the Turks decided they had retreated long enough and began counter-attacking.

Meanwhile the Turks had another problem on their hands. The Arab revolt and its brilliant sabotage operations did not involve cavalry, so do not concern us here. But, led by T. E. Lawrence, those sabotage activities, particularly along the Hedjaz railway, certainly weakened the Turks, both materially and in their will to fight. When the Allied forces closed round Jerusalem in December 1917 the Mayor of the city came out under a flag of truce and surrendered the keys. It was an historic moment. The Holy City had not been in Christian hands for six hundred years. Allenby made his official entry on 11 December. In appearance he lacked something of the presence that such an event might have required, for he was dressed in worn service khaki and he merely carried a cane. But his entry was made through the Jaffa Gate which, by tradition, is only opened to the conquerors of the Holy City.

The capture of Jerusalem was not, of course, the end of the campaign but it had several important effects. It signified the end of all danger to Mesopotamia, it encouraged the Arabs to continue their efforts to harass the Turkish lines of communication, it disposed of the boasted invincibility of the Yilderim, and it was an event of enormous moral significance. But the Turks were by no means finished, even in this area. They counter-attacked in an attempt to recover Jerusalem. Their efforts were unsuccessful but they displayed remarkable courage. They lost over 1000 soldiers killed, and 500 taken prisoner, for no territorial gain whatever.

At this point Palestine assumed greater importance in the eyes of the Allied High Command. Previously it had been regarded as an area of minor strategic value using troops which could have been more usefully employed in France. But now Allenby's successes had opened up the possibility of knocking Turkey right out of the war. After the humiliation of the Dardanelles, this would be some consolation to hurt pride, but the Dardanelles disaster had occurred three years earlier and the principal consideration now was to destroy one of Germany's most valued allies. The Germans were well aware that the Turks were wilting under Allied pressure and there were now a number of German and Austrian troops fighting alongside the units in Palestine.

Allenby was instructed to launch a further offensive with the objective of capturing Damascus and Aleppo. After a short period of regrouping, he set about his task. He was promised reinforcements, which duly arrived. Later, after the German March offensive in France, Allenby had to exchange some of his veteran troops for less experienced soldiers, but that time was not yet. In February he moved north-east of Jerusalem and captured Jericho on the 21st. He also succeeded in crossing the Jordan and establishing a bridgehead at Goraniye. This effectively secured his right flank against a sudden Turkish attack, and added further protection to Jerusalem. But any advance further north would have to confront a formidable, well-prepared Turkish force which was positioned on the Plain of Sharon between the hills and the sea. That area was only ten miles wide and a tremendous effort would be needed to break through, unless an alternative plan could be devised.

Allenby decided that no other strategy was possible but that the Turks might be deceived into thinking that the attack would not come from Allenby's left at all, but from his centre and right. To this end he made a forceful thrust in the direction of Amman during the last two weeks in March. Bad weather and the rocky terrain of the mountains of Moab delayed this thrust, and although it reached El Salt it failed to capture Amman. As this occurred just when the German offensive in France was looking its most dangerous, Allenby had to send off two complete divisions and a number of separate battalions to help plug the gap. Among the troops sent were nine Yeomanry regiments. As the troops which replaced them were, for the most part, inexperienced, Allenby now had to embark on a period of training before these new troops were available for a major assault. Nevertheless he kept up the deception plan by pushing 21 Corps along into the foothills of Judea. The plan involved keeping a force of cavalry in the Jordan valley during the summer. Being shelled by Turkish long-range guns was the least of its problems. More pressing was an average daytime temperature of over 110° Fahrenheit, hot winds full of choking dust, and a particularly vicious brand of malaria. The floor of the valley, which is 1,200 feet below sea level, is powdery dust, stones, rocks; its denizens are snakes and scorpions. The depth of the valley makes the atmosphere heavy and humid; not surprisingly it is known as 'the Valley of Desolation'. This is the sort of countryside where miracles may be seen to happen. Major Hopkins recalls, in the 1960s, seeing a bush suddenly begin to burn. It had grown during the wet season, then dried, and in the heat of the day suddenly ignited like paper left too near a fire.

For what consolation it was to the DMC, their presence there certainly convinced the Turks that the next assault must come along this flank. During that summer the Australian Light Horse adopted the sword as their principal weapon, although the Anzac Division still held on to their rifles. There was nothing to laugh about in the Jordan Valley, but an Australian trooper was heard to remark: 'I reckon God made the Jordan Valley but when he saw what he'd done he threw stones at it!'

The main attack was planned for September. It was preceded by various deceptive moves, such as had been used for the earlier attacks on Beersheba and Gaza, but this time the real attack was to be on the left, and the deception force on the right.

New bridges were made over the Jordan. 'Dummy horses were erected on dummy horse lines in dummy camps.' Troops were sent up on foot by day, only to be brought back in lorries at night to do the same journey the following morning. The rumour that the Jordan Valley was to be reoccupied spread with great speed and was commented on with such forthrightness that even the deafest spy must have heard it.

The Turks were heavily concentrated on a line running from Arsaf on the coast, to El Salt inland. Approximately forty miles behind ran the Haifa–Beisan railway. Some five miles north of that lay Nazareth, where the German area commander had his headquarters, and south of the railway line was the Plain of Esdraelon. In the middle of the plain is the ruined fortress city of Megiddo (or Armageddon), which is now known by its Arabic name of Lajjun. Megiddo was a point of great strategic importance, for various routes crossed there. It lies at the entry to the Musmus pass. Close by is Jezreel where Jehu drove furiously, where also he came to Jezebel, a woman of evil repute who called from her tower, 'Is it peace, Jehu?' Jehu did not reply. He merely said, 'Throw her down.' 'And when they went to bury her they found no more than the skull and the feet and the palms of her hands.' (II Kings, Ch. 9.)

The dramatic, inglorious death of Jezebel symbolized the importance of this place in men's minds. It was where evil would be defeated – whether the evil was represented by armies from Egypt, from the west, or from the east, was of no importance. But those with a good cause were not always successful at Armageddon. Saul was killed fighting the Philistines, many Crusaders died in a great battle against Saladin's Saracen army. However, in the Book of Revelation, the last book in the Bible, there is an account of how the forces of evil will be destroyed. Verse 16 of Chapter 16 states: 'And he gathered them together into a place called in the Hebrew tongue Armageddon', and the chapter continues with their destruction. In September 1918 when the Turks were concentrated around Armageddon and the Allied forces, who had returned Jerusalem to Christian control, were facing them, it seemed to many as if this really would be the last great battle of the world.

At 4.30 am on 19 September, 1918, five Allied divisions came swiftly forward in an attack which was covered by creeping artillery barrages. Some 50,000 shells were dropped on the Turkish lines and beyond them the Royal Air Force was busy destroying the Turkish communications. As the infantry reached its objectives and began to wheel inwards, the cavalry raced through the gap this move created. Three complete mounted divisions crashed through and came curving into the Turkish rear areas. One reached Jenin, another Megiddo, and a third Nazareth. It was an astonishing and overwhelming victory. As the Turks fell hastily back trying to escape the encircling sweeps of the cavalry, they merely hastened their own arrival into captivity. Two Turkish armies were sliced to ribbons. Four days after the beginning of the attack Haifa was captured by an Indian cavalry unit. By now the Turks on the other flank were beginning to retire. They had left it too late. The Turkish Fourth Army made a desperate effort to extricate itself but only did so for the loss of 5,00 men taken prisoner and twenty-eight guns. The 2nd Corps was cut off south of Amman and surrendered to the British in preference to trying to fight a last battle against the Arabs.

Damascus was 120 miles away. As the cavalry raced forward to capture it before defences could be organized, they overtook Turkish stragglers from the Fourth Army.

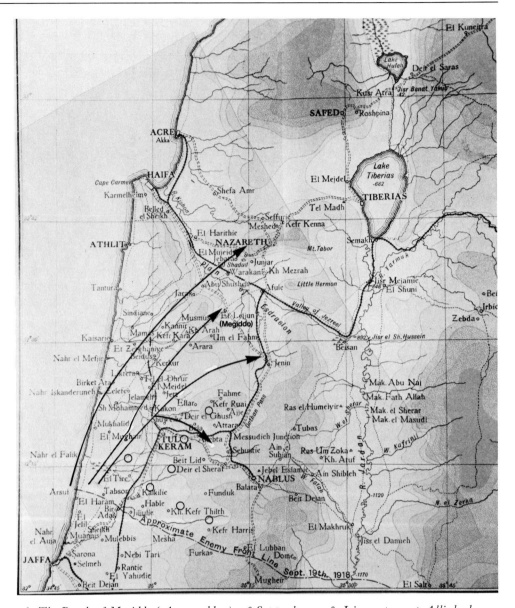

6 *The Battle of Megiddo (Armageddon), 18 September 1918. Lines represent Allied advances and circles mark main Turkish positions.*

But the garrison in Damascus had no stomach for a fight and as the cavalry came up on 30 September the Turks tried to escape to Beirut. They were caught in the Barada gorge and after being raked with machine-gun fire from the sides, decided to surrender. That made another 4,000 prisoners. The DMC rode on. They were in Homs on 15 October, in Hama on 20 October, and in Aleppo on the 26th. In five weeks they had covered 300 miles. Five days after the cavalry reached Aleppo the Turks were happy to accept terms of unconditional surrender. By then they had also been soundly defeated south of Mosul as well.

It was not of course as easy as it sounds here. The Turks are brave fighters under any conditions, and even when they were outnumbered, outgunned, and outgeneraled, they did not give up easily. Although taken by surprise at Megiddo itself, they hastily deployed an infantry battalion and a number of machine-guns to counter the advancing Allied troops.

The 2nd Lancers led the Allied attack. They had armoured cars as well as horses and they used the cars to start a machine-gun battle immediately ahead of the Turks. While this was proceeding, two squadrons of horse made a sweep to the right, and then charged in on the Turkish left flank, using their lances. Forty-six Turks were killed, mostly by lance thrusts, and another 500 were taken prisoner. Although this bloody encounter was brief it was very important, for the Turks were on their way to block the Musmus Pass. Had they reached it the whole Allied plan would have been disrupted.

At Jenin large quantities of German beer, wine, and tinned food were captured. A truck containing two locked boxes was found, and two troopers were detailed to guard them until they could be investigated. They sat on the boxes, complaining at the

The Palestine Campaign. The Barada Gorge (1 October 1918).

The British Desert Mounted Corps
aided by
The Arab Forces of King Hussein
captured
Damascus Homs and Aleppo.
October 1918.

Inscription cut on the rock cliffs of the Dog River, near Beirut, amongst those of Rameses II, Nebuchadnezar, Senacherib and other early conquerors of Syria.

boredom of it all. When the boxes were opened and found to contain gold coin to the value (today) of some £200,000, the bored guards complained ever more loudly.

There were spirited actions around Haifa and Mount Carmel. The former was a triumph for the Indian cavalry and the Jodhpur Lancers in particular. Four squadrons charged directly at enemy machine-guns and overran the position: two of them cleared the inner area of Turks and Germans. The Mysore Lancers completed the victory.

There had been a serious potential problem from the battery of Turkish guns at Karmelheim about two miles south-east of Haifa. The Mysore Lancers and Sherwood Rangers were allotted the task of destroying them. Only one squadron of the Mysore Lancers was available and this, after detaching men for duties with machine-guns and Hotchkiss rifles, was down to fifteen lancers. Nevertheless the gallant fifteen charged and killed the crews of two of the guns. That accomplished, it looked as if they were about to experience a change of fortune, for Turkish reinforcements had come up; however the Sherwood Rangers arrived at the critical moment and completed the victory.

Although large numbers of Turks had been killed or taken prisoner, and large expanses of territory had been overrun, this did not mean that the battle was over. Some detachments of Turks were putting up a lively resistance, and some of the prisoners, having surrendered, changed their minds and tried to escape. The fact that the prisoners were numbered in thousands made the task of guarding and feeding them very difficult. There was also much treachery. At Deraa a machine-gun post was manned entirely by Germans. As the Australians approached, a machine-gunner stood up and shouted 'We surrender'. The Australians stood up also and walked forward, only to be mown down by long bursts of fire from the position. Not all were killed and the survivors worked round the flanks and got in behind. Not a German survived.

An even more blatant example of perfidy occurred when a German officer raised a white handkerchief and, when an Australian officer approached, shot him dead from point-blank range. The Australians rushed the fort, ignored further pleas for clemency and bayoneted the 150 German occupants. They refused to bury the corpses and left them exactly where they were.

Some casualties occurred through over-confidence. At Irbid the 2nd Lancers attempted a charge on a force whose numbers and arms were not known. Their charge was abruptly stopped by long bursts of machine-gun fire; they lost two whole troops in the process. Though it was not the fault of the regiment, the fact that an attack had been ordered at the end of a long day, without covering fire or even reconnaissance, illustrated the point made earlier in this book that a cavalry force can ride unscathed through a battle, but meet nemesis when it is over if it has become over-confident and careless. As we saw, Prince Edward or Prince Rupert might have made that mistake here, too: Alexander or Darius, however, would not have done.

The following day, 27 September, the Turks had disappeared from Irbid. The Dorset Yeomanry was detailed to follow up and report on the Turks' new position and strength. The Dorsets caught up at El Remte but the Turks appeared still to be retreating. The Dorsets were told to keep in contact while a larger force was brought up to reinforce them, but before this could happen the Turks stopped retiring and delivered a brisk counter attack on the Dorsets. The Yeomanry was forced some way back before it could disengage; however, once it had done so the leading squadron reformed and swept back on to the Turkish line in a further charge. The effect was remarkable. Many of the enemy were killed with the sword and the remainder fell back into the village. The Dorsets pushed on, but were soon held up by concentrated and sustained machine-gun fire. But during the night the Turks moved back once more.

The final stages of the campaign were by no means the easiest. Every soldier and every horse was tired. Short rations, lack of water, and insufficient rest had taken their toll. Malaria and influenza were thinning the ranks of the effectives: some units were unable to carry out their assigned tasks through lack of numbers. But they pressed on. The Intelligence estimate that there were some 20,000 Turks and Germans at Aleppo was however enough to make the boldest man thoughtful. The last charge of the war was made by the Mysore Lancers, near Haritan. It was over rocky ground and the squadron had to wheel off when it ran into heavy machine-gun fire, but before that happened had killed a number of the enemy with the sword. The Turks, who had 3,000 infantry and 400 cavalry here, then retreated in good order: subsequently it was learnt that they believed that they were opposed by numbers equal to their own. A large force of Turks succeeded in retreating towards Istanbul but as the Armistice was signed within a few days this was of no consequence.

Field Marshal Viscount Allenby of Megiddo and Felixstowe, G.C.B., G.C.M.G. A general of exceptional quality who accepted only the highest standards and who was held in awe by many.

The record length charge of the war was made by the Australians near Homs. On 2 October they had sighted a large enemy column moving towards Khan Ayash; from there it could have taken shelter in the hills and made a continuing nuisance of itself. It was six miles away when spotted, but the Australians began the charge at once. There was no cover on the plain and the Turks, who had rifles and machine-guns, fired steadily and coolly at the advancing cavalry. In the last few yards the Australians quickened to a bone-splintering final charge. They killed a number of Turks with the sword before the others, to the number of 1,500, surrendered. The fact that they also captured twenty-six machine-guns gives some idea of the volume of fire they had had to ride through in what may have been the longest charge in the history of cavalry warfare.

Although all who took part contributed to the success of this brilliant campaign in Palestine and Syria, no one would hesitate to acknowledge that it was principally due to the military genius and leadership of Allenby. His own experience of military operations stretched back to the Bechuanaland Campaign of 1884, the Boer War of 1899–1902, and the Western Front from 1914–17. His nickname, 'The Bull', says something of his temper (when he was enraged the word went round, 'The Bull is loose'), but he was also sensitive, and an expert on flowers and ornithology. His only son was killed during the fighting in France: he was greatly saddened but he never allowed this loss to affect his concentration. When he wished he could talk fluently and interestingly on a variety of subjects, principally politics. He knew his own faults, and if he was over-harsh he would make up for it by kindness and in other ways.

It was said of him that he never nagged but that occasionally, if his orders were not obeyed properly, he would explode. All ranks trusted him, for they knew that he would make less mistakes than any other commander. After the war was over he became High Commissioner in Egypt and handled his political tasks as competently as he had his former military ones. He died in 1936. He was the last great cavalry commander.

14

The Last Phase

The arrival of the tank on the battlefield, rather than the killing efficiency of the machine-gun, eventually concluded the story of cavalry warfare. Until the time when reconnaissance and mobility could be provided by an armoured vehicle, there appeared to be no alternative to using cavalry in certain traditional roles, however great the cost. We have seen how thousands of cavalrymen were kept in readiness to exploit the breakthrough on the Western Front that never came till the war was virtually over. Even after the war, when tanks and armoured cars were still slow and unreliable, the superior mobility and speed of the horse seemed indispensable. That point of view appeared to be reinforced by Allenby's successes. Trench warfare in France had been one aspect of the war; Palestine and Syria had shown that in open country the horse still had many advantages. This view was reinforced by the fact that you did not even have to have special horses. The walers had not been bred for cavalry work but they performed magnificently. Even more remarkable was the information that some of the Yeomanry mounts were old hackneys, some apparently twenty-year-olds; these had been issued to units as emergency mounts while the regiments were in England, had gone abroad with them, and finally arrived in Damascus as proudly as their younger and better-bred neighbours. In the wave of goodwill towards the cavalry, it is hardly surprising that when the inevitable post-war retrenchment came the cavalry generals were able to ensure that the regular establishment for cavalry regiments was only cut by two – from thirty to twenty-eight. The fact that Field-Marshal Haig, in spite of the appalling slaughter caused by metal against flesh on the Western Front, still believed there was an important rôle for horse cavalry on future battlefields, slowed down the process of mechanization.

But by the 1930s the departure of the horse was seen as inevitable. The 11th Hussars and 12th Lancers had already been converted to armoured car units. By 1938 all regiments had been mechanized except the Household Cavalry, Royal Dragoons and Scots Greys, of which the latter two were in Palestine. It was not, of course, the easiest of transitions. Cavalrymen enjoyed dashing around in fast, powerful motor cars but the patient investigation of what went on inside the engine had less appeal for them. And there was nothing very sporting about a tank. You could not ride it in a point-to-point and the uniform you wore when you went to battle in it was not the sort of clothing which Beau Brummel would have approved. In the circumstances it is astonishing how well the regiments adapted themselves to this new mount, set

196

themselves to learn its little tricks and see what it could do when given a proper run over difficult country. The ultimate accolade was bestowed on the tank in the Western Desert in 1942 and 1943, when its users treated it with the consideration, imagination and trust normally given to a favourite and talented horse.

Commanding officers adapted themselves at varying speeds. Some had begun their conversion to armoured regiments by merely having their horses taken away and with nothing given to replace them. When the new vehicles finally arrived their users were already prejudiced against them. Horses would not have arrived late, it was felt.

But cavalry was still in existence at the start of the Second World War. One young man who had volunteered for the cavalry found himself assigned to patrol the cliffs of Dover, sword in hand, in case the Germans invaded. (Some of the Home Guard had been issued with pikes in 1940.) After this period of deterring the German stormtroopers, the young cavalryman was posted to Weedon, Northamptonshire, where he was astonished to find the cavalry training depot still in existence. After a time however, he learnt that there would be no more horsed cavalry regiments and that he should volunteer for something else. He chose the Fleet Air Arm.

But in certain theatres the horsed cavalry *was* still being used. The Warwickshire Yeomanry were sent to Palestine in 1940. The 5th Cavalry Brigade (the North Somerset Yeomanry, the Yorkshire Dragoons and the Cheshire Yeomanry) took part in the Syrian campaign against the Vichy French in 1941. They had sabres and rifles and were mounted on hunters.

In the twentieth century the tank has replaced the horse. These Light Tanks, Mark VI, were issued to cavalry regiments which had been assigned reconnaissance and protection duties, i.e. 4th/7th Dragoon Guards, 5th Dragoon Guards, 13th/18th Hussars, 15th/19th Hussars and certain yeomanry regiments.

In June of that year the Vichy French, who were collaborating with the Nazis, held an important bridge over the river Litani. The Cheshire Yeomanry made ready to charge looking, apart from their uniforms, much as they would have looked a hundred years earlier. The Vichy French withdrew. Subsequently the Cheshire Yeomanry were converted to Royal Signals, like their contemporaries, the Middlesex Yeomanry. The very last recorded British cavalry unit to operate in this area was the Yorkshire Dragoons.

Thus cavalry warfare ended, appropriately, in the lands in which it had begun. The Assyrians, the Hittites, the Babylonians, the Parthians, all came from the surrounding territories and in their turn had fought, with cavalry, for the strategic advantages of land routes. The Mongols were defeated by the Mamelukes in Jezreel, and Napoleon himself had to rescue one of his sorely pressed generals from the Turks when he would have much preferred to continue his siege of Acre. It is a theatre which has known war not merely for a few centuries but for thousands of years; and sadly, still does.

There was however one later charge which, although not a normal cavalry action, needs mention on account of the courage with which it was launched. In March 1942 a detachment of the Burma Frontier Force was on reconnaissance duties north of Rangoon when it ran into an ambush set by a large force of Japanese infantry. The Frontier Force was hopelessly outnumbered but it charged. The odds were too great, and the cavalry force was wiped out. Few people have ever heard of it but of its kind it was as heroic a charge as that of the Light Brigade.

Apart from a few unofficial troops of horses used in North Africa and Italy, that was the last of the British cavalry. It was not the last of cavalry as such, for the Germans had five cavalry divisions and the Russians had thirty divisions and numerous brigades in 1941, and kept most of them in use for the whole of the war. Nevertheless the principal use for horses between 1939 and 1945 was for transport and for this they were employed in their thousands.

In the 1980s the tradition of the cavalry is kept alive by saddle clubs, by race meetings, by hunting, by polo, and by Horse Shows. Every September at the Royal Military Academy Sandhurst there takes place a Horse Show which could not be staged in a more attractive setting. And every time an intake is commissioned there are two horsemen on parade (admittedly both belong to the Foot Guards) and one of them, the Adjutant, rides his horse up the steps, as the newly-commissioned young officers walk into the Great Entrance of the Old Building. Everyone is nervous except the horse – and perhaps its rider – when this delicate ceremony takes place. It all helps to keep a tradition alive, a tradition that horse and man have had a brave and enduring partnership in many battles and many long marches. They have fought together, suffered together, triumphed together, and often died together.

> Then hey for boot and horse, lad
> And round the world away
> Young blood must have its course, lad
> And every dog its day.

Barrack Life in the Army

The peacetime life of the British soldier in the standing army created in 1660 was neither comfortable nor pleasant. The cavalryman was slightly better off than the foot-soldier but both were so badly paid that they had barely a few pence a week to spend. In the early days there were no proper barracks: instead troops were housed in former defence works, such as coastal castles, or put in unsavoury billets in public or private houses. The miseries of cold, hunger and discomfort would be alleviated by as much drink as a soldier could obtain, legally or illegally.

Some soldiers had been persuaded to join the army by a taste for adventure – or by the blandishments of the recruiting sergeant. However, a large proportion of the intake consisted of vagrants, paupers and criminals. In consequence, discipline was extremely brutal, often involving the lash (which continued in use till the early nineteenth century). Light punishment was twenty-five lashes; a hundred and upwards was common, the maximum was 1500. These punishments were inflicted in the open air and were witnessed (compulsorily) by the regiment. Flogging was considered preferable to a prison sentence or to being shot. The military attitude to discipline was, of course, in accordance with contemporary views. Although a flogging necessitated a period for recovery in 'hospital', medical attention was crude, unskilled, and often fatal. One bowl of water was used to wash several men's wounds.

A number of soldiers married and set up home with their wives in barracks. 'Home' would be behind a curtain in the corner of the barrack room. But at least they were together. When the regiment went on active service, only six wives per hundred men were allowed; these would be transported, the rest would follow as best they could.

Wives, whether of officers or men, never lacked hardiness. Soldiers' wives were probably as enduring, and often as foul-mouthed, as their husbands. On occasion, in following the regiment, they would march hundreds of miles, dragging young children with them. Some were accomplished thieves; more than one was publicly flogged for crimes. On campaigns some wives were put to work as nurses in field hospitals without any training for their tasks.

Married men drew a ration for their wives. As most men slept two to a bed a wife's accommodation was no problem. They were allowed two blankets each, a pound of candles a week, and a clean towel about once a month.

From the squalor and deprivation of his living conditions the soldier emerged miraculously tidy, and picturesque. Dress regulations for December 1798 read:

'The regiment will appear powdered every day . . . particular attention is to be paid to the hair on the Parades as it is introduced as a practice to produce the most correct uniformity.'

Hair was allowed to grow until it could be plaited into a queue, which was then greased and powdered. Needless to say, the queue had to be of the right length and thickness. When it was dressed the skin was pulled back so tightly that the soldier who did not keep his eyes closed could not shut them again without pain; the process was meant to ensure that men did not close their eyes when on sentry duty. Meticulous regulations were not invariably the result of the vain whim of some commanding officer: they also had a basis in the fact that if a man is made to keep his public appearance, dress, and weapons to perfection the accurate attention to detail which the process requires will be reflected in his abilities on the battlefield. There was also, of course, the fact that endless burnishing and cleaning kept men out of mischief. Absurd though many of these practices were, the tradition of meticulous, fanatical smartness is still preserved in many regiments. It is commonly found that the regiments which tend to be smartest in turnout and drill are often the best at fighting. Often, too, they prove the most adaptable when a new weapon is introduced. Smartness was not reflected in personal cleanliness. Hair often swarmed with lice. Up till a hundred years ago only one barracks in the United Kingdom had a soldiers' bath.

Soldiers were despised by the civilian population, often including their own families, and neglected by the government except in times of national peril. Yet there were always volunteers. One of the most remarkable was William Robertson who joined the 16th Lancers on 13 November 1877. He was seventeen years, nine months old at the time and the minimum age for enlistment was eighteen, but he was tall for his age and the sergeant wrote his age down as eighteen and two months. Forty-three years later he was Field Marshal Sir William Robertson, Bart. His account of his early days in the army gives a comprehensive picture of what was involved when a young man took 'the Queen's Shilling' in 1877.

> The life of a recruit in 1877 was a very different matter from what it is now. The system introduced in 1871–72 by Mr Cardwell – one of the greatest War Ministers the country has ever had – under which men enlisted for twelve years' regular service, had not yet had time to get into full swing. Regiments were, therefore, still composed mainly of old soldiers who, although very admirable comrades in some respects and with a commendable code of honour of their own, were in many cases – not in all – addicted to rough behaviour, heavy drinking, and hard swearing. They could not well be blamed for this. Year in and year out they went through the same routine, were treated like machines – of an inferior kind – and having little prospect of finding decent employment on the expiration of their twenty-one years' engagement, they lived only for the present, the single bright spot in their existence being the receipt of a few shillings – perhaps not more than one – on the weekly pay-day. These rugged veterans exacted full deference from the recruit, who was assigned the worst bed in the room,

given the smallest amount of food and the least palatable, had to 'lend' them articles of kit which they had lost or sold, 'fag' for them in a variety of ways, and, finally, was expected to share with them at the regimental canteen such cash as he might have in the purchase of beer sold at 3d. a quart.

It so happened that I joined the regiment on pay-day, and accordingly the greatest number of my newly-found companions spent the evening at the canteen – then a mere drinking saloon – or at public-houses in the town. On return to quarters, if not before, old quarrels were revived or new ones were started, and some of them had to be settled by an appeal to fists. One of these encounters took place on and near the bed in which I was vainly trying to sleep, and which was itself of an unattractive and uncomfortable nature. Argument and turmoil continued far into the night, and I began to wonder whether I had made a wise decision after all. I continued to wonder for several nights afterwards, and would lie awake for hours meditating whether to see the matter through, or get out of bed, put on my plain clothes (which I still had), and 'desert'. Fortunately for me another occupant of the room removed the temptation these clothes afforded, for, having none of his own, he one night appropriated mine, went off in them, and never came back.

The barrack-room arrangements for sleeping and eating could not be classed as luxurious. The brown bed-blankets were seldom if ever washed; clean sheets were issued once a month; and clean straw for the mattresses once every three months. Besides the beds, the only other furniture consisted of four benches and two deal tables. The men polished their boots on the former, and the latter were used for cleaning the remaining articles of kit as well as for dining-tables. Tablecloths there were none, and plates and basins (paid for by the men) were the only crockery, the basin being used in turn as a coffee-cup, tea-cup, beer-mug, soup-plate, shaving-mug, and receptacle for pipe-clay with which to clean gloves and belts.

The food provided free consisted of one pound of bread and three-quarters of a pound of meat, and nothing more of any kind. Groceries, vegetables, and all other requirements were paid for by the men, who had a daily deduction of $3\frac{1}{2}$d. made from their pay of 1s. 2d. for that purpose. The regulation meals were coffee and bread for breakfast; meat and potatoes for dinner, with soup or pudding once or twice a week; tea and bread for tea. If a man wished to have supper or something besides dry bread for breakfast and tea he had to purchase it from the barrack hawkers or canteen. Putting the cost of this at $4\frac{1}{2}$d. a day, he thus had to expend a total of eightpence a day on his food, besides which he was subjected to a further daily charge of a penny for washing. This left him fivepence a day or about three shillings a week, and even this was not all clear pocket-money, for after the first free issue he had to keep up the whole of his underclothing as well as many articles of uniform, and also supply himself with cleaning materials, such as polishing paste for brasses, oil for steel equipment, and soft-soap for saddlery.

The 'kit' with which I was issued free of cost consisted of a valise, stable-bag, hold-all (containing knife, fork, spoon, razor and comb, shaving, hair, lace, button, clothes and boot-brushes), three baggage straps, tin of oil, tin of blacking, tin of brass paste, cloak, cape, lance-cap and plume, two forage caps, tunic, jacket, overalls (trousers), pantaloons, canvas ducks, jack-boots and spurs, ankle-boots, braces, three shirts, three pairs of socks, two pairs of pants, two towels, and a piece of soap. Finally, I was given a lance, sword, pistol, cartridge-case, cap-case, and numerous belts – an amount of armament that completely staggered me.

Uniform was of a very unpractical kind, especially the undress part of it. This comprised skin-tight overalls, an equally tight 'shell-jacket' cut off short above the hips, and a forage cap of about the size of a breakfast saucer, and kept in its place immediately above the right ear by a narrow chin-strap worn under the lower lip (never under the chin in the cavalry, except on mounted parades). There were no 'British-warms' or woollen 'jumpers' as to-day, and cloaks were not allowed to be worn when off duty without a regimental order to that effect. This order was never given except when the weather was very inclement. Later on the forage cap became a 'free issue', and was thoroughly disliked by everybody because of its ugly shape and abnormally large size as compared with the regimental pattern.

The first occasion on which it was worn by the regiment was at an inspection by the Duke of Cambridge at York in 1881, when an unofficial hint was sent round the barrack-rooms beforehand that it was to be put well on the top of the head, and generally made to appear as hideous as possible. Every one did his best, or rather his worst, to comply with the hint, and when the Duke – never in too good a temper early in the day – came on parade, the sight of the disfigured regiment nearly gave him a fit. It was alleged that he went back to the Horse Guards and wrote a furious letter to the War Office condemning the cap, but it remained the regulation article for some years afterwards, although the original pattern was still allowed to be worn off parade, and at the expense of the owner.

The cavalry recruit was kept hard at work, riding-drill, stables, foot-drill, gymnastics, and school following each other in bewildering fashion from six in the morning till six in the evening, without any appreciable interval for rest. Riding-school was the terror of most recruits, few of whom had ever before been across a horse. For some weeks no saddle was allowed, no stirrups for some months, and the chief aim of the instructor, or 'rough-rider', was not to give his pupil confidence but as many falls as possible. The 'rough-rider' deserved his name, for he was as rough with a young horse as with a young recruit. He seldom possessed a decent pair of hands, and his system of training a horse was of the break-down rather than the break-in type. These unintelligent methods have long since passed into oblivion.

A robust constitution was required in winter to withstand the cold and draughty stables and the biting winds which swept across the barrack square during foot-drill, where the shivering recruit would struggle to grasp the explanations of drill gabbled out by his instructor, and painfully endeavour to master the mysteries of the 'goose-step' and the art of drawing swords 'by numbers'. I succumbed twice during my first winter, once being in hospital for two months with rheumatic fever brought on by exposure.

When a man 'reported sick' he was marched at about nine o'clock in the morning to the medical inspection room of his regiment, and after waiting about in all weathers for an indefinite time was seen by a medical officer. If considered a case for admission he was given an aperient, whether he wanted it or not, in the shape of half-a-pint of vile-tasting liquid known as 'black-strap'. He was next marched off to hospital, which might be anything up to a mile or more away, and there he was interviewed by another doctor before being 'admitted' to hospital. Next he was told off to a ward, where he might hope to arrive about mid-day, after having been on the move for some three or four hours. In the afternoon he would put on his hospital clothing, give his own into store, and lie down to await the visit of the medical officer in charge of the ward on the following morning. He was then again examined, treatment was prescribed, and if all went well he received it during the afternoon, or some thirty hours after he first set out from his barrack-room . . .

Permission to be out of barracks after 'watch-setting' – half-past nine at night – was sparingly granted, and all-night passes were practically never given. The 'roll' was called at watch-setting, when every man not on leave had to answer his name, and to make sure that none went out afterwards one and sometimes two 'check' roll-calls were made by the orderly sergeant-major at uncertain hours during the night. Each orderly-sergeant handed in at watch-setting a statement showing the number of men sleeping in each of his troop rooms, and equipped with this the orderly sergeant-major, accompanied by the corporal of the guard, visited the rooms and counted the sleeping occupants. It was a favourite device of absentees, before going out, to fold up their bed as in day-time, so that the visiting sergeant-major might perhaps not notice their absence; while others would try to deceive him by leaving a made-up dummy in their beds. 'Breaking out of barracks' was the crime, and twenty-eight days' confinement to barracks was usually the punishment for this form of absence.

To 'break out' of barracks was a simple matter at Aldershot, for although the gates at the end of them were kept locked after watch-setting, and had high walls on either side, an unenclosed public road ran along the front which was accessible to everybody. This was not the case with all barracks, most of them being surrounded by high walls, topped with broken glass. When we were at Brighton, where the walls were of this kind, an amusing incident occurred in connection with a man who was trying to get back again after successfully breaking out. Not being able to scale the walls, he hit on the idea of returning in an officer's brougham, which was being brought back to barracks by a friendly coachman after depositing the officer and his wife at their house in the town. Unfortunately the military police sergeant looked inside the brougham before allowing it to leave the barrack gate, and the offender accordingly found himself in a worse predicament at orderly-room next morning than if he had walked into barracks and surrendered.

Of all days of the week Sunday was the most hated – a sad confession to make, but none the less true. After morning stables there was a general rush, often with little or no time for breakfast, to turn out in 'full dress' for 'divine service' – attendance at which was compulsory. On return to barracks there was another scramble preparatory to the commanding officer's inspection of stables, horses, saddlery and barrack-rooms. From early morning till half-past one in the afternoon there was more work to be done, more grumbling and swearing, and more fault-finding than on any other day, all of which could have been avoided had the inspections been carried out on a week-day. The reason they were made on Sunday was certainly not because there was no time for them on other days. The real reason probably was that Sunday was the most convenient day for the officers, as it left them greater leisure to follow their social and sporting pursuits during the week. It was only natural that the men should resent being hustled about and made to do unnecessary work on the one day of the week observed by everybody else in the country as a day of rest.

Divine service was not held for all denominations at the same time, but at hours suitable to local facilities. It might be at any time between eight o'clock and noon, and therefore it was not uncommon for men, on moving to a new station, to ask to change their religion if by so doing they would attend church or chapel at such an hour as would enable them to escape from the detested inspections. Many amusing stories are told about these changes, one being of a man who asked his sergeant-major to enter him in the books as belonging to the 'Plymouth Brethren'. He was promptly told that no such religion was officially recognised, and that he would be put down as a Roman Catholic!

On Christmas Day, 1877, I was detailed for my first military 'duty', that of stable-guard or looking after the troop-horses out of stable-hours. The custom was to employ the most recently joined recruits on this particular day, so that the old soldiers might be free to make the most of their Christmas dinner, which was provided by the officer commanding the troop, and included a variety of eatables never seen on any other day, as well as a liberal supply of beer. The casks containing the beer were brought some time before to the barrack-room where the dinner was to be held, and were there placed under charge of a man who could be depended upon to see that they were not broached before the appointed hour. Had this happened – as it sometimes did – rather awkward incidents might have occurred when the officers visited the room just previous to the dinner to wish the men a merry Christmas and to receive similar wishes in return. If any individual did, by some means or other, contrive to start his festivities too early, efforts were made to keep him in the background until the officers had left.

It was the practice to see that all members of the troop who were absent on duty should be specially well-cared for, and in my case the dinner brought to the stable consisted of a huge plateful of miscellaneous food – beef, goose, ham, vegetables, plum-pudding, blancmange – plus a basin of beer, a packet of tobacco, and a new clay pipe!

At night the horses were looked after by a 'night-guard', which paraded about five or six o'clock in the evening and came off duty at *réveille* on the following morning. It was mainly composed of recruits and other men who were required to attend training or do other work during the day-time. The chief duties of a 'sentry' of the night guard were to perambulate outside the stables, tie up any horse that might get loose (some of the old troop-horses were extraordinarily clever at slipping their head collars and finding their way to the corn-bin), see that the doors were kept closed, and, in the phraseology of the 'orders', 'call the corporal of the guard in the event of fire or other unusual occurrence.' The sentry was armed with either a sword or a carbine (no ammunition), though what assistance he was supposed to derive therefrom in the performance of his duties no one ever understood.

The nights were sometimes intensely cold and always interminably long, although the two hours 'on' sentry were followed by four hours 'off', and to the tired recruit the bales of forage offered tempting resting-places. That way lay danger if not disaster, for once he succumbed to the temptation to sit down it was a hundred to one that he would fall asleep, and if he did he might wake up to find himself confronted by an officer or non-commissioned officer going the 'rounds', with the result that he would be made prisoner and tried by court-martial. The punishment for this crime was invariably two months' imprisonment, and although young soldiers must be made to realise their responsibilities when on sentry, a little more consideration in dealing with tired lads not yet out of their teens would not have been misplaced. I have known more than one lad ruined for life because of undue severity of punishment for a first offence.

Forty years ago every offence, however trivial, was classed as a 'crime', and the 'prisoner' was interned in the 'guard-room'. The latter, in the case of the cavalry barracks at Aldershot, was about fifteen feet square, indifferently ventilated, and with the most primitive arrangements for sanitation. No means of lighting it after dark were either provided or permitted. Running along one of its sides was a sloping wooden stage, measuring about six feet from top to bottom, which served as a bed for all the occupants, sometimes a dozen or more in number; at the top was a wooden shelf, slightly raised above the level of the stage, which acted as pillow; and no blankets (except in very cold weather) or mattresses were allowed, except for prisoners who had been interned for more than seven days. Until then their only covering, besides their ordinary clothes – which were never taken off – consisted of their cloaks, and they had to endure as best they could the sore hips and shoulders caused by lying on the hard boards. I shall describe presently how I once came to be incarcerated in this horrible place for a period of three weeks, and will only say here that I was exceedingly glad when the first seven days were completed.

A prisoner charged with committing an offence was kept in the guard-room until he could be brought before the commanding officer, no other officer in the regiment having power to dispose of his case, and if he were remanded for a court-martial, as he not infrequently was, he might be interned for several days before his trial took place. In the meantime he would have for company all classes of prisoners thrust into the room at any hour of the day or night, some for drunkenness, some for desertion, some

for insubordination, and some for no offence at all which merited
confinement. This was not a healthy atmosphere in which to bring up young
soldiers, to many of whom the shady side of life was as yet unknown, and, as
will be shown later, a more sensible and humane system was eventually
adopted. It should not be forgotten that these harsh and short-sighted
methods were more or less common to the age, and were not confined to the
army.

The 'Articles of War', based on the 'Mutiny Act', constituted the law
which then governed the soldier. The Articles contained a list of all military
offences, with their punishments, and were read out to the men once a
month after 'muster parade'. Originally – they dated back a long time – they
were of excessive severity, inflicting death or loss of limb for almost every
crime. They were not much more lenient in my early days from what I can
remember of them, the termination of most of them being to the effect that
'any soldier committing this offence shall, on conviction by court-martial,
be liable to suffer death or such less punishment as may be awarded.' In 1879
the Articles of War and Mutiny Act were consolidated in the 'Army
Discipline and Regulations Act'. This was repealed in 1881 and re-enacted
with some amendments in the present Army Act, which is brought into
operation annually by another Act of Parliament.

'Muster parade', I may explain, was held on the last day of each month,
and was the only parade at which every officer and man had to be present.
The paymaster was the important person, as he had to satisfy himself that
every one for whom he had issued pay was actually serving in the regiment.
It appears to have been a relic of the days when commanding officers
received a lump sum of money for a given number of men, and could not be
trusted to have that number in the regiment.

A man sentenced to undergo imprisonment, even if for some such
short period as forty-eight hours, had his hair closely cropped off, and was
thus made to look like a convict for several weeks after his discharge.
'Confinement to barracks' included 'punishment drill' for four separate
hours each day except Sunday, and this again seemed to have been designed
to destroy any shred of self-respect the unfortunate defaulter might possess.
The 'drill' consisted in being turned and twisted about on the barrack
square, in quick time and with only a few short pauses during the hour, the
men carrying their full kit, strapped on their shoulders, besides the lance and
sword – a total weight of some 40 or 50 lbs. The drill could be made, and
frequently was, according to the fancy of the sergeant in charge, extremely
exasperating and fatiguing, and in order to escape from such degrading
drudgery men would sometimes deliberately commit a second and more
serious offence so as to be sent to prison. In the cavalry it was not feasible, as
in the infantry, to spare the men for four hours a day from their other duties,
and as a rule the punishment took the form of one hour's drill and one or
two of employment on 'fatigue duties'.

In August 1878 – or about nine months after joining – I was 'dismissed' recruit-drill, this being the length of time usually taken to become
classified as a trained cavalry soldier. The recruit training included a 'course'

of musketry of about three weeks' duration, most of the time being devoted to the deadly dull exercise known as 'bob and joe' – the bringing of the carbine from the 'ready' to the 'present' and *vice versa*. Forty rounds of ball ammunition, no more and no less, regardless of requirements, were allowed for each and every recruit to make himself a proficient shot. The result was that not one in twenty was proficient, or anything like it. I remember that I carried off the prize for the best shot of my batch, the prize being three shillings!

As a trained soldier I now became available for 'day-guard', which furnished the full-dress sentry on the barrack gate and was responsible for the safe custody of the prisoners in the guard-room. It was composed of a corporal, a trumpeter, and five men, and was paraded for inspection by the regimental sergeant-major. The parade of this guard was one of the chief events of the day, for from amongst the five men the sergeant-major selected the two whom he thought to be the smartest and best turned out to act as 'orderlies' to the commanding officer and adjutant. To be thus selected was the ambition of the whole five, for while the three had turn about to spend the next twenty-four hours on sentry on the barrack gate, the chosen two passed their night in bed and had little to do during the day. I was lucky enough to be selected at my first two attempts, though I was not equally fortunate on all other occasions.

Being considered, I suppose, to be a promising and trustworthy lad, I was detailed in the summer of 1878, in company with another man and a corporal, to form the 'escort' for bringing back from London a notorious deserter who had been arrested there by the civil police. He had been a burglar by profession before becoming a soldier, and notwithstanding the size of the escort he managed, with the assistance of some of his friends who appeared on the scene, and favoured by darkness, to make his escape while we were passing through the purlieus adjacent to Waterloo station. Crestfallen, we returned to Aldershot minus our prisoner. The corporal was at once placed 'in arrest', whilst I and my companions were consigned to the guard-room, there to await trial by court-martial, and in all probability to be sentenced to not less than six months' imprisonment. At the end of three weeks the General commanding the Cavalry Brigade exercised, as I thought and still think, a sensible discretion by releasing us. Had he brought us to trial, the chances are that I would have followed in the steps of many another soldier of those days and have become a hardened offender against military law, a disgrace to myself, and a burden to the country.

This was my first 'crime', and the second followed a week or two later. It consisted in allowing a led horse to break loose at exercise, and for this I was duly 'reprimanded' by the commanding officer (Whigham) and warned that stern punishment would be meted out the next time I misbehaved. My future prospects were therefore beginning to appear somewhat gloomy, but thanks to the good sense of Graham, my troop commander, neither of the two offences were allowed to count seriously against me. He realised that such neglect as there might have been was attributable to nothing worse than youthful inexperience, and early in 1879 he took advantage of the temporary absence of the colonel to recommend me to the acting commanding officer for promotion to lance-corporal, this obtaining for me the first step towards the rank of Field-Marshal.

Military training lagged far behind, notwithstanding the many lessons furnished by the Franco-German War of 1870, and was still mainly based on the system inherited from the Peninsula and Crimean campaigns. Pipe-clay, antiquated and useless forms of drill, blind obedience to orders, ramrod-like rigidity on parade, and similar time-honoured practices were the chief qualifications by which a regiment was judged. Very few officers had any ambition beyond regimental promotion. 'Squadron leader' was a name and not a reality, for beyond commanding it on parade this officer had no responsibility or duty of any kind connected with the squadron as such. In all other respects each of the two troops which then formed a squadron was a separate and independent unit, the troop commander being subordinate only to the regimental commanding officer. Once a week or so the latter held his 'field-day', when the regiment as a whole attended parade and spent the greater part of two or three hours in carrying out a series of complicated drill-book movements: equally good results could have been secured in half the time, and with half the expenditure of horse-flesh and strong language. For the remainder of the week training, as understood in those days, was the preserve of the adjutant, whose parades were attended only by those officers who were junior to him in rank, and by a comparatively small proportion of the men. For the drill of recruits on foot the adjutant was also responsible, and in riding drill the ridingmaster was supreme. Troop officers had no responsibility for either one or the other.

As already mentioned, Lancer regiments carried sword, lance, and a muzzle-loading horse-pistol, and about half-a-dozen men in each troop, known as scouts or skirmishers, had a carbine as well. They had a very sketchy knowledge of the use of this weapon, and, like every one else, but a hazy idea of either scouting or skirmishing. Later, carbines were issued to all men, and the horse-pistols were withdrawn; but for some years musketry was universally hated and deemed to be a degradation and a bore. In no case could it have been made of much value, since the annual allowance of ammunition was fixed at forty rounds a man, and thirty rounds of these were fired at distances between 500 and 800 yards.

Manoeuvres as practised in more recent years were practically unknown, though there was a legend amongst the old soldiers that they had taken place at Cannock Chase some years before I joined. The nearest approach to them was the 'field-day' held, perhaps half-a-dozen times during the year, by the Commander-in-Chief, the Duke of Cambridge. The first one I attended was held on the ground at the back of the Staff College, the whole of the Aldershot garrison – about a division – taking part in it. I remember that towards the end of the battle – a field-day always entailed a 'battle' – my squadron was ordered to charge a battalion of the opposing infantry. Down came our lances to the 'engage', the 'charge' was sounded, and off we went at full speed, regardless of everything except the desire to make a brave show worthy of our regimental predecessors who had delivered the immortal charge at Aliwal some thirty odd years before. The enemy received us in square, with fixed bayonets, front rank kneeling and rear rank standing, the orthodox method of dealing with a cavalry charge. Finding our opponents too strong – or for some other reason – the order was given 'troops right-about wheel', and so near were we that, in wheeling, the outer flank was carried on to the infantry and one of the horses received a bayonet in his chest. Being too seriously injured to live he was shot, but in other respects we were congratulated on having accomplished a fine performance. No doubt it was magnificent, but it was not the way to fight against men armed with rifles.

These defective methods of training in general were due in a large measure to the system of voluntary enlistment, under which recruits were received in driblets throughout the year, and, more especially perhaps, to the fact that the four different arms were kept severely apart from each other. Cavalry training was the business of the Inspector-General of Cavalry at the Horse Guards, the local General having little or no say in the matter. Artillery were mainly stationed at Woolwich and engineer units at Chatham, each having, like the cavalry, its own special Generals and staffs and its special representatives at the Horse Guards. Combined training of the different arms, without which it is nonsense to expect intelligent co-operation in war, was therefore impossible.

There may have been, and probably were, other obstacles in the way of improvement, but one would think that most of them could have been surmounted, given more impetus from the top. It was not forthcoming, and for this the Duke of Cambridge, Commander-in-Chief from 1856 to 1895 (thirty-nine years), must be held accountable. He was a good friend of the soldier and extremely popular with all ranks in the army, but he was extraordinarily conservative in his ideas on the training and education of both officers and men. He seems to have believed, quite honestly, that the army as he had found it, created by such a master of war as the Duke of Wellington, must be the best for all time, and he had not realised the changes which had since taken place in the armies of Europe. I have been told that he once took the chair at a lecture given to officers of the Aldershot garrison on the subject of foreign cavalry, when he proved to be a veritable Balaam in commending the lecturer to the audience. 'Why should we want to know anything about foreign cavalry?' he asked. 'We have better cavalry of our own. I fear, gentlemen, that the army is in danger of becoming a mere debating society.'

Many of the younger generation of officers were fully alive to the fact that better organisation, education, and training were necessary, the most notable amongst them being Lord Wolseley, the best-read soldier of his time. From 1882 onwards he was the moving spirit in the path of progress, and thanks to his energy and initiative, and to the support he received from Sir Evelyn Wood and other keen-sighted soldiers, apathy and idleness began to go out of fashion, and hard work became the rule; study was no longer considered to be 'bad form', but a duty and an essential step to advancement; hunting on six days of the week was no longer admitted to be the only training required by the cavalry leader; and in general the professional qualifications of our regimental officers began to reach a much higher standard.

Appendix 2

The Introduction of Polo

The game of Polo was introduced into England in 1870 by officers of the 10th Hussars, from a description of the game as played by the Manipuri tribe in India which appeared in the *Field* newspaper. Lord Valentia, Mr E. Hartopp, and Mr George Cheape of the 11th Hussars, attached to the regiment, were the originators.

The first game which was ever played took place at Aldershot on a piece of ground near Caesar's Camp. Amongst those who took part in it on this day were Lt Hartopp, The Hon Thomas Fitzwilliam, Lt Edward Watson, etc. The officers rode their chargers, and golf sticks and billiard balls were used: later on it was found that a cricket ball, whitened, was more suitable for the purpose.

The 9th Lancers adopted the game the following year, and assisted materially by introducing an improved stick.

(From *Memories of the Tenth Hussars*: R. S. Liddell)

Concerning Lord Cardigan

James Thomas Brudenell, Seventh Earl of Cardigan, and Baron Brudenell, K.C.B., was born at Hambledon, Herts, on October 16, 1797. After spending a few terms at Christ Church, Oxford, he was elected for Parliament shortly before he came of age. He sat for Marlborough from 1818 to 1829, until the Duke of Wellington's Administration brought in the Catholic Emancipation Bill. Differing from Lord Ailesbury, by whose influence he had first been brought into public life, Lord Cardigan then resigned his seat for Marlborough and sat for Fowey in Cornwall. On the passing of the Reform Bill, he, together with Lord Milton, contested the Northern Division of Northamptonshire, being returned after a keen contest. Whilst representing Marlborough, an incident rare in Parliamentary history occurred, Lord Brudenell being obliged to vacate his seat on his acceptance of a Cornetcy in the 8th Hussars. He was re-elected. It is only the original commission that vacates a seat. A man generally enters the army some years before he does the House of Commons, but Lord Brudenell did not enter the army until he was twenty-seven or twenty-eight years of age. His promotion was, owing to the purchase system then in vogue, very rapid. He became Lieutenant in January 1825, Captain in June 1826, Major in August 1830, Lieutenant-Colonel in December 1830. In 1832 he was promoted from half-pay to the Lieutenant-Colonelcy of the 15th Hussars. On January 16, 1834, he quitted the 15th on account of a personal quarrel with Captain Wathen. This quarrel had resulted in a Court-Martial which terminated unfavourably to Lord Brudenell.

In May 1836 Lord Brudenell was appointed to the command of the 4th Light Dragoons, exchanging with Lieutenant-Colonel Childers into the 11th Light Dragoons on March 25, 1837. He joined his new regiment at Cawnpore on September 10, 1837, and on October 23 of the same year he succeeded to the command upon the resignation of Lieutenant-Colonel Brutton. On returning to England with the regiment in 1838 he found that his father had died, and that he had succeeded to the earldom. The 'Dictionary of National Biography' tells us that 'Lord Cardigan spent £10,000 a year on the regiment, which became the smartest cavalry regiment in the service.' It is said among other acts of liberality he added from his own pocket to the price allowed by Government for each remount. This caused the regiment to be

---

[1] This account of Cardigan appeared in the history of the 11th Hussars. The reader will note that the famous charge does not even receive a mention.

beautifully mounted, a fact that told greatly in their favour in the earlier days of the Crimean War, before lack of forage had told its tale. We are also informed that he spent large sums in causing the accoutrements of the men to correspond with his idea of what a light cavalry regiment should be.

In 1840, whilst the regiment was stationed at Canterbury, some officers of the 'Eleventh' galloped their horses when coursing into the paddock of a miller named Brent. Mr. Brent complained to Lord Cardigan, who offered to pay for the damage, but this procedure did not commend itself to Mr. Brent who required the punishment of the offenders. A somewhat acrimonious dispute ended in Lord Cardigan challenging the miller to a duel with pistols, which the latter refused. Later Lord Cardigan caused the officers to send an apology to Mr. Brent.

On May 18 of the same year, occurred his Lordship's quarrel with Captain John Reynolds of the 'Eleventh' in what is known as the 'Black Bottle Incident'. Briefly the cause was as follows: On the day in question Major-General Sir J. W. Sleigh, Inspector-General of Cavalry, had inspected the regiment and dined with them that evening. During dinner Captain Reynolds ordered a bottle of Moselle. This was placed by his servant in a black bottle on the table beside him. On the following day Lord Cardigan sent a message by the Mess President, Captain Inigo Jones, to Captain Reynolds, in which he objected in the strongest manner to Captain Reynolds' behaviour in allowing a black bottle to appear on the table during dinner. This led to friction between Lord Cardigan and Captain Jones on the one side and Captain Reynolds on the other. The quarrel was not allayed until the question had been referred to the Horse Guards.[1] This matter had scarcely been concluded when in August arose a still more serious affair. Captain Richard Anthony Reynolds considered himself insulted by a remark made it was alleged by Lord Cardigan during an entertainment at his Lordship's private house at Brighton, and which had reference to the two Captains Reynolds. This remark Captain Reynolds resented to such a degree that on August 27 he addressed a private letter to Lord Cardigan on the subject. Lord Cardigan directed the Adjutant to reply that any communication Captain Reynolds wished to make to him must be official. Captain Reynolds replied as follows:

Brighton, August 28, 1840.

My Lord, – Having in my letter to your Lordship of yesterday stated to your Lordship that a report had reached me that your Lordship had spoken of me in such manner as I deem prejudicial to me, considering the position in which I am placed, and having in the most respectful manner requested your Lordship to allow me to contradict such report, and your Lordship having this morning positively refused to give me my answer; I beg to tell your Lordship that you are in no wise justified in speaking of me at all at a public party given by your Lordship, and more particularly in such manner as to make it appear that my conduct has been such as to exclude me from your

---

[1] The quarrel between Lord Cardigan and Captain Reynolds was continued until 1865. A reconciliation was effected in that year between these two old enemies, details of which follow.

Lordship's house. Such assertion is calculated to injure me. Your Lordship's reputation as a professed duellist, founded on having sent Major Jenkins to offer satisfaction to Mr. Brent, the miller, of Canterbury, and your also having sent Capt. Forrest to London, to call out an attorney's clerk, does not admit of your privately offering insult to me, and then screening yourself under the cloak of Commanding Officer, and I must be allowed to tell your Lordship that it would far better become you to select a man whose hands are untied for the object of your Lordship's vindictive reproaches, or to act as many a more gallant fellow than yourself has done, and waive that rank which your wealth and Earldom alone entitle you to hold.

I am,
    My Lord,
        Your Lordship's obedient servant,
            RICHARD ANTHONY REYNOLDS.

The Rt. Hon. The Earl of Cardigan,
47, Brunswick Square, Brighton.

For this letter Captain Reynolds was on September 25 tried by Court-Martial, Sir H. Pakenham presiding. Lord Cardigan was assisted by Mr. Serjeant Wrangham, and Captain Reynolds by Mr. Watson. Fourteen military officers formed the Court, and Major Peppin acted as Judge Advocate. The Court-Martial lasted until October 5, and ended in Captain R. A. Reynolds being cashiered. Meanwhile, on September 3, an anonymous letter signed 'H.T.' had appeared in the *Morning Chronicle* animadverting in severe terms on Lord Cardigan's conduct. The writer was discovered to be Captain Harvey Tucket of the 11th Hussars. As a result of this letter a duel was fought on Wimbledon Common between Lord Cardigan and Captain Tucket. At the second shot Lord Cardigan wounded his opponent severely but not fatally. Charged with duelling his Lordship was first brought before the Wandsworth magistrates. Later he appeared before the Court of Queen's Bench, and finally on February 16, 1841, he was tried by the House of Lords and acquitted. Captain Douglas, Lord Cardigan's second in the duel, was in March tried on the same charge at the Old Bailey and likewise acquitted. Owing to these and many other causes, no man of his time in England seems to have excited greater interest in the public mind than did Lord Cardigan. It is related that when, in 1854, he was ordered to the East in command of a brigade of light cavalry, the community in general, from club to pot-house, marvelled as to how he would behave. Their remembrance of him satisfied all that he had a taste for gunpowder, but they had no experience as to how he could wield the sword. The deduction drawn was, however, favourable to their old acquaintance, and many longed for a battle to take place, if for no other reason than to satisfy themselves as to how far they had judged him correctly. Upon his return from the war he was fêted by the Lord Mayor of London and by the Corporations of many provincial towns, receiving an enthusiastic welcome. It is sad, however, to relate that his impulsive nature again too often got the better of his more mature judgment, and that the speeches he delivered on these occasions have been the subject of severe criticism. In 1855 he became Inspector-General of Cavalry, a post he retained until 1860. That his mind, unexpanded by recent events, had lost none of the vigour of its observance of the strictest details of military exactitude we have ample proof. In this connection the following letter from the officer commanding a very well-known cavalry regiment to one of his officers, in charge of a detachment of the same regiment, is interesting. It runs:

Birmingham, August 30, 185–.

My dear H. – Lord Cardigan finished his inspection of the Regt. yesterday afternoon. I am sorry to say he did not appear to be well satisfied with anything with perhaps the exception of the Rides in the School.

He is to be in Manchester on Wednesday and I think it probable he will go to Coventry about the end of the week.

He is particular about having an Officer awaiting his arrival. You had better have one told off for him, also a Sergeant as an Orderly, both in full dress. He found great fault with the appearance of the Men's overalls on foot parade, he does not approve of the leathered overalls being worn on foot Parades and he appears to expect that each man should have a good pair without leather for those Parades.

I hardly see how that system is to be carried out. From the short notice I had of his coming I had not time to get the Men's clothing cleaned, which made it look worse than it otherwise would, you will be able to get yours in better order. Non-commissioned officers are not to be used as Serrifiles. In advancing in Parade order on foot, Serrifiles are not to come to the front on the command 'rear rank take order'. But mounted men do.

Lord Cardigan is very particular in questioning the Captains and Officers in Command of troops, on all subjects, the age, number, and the different Regiments the horses come from, Messing, etc. etc.

I suppose the Officers at Coventry are all supplied with the Regulation Books, each Officer has to produce his own. *All* the Sergeant-Majors must ride in the Officers ride. I was obliged to have Hickman brought into the Riding School.

On the mounted parade the dressing of the two ranks at open order gave us the greatest trouble, the lines always got worse instead of better and the men got confused. I did all my formations from the Column from the Halt. In the Carabine Exercise all the words of command for loading must be given by the Officer who puts the men through it, most probably you do so already.

His Lordship was pleased with the Officers' chargers, he said they were a very good lot.

That is all I can remember at present, but something else may occur to me before he inspects your Detachment.

Altogether I had not a very pleasant day of it yesterday.

Believe me,
Yours very truly,
J. WILKES.

P.S. – At your field days had you a Non-commissioned told off to dress the base in changes of position, close Column manoeuvres, etc. etc. – J.W.

In 1885 Lord Cardigan was nominated a K.C.B. In 1860 he reached the summit of his ambition, becoming Colonel of the 11th Hussars. In 1861 he became a Lieutenant-General, and in this year he published a book called 'Cavalry Brigade Movements'. In 1863 we find him once more engaged in litigation. The action was one brought by him against Major Calthorpe, an officer who had served on Lord Raglan's Staff in the Crimea. This officer, in a military work dealing with the Crimean campaign, reflected adversely upon Lord Cardigan's handling of the Light Brigade at Balaclava. Lord Cardigan was twice married; in 1826 to Elizabeth Jane Henrietta, eldest daughter of Vice-Admiral Richard Delap Tollemache, and after her death in 1858, to Adeline Louisa Mary, only daughter of the late Mr. Spencer Horsey de Horsey, M.P. He had no children by either marriage.

The latter years of his life were spent at Deene Park, and here on March 28, 1868, he brought a dazzling if somewhat chequered career to a close; a fall from a young horse he was riding caused his death. By the 11th Hussars his name will long be cherished as one to whom the interests of that Regiment were always a primary consideration, and under whose rule a very high standard of perfection was attained. On the other hand, it must be admitted that his somewhat domineering manner, his strict adherence to what he considered 'light cavalry form' brought him into frequent conflict with a section of his officers. These, while zealous in attention to their duties, considered that when the toils of the drill-ground had been exchanged for the social intercourse of the mess or the hunting-field, the bands of discipline might be somewhat relaxed. The offending section, known as 'The Rebels', had as their leader Captain William Forrest, afterwards Colonel of the Regiment. Many are the amusing anecdotes which in later years General Forrest loved to relate, concerning this (to the officers) somewhat troubled period in the history of the Regiment. By the country at large it may be said, without fear of contradiction, that the name of 'Cardigan's Light Brigade' will be affectionately remembered when the trivialities and failings that sometimes marred the private life of a most gallant cavalry officer have been long forgotten.

The Reconciliation between Lord Cardigan and Captain Reynolds

When I was a youngster[1] I was always keen to hear stories from my father about the regiment in which I, as a child – I was only five years old when my father retired from the Service – could count so many friends. One, however, told me many years afterwards, when I was old enough to appreciate its importance and its infinite pathos, made a deep impression on my mind. The 'Black Bottle' affair is too well known to all officers of the 'Eleventh' to call for any description from me, but it was always a source of keen regret to my father that the two actors in it, Lord Cardigan and Captain Reynolds, should have remained estranged for so many years after their bitter quarrel.

[1] Major-General Desmond D. J. O'Callaghan, C.V.O.

At a regimental dinner, about the year '65, some of the seniors (Peel, Dallas?), approached my father and begged him to try and bring about a reconciliation between the two. 'You,' they said, 'are now almost the *doyen* of the regiment, and are, moreover, a friend of both. You also have more influence over his Lordship than any of us. Tell them that it is the unanimous wish of the Regiment; anyhow, do your best.'

With some misgivings my father went up to Reynolds and repeated the words of what might be called the deputation, and to his great relief Reynolds at once agreed. Lord Cardigan came late, and in considerable fear and trembling, my father, after the usual greeting, said, 'I have a great favour to ask of you.' 'Anything about the boy?' (I should explain that it was mainly owing to his Lordship's good offices that I obtained my nomination for a cadetship in the R.M.A.). 'No,' replied my father, 'I am deputed by the regiment to ask you to forgive old scores and to shake hands with Reynolds.' 'You ought to know me better than to ask such a thing,' said Lord Cardigan angrily, 'quite impossible.' 'But,' urged my father, 'you are both old men, why nurse this miserable quarrel to the grave?' 'Will he come to me?' 'Yes, he is only too anxious to do so.' 'Bring him up, O'Callaghan,' and my father beckoned to Reynolds, who walked quickly up. They grasped each other's hands but neither could speak, and as dinner was announced at the same moment, the two old men, still hand in hand, walked silently into the dining-room and sat down next each other.

Lord Cardigan died in '68, and it is possible that this was the last, or nearly the last, regimental dinner that he attended.

As an interesting sequel to the above, I may be permitted to describe an incident which happened to myself some years afterwards, when quartered at Shoeburyness. As a captain on the experimental staff I had rather better bachelor's rooms than the ordinary duty officer, and possessed a spare bedroom. This I gladly placed one evening at the disposal of our Brigade Major, Captain, now Colonel Mitchell, who expected a relative of his wife's to stay with them, and for whom he could not, without much difficulty, find room in his own house. A handsome and particularly courteous old gentleman arrived in due course, accompanied by Mitchell, and after seeing to his traps, strolled with me into my sittingroom. 'Why,' he exclaimed, 'there's the old "Eleventh" and that's O'Callaghan and his old charger, Chalk!' 'Yes, Sir,' I said, 'that is a portrait of my father.' 'Is your name O'Callaghan?' 'Yes, Sir.' 'Why, God bless my soul, my dear boy, *I'm Black Bottle!*'

So unexpected a link with the past was naturally of intense interest to myself, and although those who knew and have spoken to the two men to whom a foolish but deplorably bitter quarrel had given such notoriety must daily diminish in numbers, I venture to think that there are yet many to whom this brief account of what might be described as the burial of an enmity and the epitaph over its grave may not be uninteresting.

Dress and Appointments of a Cavalry Regiment, the 5th Lancers

In the mid-nineteenth century the 5th Lancers, a typical cavalry regiment, had the following establishment:

8 TROOPS

1	Colonel
1	Lieutenant Colonel
1	Major
8	Captains
8	Lieutenants
8	Cornets
1	Pay Master
1	Adjutant
1	Riding Master
1	Quarter Master
1	Surgeon
1	Assistant Surgeon
1	Veterinary Surgeon
1	Regimental Sergeant Major
8	Troop Sergeant-Majors
1	Quarter Master Sergeant
1	Pay Master Sergeant
1	Armourer Sergeant
1	School Master (to be appt. by U.S. of S.)[1]
1	Saddler Sergeant
1	Farrier Sergeant
1	Hospital Sergeant
1	Orderly Room Clerk
24	Sergeants
1	Trumpet Major
8	Trumpeters
32	Corporals
8	Farriers
537	Privates
661	Total
428	Troop horses

[1] Under Secretary of State.

The dress and appointments of the Regiment at this period were as follows:

Tunic of blue cloth, double breasted, scarlet facings, two rows of buttons, seven in each row, the distance between the rows being eight inches at the top and four at the bottom, lapels of Regimental facings to be worn doubled back, excepting on the line of march or in bad weather, skirt nine inches in height, and lined with black, collar two inches deep of Regimental facings and rounded in front with the following distinctions of rank.

> *Colonel* Collar laced all round with gold lace one inch wide. Silver crown and stars embroidered on each side.
>
> *Lieut. Colonel* Laced as above and badge of a crown.
>
> *Major* Laced as above and badge of a star.
>
> *Captain* Collar laced on upper edge with crown and star.
>
> *Lieutenant* Laced as above with badge of star.
>
> *Cornet* Laced as above with badge of star.

The waist of the tunic to be long; plain pointed cuff of the Regimental facings; on each shoulder a double gold cord, a welt of the Regimental facings down the sleeve and back seams, down the edge and front and round the skirt. Trousers of blue cloth with two gold lace stripes down each outward seam, each stripe $\frac{3}{4}$ inch wide leaving a light between.

Girdle of gold lace two and a half inches wide, with two crimson silk stripes.

Sword, steel mounted, half basket hilt, blade slightly curved, thirty five and a half inches long, and one and a quarter inches wide. Scabbard steel.

Belts, gold laced, with crimson silk stripes up the centre and edged with scarlet morocco.

Pouch of scarlet morocco with solid silver flap.

Gauntlets, white leather.

Cap, the square top Lancer cap covered with scarlet cloth and trimmed with gold lace, with gold lines to fasten round the neck and green horse hair plume.

Saddlery, Hussar pattern saddle with brass head and cantle. Buckles on bridge and ornaments of brass.

Sheepskin of black Ukraine lambskin with leather seat, trimmed with scarlet cloth.

Shabraque of blue cloth cut round before and behind, three feet eleven inches in length, two feet four inches in depth, trimmed with gold overall lace. Device on the fore corners V.R. and crown in gold, on the hind corners crown over harp within garter, with words 'Quis Separabit' round it, and the lances crossed under the garter.

The Regiment was mounted on strong well bred horses of various colours purchased from dealers in Ireland.

The average height of the horses was 15 h. 3 in.
The average height of the men was 5 ft 7 inches.
Total average weight of a lancer in marching order was 17 stone 7 lbs.

Prices of Commissions in the 1st Troop of Horse Guards as fixed in 1766.

	Prices (£)	Difference in Value between the several Commissions in Succession
First Lieut Colonel	5,500	400
Second Lieut Colonel	5,100	800
Cornet and Major	4,300	200
Guidon and Major	4,100	1,400
Exempt and Captain	2,700	1,200
Brigadier and Lieut. or Adjt. and Lieut.	1,500	300
Sub Brigadier and Cornet	1,200	1,200
		£5,500

Rates of Pay per Diem of the Officers of the Life Guards, Royal Regt. of Horse Guards, and of the Reduced Troops of Horse Grenadier Guards.

	Life Guards	Royal Regt. of Horse Guards	Reduced Troops of Horse Gren. Guards
Lieutenant Colonel	1 11 0	1 9 6	1 10 0
Supernumary Lieut Col.	1 7 0	—	—
Major	1 6 0	1 7 0	1 5 0
Supernumary major	1 4 –	—	—
Lt. & Captain	—	—	0 19 6
Guidon & Captain	—	—	0 18 6
Captain	0 16 0	1 1 6	—
Lieut	0 11 0	0 15 0	—
Cornet	0 9 6	0 14 0	—
Sub Lieutenant	—	—	0 12 6
Chaplain	0 6 8	0 6 8	0 6 8
Adjutant	0 11 0	0 5 0	0 9 6
Surgeon	0 8 0	0 6 0	0 8 0

Appendix 6

The Desert Mounted Corps

Yeomanry Division

6th Mounted Brigade: Dorset, Bucks, and Berks Yeomanry Regiments.

8th Mounted Brigade: 1st City of London and 1st and 3rd County of London Yeomanry Regiments.

22nd Mounted Brigade: Stafford, Lincoln, and East Riding Yeomanry Regiments.

Artillery: 20th Brigade R.H.A. (Berks, Hants, and Leicester Batteries) and Divisional Ammunition Column.

Australian Mounted Division

3rd Australian Light Horse Brigade: 8th, 9th, and 10th Regiments Australian Light Horse.

4th Australian Light Horse Brigade: 4th, 11th, and 12th Regiments Australian Light Horse.

Artillery: 19th Brigade R.H.A.

Corps Reserve

7th Mounted Brigade: Sherwood Rangers, South Notts and Herts Yeomanry Regiments, with Essex Battery R.H.A., and Brigade Ammunition Column.

Imperial Camel Corps Brigade: Two Australian and one British Camel Battalions, with the Hongkong and Singapore Mountain Battery R.G.A.

After the reorganization consequent upon the despatch of many of the Yeomanry regiments to France, in April and May 1918, and the arrival of Indian Cavalry Regiments from Europe, the Corps was expanded into four divisions:—

4th Cavalry Division

10th Cavalry Brigade: Dorset Yeomanry, 2nd Lancers, 38th Central India Horse.

11th Cavalry Brigade: 1st County of London Yeomanry, 29th Lancers, 36th Jacob's Horse.

12th Cavalry Brigade: Stafford Yeomanry, 6th Cavalry, 19th Lancers.

Artillery: 20th Brigade R.H.A. and Divisional Ammunition Column.

5th Cavalry Division

13th Cavalry Brigade: Gloucester Yeomanry, 9th Hodson's Horse, 18th Lancers.

14th Cavalry Brigade: Sherwood Rangers Yeomanry, 20th Deccan Horse, 34th Poona Horse.

15th (Imperial Service) Cavalry Brigade: Jodhpur, Mysore and 1st Hyderabad Lancers.

Artillery: 'B' Battery H.A.C. and Essex Battery R.H.A. with Divisional Ammunition Column.

Swords were issued to the Australian Mounted Division at the beginning of August 1918, and the men had about six weeks' training in the use of them before the operations commenced. The Australian troopers took to their new weapon enthusiastically, and showed, later on, that they knew how to use it.

Select Bibliography

The most comprehensive work on the later British cavalry is *A History of the British Cavalry* by the Marquess of Anglesey, published by Leo Cooper/Secker and Warburg. This is a four-volume study, which begins in 1816, i.e. after Waterloo, of which so far three volumes have been published, taking the story up to 1898. The series gives a detailed account of the activities of cavalry, both in the field and in barracks, and is unlikely to be equalled. It is strongly recommended.

Ascoli, David *A Companion to the British Army* Harrap 1983

Brereton, J.M. *The Horse in War* David & Charles 1976

Carman, W.Y. *Simkin's Uniforms of the British Army: the Cavalry Regiments* Webb & Bower 1982

Chappell *British Cavalry Equipment 1800–1941* Osprey 1983

Chenevix-Trench, C. *A History of Horsemanship* Doubleday & Co 1970

Childers, Erskine *War and the Arme Blanche* E. Arnold 1910

Dennison, G.T. *History of the Cavalry* Macmillan 1877

Haig, Douglas *Cavalry Studies* Hugh Rees Ltd 1907

Hills, R.J.T. *The Royal Dragoons* Leo Cooper 1972

Lawford, James *Wellington's Peninsular Army* Osprey 1973

Luard, John *History of the Dress of the British Soldier* W. Clowes 1852

Mileham, P.J.R. *The Yeomanry* Yeomanry Association 1983

MacMunn, Sir George *History of the Guides* Gale and Polden 1950

Rimington, M.F. *Our Cavalry* Macmillan 1912

de Watteville, H. *The British Soldier* Dent 1954

Wavell, A.P. *The Palestine Campaign* Constable 1927

Wilkinson-Latham, R.C. *Cavalry Uniforms* Blandford Press 1969

Young, Peter *The British Army* Kimber 1967

Younghusband, Sir G. *A Soldier's Memories* Herbert Jenkins 1917

Also:

Military Operations: France & Belgium, 1914, 1915, 1916, 1917, 1918 H.M.S.O.

Military Operations: Egypt & Palestine, Vols I & II H.M.S.O.

Index